The United Nations, Peace Operations
and the Cold War

The United Nations, Peace Operations and the Cold War

2nd edition

Norrie MacQueen

Longman
is an imprint of

Harlow, England • London • New York • Boston • San Francisco • Toronto
Sydney • Tokyo • Singapore • Hong Kong • Seoul • Taipei • New Delhi
Cape Town • Madrid • Mexico City • Amsterdam • Munich • Paris • Milan

PEARSON EDUCATION LIMITED

Edinburgh Gate
Harlow CM20 2JE
United Kingdom
Tel: +44 (0)1279 623623
Fax: +44 (0)1279 431059
Website: www.pearsoned.co.uk

First edition published in Great Britain in 1999
Second edition published 2011

© Pearson Education Limited 1999, 2011

The right of Norrie MacQueen to be identified as author of this work has been asserted
by him in accordance with the Copyright, Designs and Patents Act 1988.

Pearson Education is not responsible for the content of third party internet sites.

ISBN: 978–1–4082–3766–3

British Library Cataloguing in Publication Data
A CIP catalogue record for this book can be obtained from the British Library

Library of Congress Cataloging in Publication Data
MacQueen, Norrie, 1950–
    The United Nations, peace operations and the Cold War / Norrie MacQueen. – 2nd ed.
        p. cm.
    Rev. ed. of: United Nations since 1945 : peacekeeping and the Cold War. London :
Longman, 1999.
    Includes bibliographical references and index.
    ISBN 978–1–4082–3766–3 (pbk.)
    1. United Nations – Peacekeeping forces – History.   2. Security, International –
International cooperation – History.   3. Peace-building – International cooperation –
History.   4. Cold War.   5. World politics – 1945–1989.   I. MacQueen, Norrie, 1950–
United Nations since 1945.   II. Title.
    JZ4971.M298 2011
    341.5'84–dc22

                                                                    2011014746

10   9   8   7   6   5   4   3   2   1
15   14   13   12   11

Set by 35 in 10/13.5pt Berkeley Book
Printed in Malaysia (CTP-VP)

For Betsy and Triona

Introduction to the series

History is narrative constructed by historians from traces left by the past. Historical enquiry is often driven by contemporary issues and, in consequence, historical narratives are constantly reconsidered, reconstructed and reshaped. The fact that different historians have different perspectives on issues means that there is also often controversy and no universally agreed version of past events. *Seminar Studies in History* was designed to bridge the gap between current research and debate, and the broad, popular general surveys that often date rapidly.

The volumes in the series are written by historians who are not only familiar with the latest research and current debates concerning their topic, but who have themselves contributed to our understanding of the subject. The books are intended to provide the reader with a clear introduction to a major topic in history. They provide both a narrative of events and a critical analysis of contemporary interpretations. They include the kinds of tools generally omitted from specialist monographs: a chronology of events, a glossary of terms and brief biographies of 'who's who'. They also include bibliographical essays in order to guide students to the literature on various aspects of the subject. Students and teachers alike will find that the selection of documents will stimulate discussion and offer insight into the raw materials used by historians in their attempt to understand the past.

Clive Emsley and Gordon Martel
Series Editors

Contents

Preface to the second edition

Since 1999, when *The United Nations since 1945: Peacekeeping and the Cold War* was first published as a Seminar Study, there has been an enormous increase in both general and academic interest in the interventionist role of the UN. This reflects both the huge increase growth in that role in terms of operations mounted after the end of the cold war (which reached a peak around the turn of the millennium) and the increasing complexity of these operations. At the end of the 1990s the record of the United Nations as an agent of successful intervention was under great scrutiny. Evidently catastrophic failures of intervention over the previous decade – in Rwanda, Somalia, Angola and Bosnia – cast the future of UN peace operations in doubt. In 1999, for example, the 'humanitarian intervention' in Kosovo was carried out by the North Atlantic Treaty Organization (NATO) without direct reference to the United Nations – though the UN was left to handle the complex post-conflict administration of the territory.

More recently, the pressures on UN resources have eased somewhat as the great ideological and territorial flux created by the end of the cold war has settled. Denunciations of the UN's shortcomings as a peacekeeper have declined. This has been helped by some conspicuous successes in, for example, East Timor and belatedly in Liberia and Sierra Leone. At the same time, the appeal of military intervention by non-UN forces has been greatly lessened after the catastrophic invasion of Iraq in 2003 and to some extent too by the uncertain trajectory of NATO's involvement in Afghanistan. A certain equilibrium has therefore been re-established in which public expectations for UN interventions are more realistic and closer to those that prevailed during the cold war years of 'traditional' peacekeeping.

In that earlier period UN interventions were, typically, in conflicts between member countries of the organisation and a reasonable degree of self-interested cooperation could be expected from the protagonists. They were, after all, sovereign states which had invited the presence of UN forces in pursuit of conflict resolution and they were keenly aware of how their behaviour would reflect on their broader international standing and prestige. United Nations interventions in the post-cold war period were rarely so straight-forward. Now UN forces were more usually to be deployed in conflicts between factions and movements *within* states. Moreover, there was usually no peace – or at least no reliable peace – to keep. The presence of United Nations forces in these conflicts was therefore designed to secure a cessation of fighting rather than to monitor pre-existing ceasefires.

This apparent discontinuity between the supposed golden age of cold war peace missions and the contemporary challenges of armed humanitarian intervention in complex emergencies resulted in a tendency to separate the UN's historical experience into categories of 'old' and 'new' peacekeeping. Yet while the two periods did produce different challenges to the United Nations, often the differences were more ones of degree than truly ones of kind. Yes, the overall pressures on UN resources – and those of the member states it had to call on to 'peacekeep' – were infinitely greater in the 1990s than they had been in the 1960s. But it is perhaps misleading to suggest that the earlier experience was much less complex than the later one. Interventions in civil conflicts – 'intra-state' rather than 'inter-state' peace operations – did not begin with the end of the cold war. Most obviously, the intervention in the Congo between 1960 and 1964 and then the Cyprus force after 1964 were interventions in essentially civil conflicts. So too was that in the Lebanon from 1978. Certainly all of these crises had international dimensions to them which provided the main political and legal justification for the UN's involvement in the first place. But they were all primarily internal conflicts. There was, in short, a great deal more continuity between the UN's experience before and after the end of the cold war than is sometimes acknowledged.

This revised and updated edition of *The United Nations since 1945: Peace-keeping and the Cold War* is intended in part to underline this continuity. Indeed, the book also emphasises the affinities between United Nations peacekeeping and its precursors in the inter-war years when international forces were deployed by the League of Nations and other multinational bodies to carry out tasks such as election supervision and international administration – undertakings which are often assumed to have been patented by the United Nations during the cold war. To these ends this new edition focuses more closely on the cold war years as such rather than the post-1945 period as a whole which was the range of the first edition. The post-cold war years are not ignored, but now, a decade on, they are con-sidered in the context of the distinct period of superpower bipolarity from the late 1940s to the end of the 1980s. The extent of this reorientation is reflected in the decision to provide this edition with a new title: *The United Nations, Peace Operations and the Cold War*. It does not, to the same extent as its predecessor, seek to cover the period 'since' 1945. It is hoped, however, that this more concentrated focus will in itself offer a sharper, historically informed perspective on the current state of the United Nations and its capacity for armed intervention. Beyond this, in keeping with the revised format of the Seminar Studies series, the new edition will offer a more lengthy and detailed narrative of the period under examination and a greater and richer range of documents. It is also written after a period in which a florescence of analytical studies has provided new knowledge and new insights into the whole subject of multilateral intervention in local conflicts.

Publisher's acknowledgements

The publishers would like to thank the following for permission to reproduce copyright material:

Document 5 from *Memories* by A. Gromyko (1989) published by Hutchinson. Reprinted by permission of The Random House Group Ltd. E-rights granted by Andrew Nurnberg Associates; Document 9 reprinted with the permission of Scribner, a division of Simon & Schuster, Inc., from *In the Cause of Peace: Seven Years with the United Nations* by Trygve Lie. Copyright © 1954 by Trygve Lie: copyright renewed by 1982 by Guri Lie Zeckendorf, Sissel Lie Bratz and Mette Lie Holst. All rights reserved; Document 10 from *Mike: The Memoirs of the Right Honourable Lester B. Pearson*, Vol. 2, 1948–1957 (Munro, J.A. and Inglis, A.I. (eds.)) (1973), pp. 245–6. © University of Toronto Press 1973; Document 11 from *View from The UN* by U. Thant, copyright © 1978 by Myint-U, as Executor of the Estate of U. Thant. Used by permission of Doubleday, a division of Random House, Inc; Document 18 from 'Letter from Frank Aiken', *Bulletin of the Department of External Affairs of Ireland*, 653, 23/3/1964. Published with permission from the Department of Foreign Affairs, 79–80 St. Stephen's Green, Dublin 2; Document 19 from 'Certain Expenses of the United Nations (Article 17, paragraph 2 of the Charter)', Advisory Opinion of 20 July 1962, *ICJ Reports* 1962. Published with permission from the International Court of Justice; Document 20 from *The Years of Upheavel*, Henry Kissinger (1982), Weidenfeld & Nicolson, a division of The Orion Publishing Group, London and Document 22 from *In the Eye of the Storm*, Kurt Waldheim (1985), Weidenfeld & Nicolson, a division of The Orion Publishing Group, London. Published with permission from the publisher; Document 23 from *Unvanquished* by Boutros Boutros-Ghali (1999), copyright © 1999 by Boutros Boutros-Ghali. Used by permission of Random House, Inc.

Plates 1–8 courtesy of the United Nations Photo Library.

In some instances we have been unable to trace owners of copyright material, and would appreciate any information that would enable us to do so.

Chronology

1920

January First sessions of the League of Nations.

1931

September Japanese attack on Manchuria (China).

December League of Nations establishes commission to investigate situation in Manchuria.

1935

January Plebiscite on future of the Saar territory overseen by League of Nations international force.

October Italy invades Abyssinia (Ethiopia). Condemned by League of Nations.

1936

February League of Nations fails to agree an oil embargo on Italy over invasion of Abyssinia.

1939

September The Second World War begins in Europe.

1941

August Roosevelt and Churchill meet and agree 'Atlantic Charter'.

1943

November Tehran conference – Roosevelt outlines his big power 'policemen' concept for post-war security.

1944

August   Dumbarton Oaks talks begin – American, Soviet, British and Chinese representatives agree outline for a new international organisation based on the principle of collective security.

1945

February   Yalta conference – the plan for the UN is discussed by Roosevelt, Stalin and Churchill.

April   Death of Roosevelt – succeeded by Harry S. Truman.

              San Francisco conference finalises preparations for the new organisation. Attended by the 'big five' (US, USSR, UK, France and China) and fifty other anti-Axis states.

May   Germany surrenders.

August   Japan surrenders.

1946

February   UN's first secretary general, Trygve Lie of Norway, takes office.

April   League of Nations formally dissolved.

1948

April   Berlin crisis.

May   British Mandate ends in Palestine – state of Israel declared and war breaks out.

June   United Nations Truce Supervision Organization (UNTSO) established for Palestine.

September   UN Mediator for Palestine, Count Bernadotte, murdered.

1949

January   United Nations Military Observer Group in India and Pakistan (UNMOGIP) established.

1950

June   North Korea invades the South across 38th parallel. Security Council demands its withdrawal. United States mobilises forces in support of the South.

July   Security Council authorises American-led 'Unified Command' to confront North Korean invaders.

September   Landings by 'UN' forces turns tide and forces North Korea back towards 38th parallel.

October   'UN' forces cross northwards over 38th parallel.

November   'Uniting for Peace' resolution passed by General Assembly.

Communist Chinese cross into North Korea to confront western forces.

1951

January   Chinese and North Korean forces push south again across 38th parallel.

April   Truman dismisses General MacArthur from command of western forces in Korea.

June   Western forces push northwards in Korea again. Ceasefire talks proposed.

1953

January   Eisenhower inaugurated as US president in succession to Truman.

March   Death of Stalin – succeeded by 'collective leadership' including Nikita Khrushchev.

April   Trygve Lie succeeded as UN secretary general by Dag Hammarskjöld of Sweden.

July   Armistice signed in Korea.

1956

July   Nasser nationalises the Suez Canal.

October   Hungarian uprising suppressed by Russians.

Israeli attack on Egypt followed by Anglo-French 'ultimatum' and air-raids on Suez Canal Zone.

US draft resolution in Security Council calling for Israeli withdrawal vetoed by Britain and France.

November   Anglo-French forces invade Suez.

General Assembly resolution establishes United Nations Emergency Force (UNEF) for Suez.

1958

February   Egypt and Syria declare themselves unified as the 'United Arab Republic'.

October   Hammarskjöld produces 'Summary Study' on lessons of Suez.

June   United Nations Observation Group in Lebanon (UNOGIL) formed in response to Lebanese government claims of Syrian infiltration.

July   US troops landed in Lebanon.

December   Lebanon crisis recedes – UNOGIL withdrawn.

1960

June Independence of Congo from Belgium.

July Congolese army mutinies – Belgian paratroops intervene.

Congolese prime minister (Lumumba) and president (Kasavubu) seek UN assistance.

Katanga announces secession from Congo.

Security Council establishes United Nations Operation in the Congo (ONUC).

September Congolese government crisis – Kasavubu dismisses Lumumba and *vice versa*. UN orders closure of airports and radio station.

Congolese army commander Mobutu announces coup and allies himself with Kasavubu. Lumumba placed under UN protection.

Khrushchev denounces 'pro-western' stance of ONUC in Security Council – calls for *troika* to replace office of secretary general.

November General Assembly recognises Kasavubu–Mobutu faction as legitimate government of Congo.

Lumumba leaves UN protection and is captured by Mobutu's forces.

1961

January Lumumba murdered after being transferred by his captors to Katanga.

John F. Kennedy inaugurated as US president.

February Security Council authorises ONUC to use force if necessary to prevent civil war in Congo.

August–September Unsuccessful UN military operations against Katanga.

September Death of Hammarskjöld *en route* to meet Katangese leaders in Northern Rhodesia. Succeeded as secretary general by U Thant of Burma.

1962

July Advisory Opinion of International Court of Justice that peacekeeping is a 'normal' expense of the UN.

October United Nations Temporary Executive Authority/Security Force (UNTEA/UNSF) created for West New Guinea.

Cuban missile crisis.

1963

January Katangese secession formally ended in face of mounting UN military pressure.

April UNTEA/UNSF completes mission in West New Guinea.

July	United Nations Yemen Observation Mission (UNYOM) deployed.
August	Partial Nuclear Test Ban Treaty signed in Moscow by US, USSR and Britain.
November	Kennedy assassinated – Lyndon Johnson becomes US president.

1964

March	United Nations Force in Cyprus (UNFICYP) formed by Security Council in response to widespread inter-communal violence.
June	Withdrawal of ONUC from Congo.
September	UNYOM completes mission in Yemen.
September–December	'Article 19 crisis' over General Assembly voting rights.
October	Khrushchev deposed. Replaced by new leadership including Leonid Brezhnev.

1965

September	United Nations India-Pakistan Observer Mission (UNIPOM) established.

1966

March	UNIPOM withdrawn from India–Pakistan border.

1967

May	UNEF withdrawn from Suez at request of Egypt.
June	'Six Day War' between Israel and Arabs.
November	UNFICYP responds to sharp deterioration in Cyprus situation.

1968

January–February	Vietnam war intensifies with 'Tet Offensive' by Vietcong.
August	Russian tanks suppress reformist movement in Czechoslovakia.

1969

January	Richard Nixon sworn in as US president.

1971

October	Communist China replaces Formosa/Taiwan in the 'China seat' at the UN following *rapprochement* between Washington and Beijing.

1972

January	Kurt Waldheim of Austria becomes UN secretary general.
May	Nixon and Brezhnev sign Strategic Arms Limitation Treaty (SALT) in Moscow.

1973

October   War in the Middle East. US and USSR cooperate in orchestrating UN response.

Second United Nations Emergency Force (UNEF II) deployed between Israeli and Egyptian armies in Sinai.

1974

June   United Nations Disengagement Observer Force (UNDOF) deployed between Israeli and Syrian armies in Golan Heights.

July–August Coup attempt in Cyprus by right-wing Greek Cypriots provokes Turkish invasion. UNFICYP interposed between warring sides. Cyprus effectively partitioned.

August   Nixon forced to resign following Watergate scandal. Gerald Ford becomes president.

1975

April   Saigon falls to North Vietnamese forces. Final American withdrawal from South Vietnam.

Civil War breaks out in Lebanon.

November   Portugal withdraws from Angola – civil war between US and Soviet backed factions. Cuban troops intervene in support of Marxist government.

1976

June   Syria moves against Palestinians in Lebanon.

1977

January   Jimmy Carter sworn in as US president.

1978

March   Israeli invasion of Lebanon. Security Council formation of United Nations Interim Force in Lebanon (UNIFIL).

September   Camp David agreement between Israel and Egypt.

1979

January   Shah of Iran deposed. Anti-western Islamist regime installed.

June   Second Strategic Arms Limitation Treaty (SALT-2) signed by Carter and Brezhnev in Vienna.

July   UNEF II withdrawn from Sinai at the insistence of the Soviet Union.

December   Soviet invasion of Afghanistan.

1981

January   Ronald Reagan sworn in as US president.

1982

January   Javier Pérez de Cuéllar of Peru replaces Kurt Waldheim as UN secretary general.

June   Israel invades Lebanon again, brushing UNIFIL aside.

August   Non-UN Multinational Force (MNF) established to oversee withdrawal of Palestinians from Beirut and act as buffer between Israeli and Syrian forces.

November   Brezhnev dies, succeeded by Yuri Andropov.

1983

October   300 US and French troops of the MNF in Lebanon killed in bomb attacks. Force withdrawn.

1984

February   Andropov dies, succeeded as Soviet president by Konstantin Chernenko.

1985

March   Chernenko dies – succeeded as Soviet president by Mikhail Gorbachev.

1987

December   Strategic Arms Reduction Treaty (START) signed by Reagan and Gorbachev in Washington.

1988

April   United Nations Good Offices Mission in Afghanistan and Pakistan (UNGOMAP) established.

August   United Nations Iran-Iraq Military Observer Group (UNIIMOG) formed.

1989

January   George H.W. Bush sworn in as US president.

First United Nations Angola Verification Mission (UNAVEM) formed.

April   United Nations Transition Assistance Group (UNTAG) for Namibia established.

November   Berlin Wall comes down.

United Nations Observer Group in Central America (ONUCA) formed.

1990

March	UNTAG completes mission in Namibia.
	UNGOMAP completes mission in Afghanistan and Pakistan.
August	Iraq invades Kuwait.
October	Unification of Germany.
November	Security Council resolution 678 authorises formation of military coalition against Iraq.

1991

January	Operation Desert Storm begins against Iraq.
February	UNIIMOG completes mission on Iran–Iraq border.
April	United Nations Iraq-Kuwait Observation Mission (UNIKOM) formed.
	United Nations Mission for the Referendum in Western Sahara (MINURSO) formed.
May	UNAVEM I completes mission in Angola ahead of schedule.
	Second Angola Verification Mission (UNAVEM II) formed.
July	United Nations Observation Mission in El Salvador (ONUSAL) formed.
September	Soviet Union formally dissolved. Commonwealth of Independent States (CIS) succeeds it.
December	Gorbachev resigns a president of CIS – hands power to Russian president Boris Yeltsin.

1992

January	Boutros Boutros-Ghali of Egypt replaces Pérez de Cuéllar as UN secretary general.
	ONUCA completes mission in Central America.
February	United Nations Protection Force (UNPROFOR) for former Yugoslavia established.
	United Nations Transitional Authority in Cambodia (UNTAC) formed.
April	United Nations Operation in Somalia (UNOSOM) established.
June	Boutros-Ghali publishes *An Agenda for Peace*.
December	United Nations Operation in Mozambique (ONUMOZ) established.
	American-led Unified Task Force in Somalia (UNITAF) deployed.

1993

January	Bill Clinton sworn in as US president.
May	UNITAF withdrawn from Somalia.

June	United Nations Observer Mission Uganda-Rwanda (UNOMUR) formed.
August	United Nations Observer Mission in Georgia (UNOMIG) formed.
September	United Nations Observer Mission in Liberia (UNOMIL) established.
	United Nations Mission in Haiti (UNMIH) formed.
October	United Nations Assistance Mission for Rwanda (UNAMIR) established.

1994

April	Genocide begins in Rwanda – majority of UN troops withdrawn.
September	UNOMUR withdrawn from Uganda–Rwanda border.
December	ONUMOZ completes mission in Mozambique.
	United Nations Mission of Observers in Tajikistan (UNMOT) formed.

1995

February	UNAVEM II wound-up in Angola. Third United Nations Angola Verification Mission (UNAVEM III) formed.
March	UN operation in Somalia ends.
	Preventive Deployment Force (UNPREDEP) replaces UNPROFOR in Macedonia.
August	NATO-led 'Operation Deliberate Force' against Bosnian Serbs begins.
November	Dayton Agreement on Bosnia signed.
December	UNPROFOR wound down in Bosnia after deployment of NATO Implementation Force (I-FOR).

UN operations established 1948–1995

United Nations Truce Supervision Organization (UNTSO)

Location:	Israeli border/Palestine
Date formed:	June 1948
Strength:	180 (mid-1990s)
Function:	Observation of ceasefires between Israel and Arab states and, later, assistance to other UN peacekeeping operations in the region. The first UN peace operation is still deployed.

United Nations Military Observer Group in India and Pakistan (UNMOGIP)

Location:	India–Pakistan ceasefire line in Kashmir
Date formed:	January 1949
Strength:	45 (mid-1990s)
Function:	To observe ceasefire between India and Pakistan following war over disputed and divided border territory of Kashmir in 1948. Remains deployed.

United Nations Emergency Force (UNEF)

Location:	Suez Canal and Sinai peninsula
Date formed:	November 1956
Strength:	6000
Function:	To supervise cessation of hostilities between Israel and Egypt and, initially, to supervise withdrawal of Anglo-French forces from canal zone. Withdrawn at the request of Egypt in May 1967 on the eve of the Six Day War. The first UN peacekeeping 'force' (as opposed to military observer mission).

United Nations Observation Group in Lebanon (UNOGIL)

Location:	Lebanese-Syrian border
Date formed:	June 1958
Strength:	600
Function:	To monitor alleged infiltration into Lebanon of hostile elements. Withdrawn in December 1958 after successful mission and easing of regional tensions.

United Nations Operation in the Congo (ONUC: *Opération des Nations Unies au Congo)*

Location:	Republic of Congo (previously Belgian Congo; subsequently Zaire then Democratic Republic of Congo)
Date formed:	July 1960
Strength:	20,000
Function:	Initially to supervise the withdrawal of Belgian forces; later to provide stability in, and ensure the territorial integrity of, the new state. Withdrawn in June 1964. By far the largest and most complex UN peace operation when first established.

United Nations Temporary Executive Authority and Security Force in West New Guinea (UNTEA/UNSF)

Location:	Dutch New Guinea/Indonesian province of Irian Jaya
Date formed:	October 1962
Strength:	1600
Function:	To provide transitional administration and security for the territory during the transfer of power in West New Guinea from the Netherlands to Indonesia. Mission successfully completed in April 1963, though transfer generates long-lasting separatist agitation.

United Nations Yemen Observation Mission (UNYOM)

Location:	Yemen
Date formed:	July 1963
Strength:	200
Function:	To supervise mutual disengagement from Yemen civil war of Saudi Arabia and United Arab Republic (Egypt). Withdrawn in September 1964.

United Nations Peacekeeping Force in Cyprus (UNFICYP)

Location:	Cyprus
Date formed:	March 1964
Strength:	1200 (mid-1990s)
Function:	To prevent fighting between Greek and Turkish Cypriot communities. After 1974 Turkish invasion, to supervise ceasefire line between Turkish/Turkish Cypriot forces and Greek Cypriot forces. Operation remains in place in absence of definitive settlement of Cyprus question.

United Nations India-Pakistan Observer Mission (UNIPOM)

Location:	India–Pakistan border west of Kashmir
Date formed:	September 1965
Strength:	100
Function:	To supervise ceasefire following 1965 India–Pakistan war. Withdrawn in March 1966.

Second United Nations Emergency Force (UNEF II)

Location: Suez Canal area and Sinai peninsula
Date formed: October 1973
Strength: 7000
Function: To supervise Israeli-Egyptian ceasefire following 1973 war and to provide a buffer between disengaging forces. Mandate terminated at Soviet insistence in July 1979 following the Camp David agreement between Egypt and Israel. Succeeded by US-organised Multinational Force and Observers.

United Nations Disengagement Observer Force (UNDOF)

Location: Golan Heights (Israeli-Syrian border)
Date formed: June 1974
Strength: 1000 (mid-1990s)
Function: To supervise disengagement of Israeli and Syrian forces following 1973 war and to provide a buffer between them. Operation remains in place.

United Nations Interim Force in Lebanon (UNIFIL)

Location: Southern Lebanon
Date formed: March 1978
Strength: 4600 (mid-1990s)
Function: To oversee Israeli withdrawal from southern Lebanon following 1978 invasion and assist return of Lebanese government authority to the area. Mandate adjusted following subsequent outbreaks of violence. Operation remains in place.

United Nations Good Offices Mission in Afghanistan and Pakistan (UNGOMAP)

Location: Afghanistan and Pakistan
Date formed: May 1988
Strength: 50
Function: To supervise peace agreement following withdrawal of Soviet forces from Afghanistan. Mission completed March 1990.

United Nations Iran-Iraq Military Observer Group (UNIIMOG)

Location: Iran and Iraq
Date formed: August 1988
Strength: 400
Function: To supervise Iran–Iraq ceasefire following the peace agreement to end of the war between the two neighbours which began in 1980. Mission completed February 1991.

United Nations Angola Verification Mission (UNAVEM)

Location: Angola
Date formed: January 1989

Strength: 70

Function: To supervise withdrawal of Cuban forces from Angola as part of linked agreement for the independence of Namibia from South Africa. Mission successfully completed in May 1991 ahead of schedule.

United Nations Transition Assistance Group (UNTAG)

Location: Namibia

Date formed: April 1989

Strength: 8000

Function: To provide security and administrative support during Namibia's transition to independence from South Africa. Linked to the withdrawal of Cuban forces from neighbouring Angola supervised by UNAVEM. Mission completed March 1990.

United Nations Observer Group in Central America (ONUCA: *Observadores de las Naciones Unidas en Centroamerica*)

Location: Costa Rica, El Salvador, Guatemala, Honduras, Nicaragua

Date formed: December 1989

Strength: 1000

Function: To supervise regional agreement to prevent cross-border movement of irregular forces and arms, in particular from and to Nicaragua. Withdrawn January 1992.

United Nations Iraq-Kuwait Observation Mission (UNIKOM)

Location: Iraq–Kuwait border

Date formed: April 1991

Strength: 1200 (mid-1990s)

Function: To monitor demilitarised zone on Iraq–Kuwait border following the expulsion of Iraqi forces from Kuwait after Operation Desert Storm. Withdrawn in 2003 following American-led invasion of Iraq.

United Nations Mission for the Referendum in Western Sahara (MINURSO: *Mission des Nations Unies pour l'Organisation d'un Référendum au Sahara Occidental*)

Location: Western Sahara

Date formed: April 1991

Strength: 2500

Function: Following agreement between Morocco and Polisario Front, to supervise disengagement of both sides' forces and to prepare elections on the future of the territory contested since Spain's withdrawal from its former colony in 1976. Operation continues in absence of political settlement.

Second United Nations Verification Mission in Angola (UNAVEM II)

Location:	Angola
Date formed:	May 1991
Strength:	350
Function:	To verify ceasefire between Angolan government and UNITA guerrillas, and to monitor national elections. Following refusal of UNITA to accept adverse election result, to assist in humanitarian relief. Withdrawn February 1995.

United Nations Observer Mission in El Salvador (ONUSAL: *Observadores de las Naciones Unidas en El Salvador*)

Location:	El Salvador
Date formed:	July 1991
Strength:	1000
Function:	To verify ceasefire between El Salvador government and leftist guerrillas, and to supervise national elections. Withdrawn April 1995.

United Nations Protection Force (UNPROFOR)

Location:	Bosnia, Croatia, Serbia, Macedonia
Date formed:	February 1992
Strength:	39,000
Function:	First deployed in Croatia and then most notably in Bosnia to secure UN 'protected areas', provide security for humanitarian aid and monitor UN-declared air exclusion zones. Wound up March 1995 after the Dayton peace agreement for Bosnia and replaced with NATO-led 'Implementation Force'.

United Nations Transitional Authority in Cambodia (UNTAC)

Location:	Cambodia
Date formed:	March 1992
Strength:	22,000
Function:	To supervise implementation of 1991 peace agreement in Cambodia; to provide an interim authority and to prepare and administer national elections. Mission completed in September 1993.

United Nations Operation in Somalia (UNOSOM I and II)

Location:	Somalia
Date formed:	April/December 1992
Strength:	28,000
Function:	To restore peace and stability by ending factional fighting in Somalia and to secure the distribution of humanitarian aid. Withdrawn March 1995.

United Nations Operation in Mozambique (ONUMOZ: *Operação das Nações*
***Unidas em Moçambique*)**

Location:	Mozambique
Date formed:	December 1992
Strength:	7000
Function:	To assist in the implementation of the peace agreement between Mozambican government and Renamo guerrillas; to administer and supervise national elections. Mission completed December 1994.

United Nations Observer Mission Uganda-Rwanda (UNOMUR)

Location:	Uganda–Rwanda border
Date formed:	June 1993
Strength:	80
Function:	To ensure no military forces or material permitted to cross Uganda–Rwanda border. Withdrawn September 1994.

United Nations Observer Mission in Georgia (UNOMIG)

Location:	Georgia (former Soviet Union)
Date formed:	August 1993
Strength:	140
Function:	Initially, to verify peace agreement between government of Georgia and Abkhaz separatists; later, to monitor operation of Commonwealth of Independent States (of the former Soviet Union) peacekeeping force in Georgia. Withdrawn after Security Council failure to agree new mandate in 2009.

United Nations Observer Mission in Liberia (UNOMIL)

Location:	Liberia
Date formed:	September 1993
Strength:	160
Function:	To support and monitor the peacekeeping efforts of the Economic Community of West African States (ECOWAS) in Liberia after the end of the civil war in 1993. Withdrawn in September 1997.

United Nations Mission in Haiti (UNMIH)

Location:	Haiti
Date formed:	September 1993
Strength:	1200 (mid-1990s)
Function:	Originally, to train and modernise Haitian security forces. After 1994 United States intervention UNMIH assisted the new government in preparation of elections. Mission ended in June 1996.

United Nations Assistance Mission for Rwanda (UNAMIR)

Location:	Rwanda
Date formed:	October 1993
Strength:	5500
Function:	Originally, to implement peace agreement between Rwanda government and rebel forces. Overtaken by genocide and subsequent civil war in Rwanda in mid-1994. Given a renewed humanitarian mandate in aftermath of this. Withdrawn March 1996.

United Nations Mission of Observers in Tajikistan (UNMOT)

Location:	Tajikistan
Date formed:	December 1994
Strength:	45
Function:	To monitor ceasefire on Tajik-Afghan border; to liaise with Organization for Security and Cooperation in Europe (OSCE) mission and to monitor Commonwealth of Independent States peacekeeping force. Mandate terminated in May 2000.

Third United Nations Verification Mission in Angola (UNAVEM III)

Location:	Angola
Date formed:	February 1995
Strength:	7000
Function:	To supervise implementation of Lusaka peace agreement of 1994 after resumption of civil war between government forces and UNITA in 1992. Replaced by new UN observer mission June 1997. UN military presence withdrawn in 1999.

United Nations Preventive Deployment Force (UNPREDEP)

Location:	Macedonia
Date formed:	March 1995
Strength:	1100
Function:	Replaces UNPROFOR in Macedonia to monitor borders to prevent spread of violence from elsewhere in the former Yugoslavia. The UN's first truly 'preventive' peace operation. Withdrawn in 1999.

Who's who

Aiken, Frank (1898–1983): Irish foreign minister 1957–69; a 'middle power' activist at the UN and advocate of Irish army participation in peacekeeping operations.

Akashi, Yasushi (1931–): Japanese diplomat who was the UN representative in Bosnia during the civil war there. Widely criticised for his reluctance to authorise robust UN action against the Bosnian Serbs.

Andropov, Yuri (1914–84): Soviet leader 1982–84; regarded as a reformer though his early death in office prevented development of distinct policies.

Annan, Kofi (1938–): Ghanaian secretary general of the UN 1997–2006. Under-secretary general for peacekeeping, 1994–95.

Assad, Hafiz al- (1930–2000): President of Syria from November 1970 (previously defence minister); negotiated deployment of UNDOF in 1974 with Henry Kissinger.

Aideed, Mohammed Farah (1934–96): Somali 'warlord'; leader of one of the largest armed factions confronting UNOSOM/UNITAF, 1992–95.

Barre, Siad (1919–95): Somali president between 1969 and 1991; supported by the US during the cold war; overthrown by opposition factions who then began to fight among themselves for control of the country.

Begin, Menachim (1913–92): Israeli prime minister 1977–83; leader of right-wing Likud Party; negotiated 1978 Camp David peace agreement with Egypt under American auspices.

Ben-Gurion, David (1886–1973): First prime minister of Israel from 1948 to 1963 and leader of Labour Party; in office during wars of 1948 and 1956.

Bernadotte, Count Folke (1895–1948): Nephew of king of Sweden; UN mediator in Palestine in 1948; he had previously acted in various mediatory roles during the Second World War; assassinated by Jewish extremists in September 1948.

Boutros-Ghali, Boutros (1922–): Egyptian secretary general of the UN 1992–97; in office during the post-cold war expansion of peacekeeping undertakings; published *An Agenda for Peace* in 1992. Hostility of the United States blocked prospect of second term in office.

Brezhnev, Leonid (1906–82): Soviet leader 1964–82; succeeded the deposed Khrushchev; ordered Soviet invasion of Czechoslovakia in 1968 though he also pursued a policy of détente with the west.

Bunche, Ralph (1904–71): Long-serving African-American UN official; involved in a range of peacemaking efforts from Palestine (where he succeeded Count Bernadotte as Mediator) to the Congo.

Burns, General E.L.M. (Eedson Louis Millard) (1897–1985): Canadian commander of UNEF from its formation in 1956 until 1959.

Bush, George H. W. (1924–): US president (Republican) from 1988 to 1992; in office during the Gulf War against Iraq and through the end of the cold war.

Cadogan, Sir Alexander (1884–1968): British diplomat and representative at Dumbarton Oaks conference in 1944; later British permanent representative at the UN.

Carter, Jimmy (1924–): US president (Democrat) from 1976–80; a foreign policy liberal by American standards, he was the driving force behind 1978 Camp David agreement between Israel and Egypt.

Chamoun, Camille (1900–87): Maronite Christian president of Lebanon during crisis of 1958 which led to creation of UNOGIL. Chamoun invited American intervention against what he claimed was a threat from Syria.

Chehab, General Fuad (1902–73): President of Lebanon between 1958 and 1964. Prior to succeeding Camille Chamoun as head of state following the crisis of 1958 in which UNOGIL was deployed, Chehab had been the widely respected commander of the Lebanon's armed forces.

Chernenko, Konstantin (1911–85): Soviet leader in 1984–85 in interval between Andropov and Gorbachev.

Churchill, Winston S. (1874–1965): British war leader during Second World War; prime minister in war-time coalition from 1940–45 and then Conservative prime minister from 1951–55; signatory of Atlantic Charter in 1941 and closely involved in the creation of the UN.

Clinton, Bill (1946–): US president from 1992; inherited American involvement in Somalia from his predecessor (George H.W. Bush); urged international intervention in Haiti in early 1990s and robust action in Bosnia.

Cordier, Andrew (1901–75): UN representative in the Congo capital Leopoldville in 1960. An American, he was accused of pro-western, anti-Lumumba bias during crisis of September of that year.

Dayal, Rajeshwar (1909–99): Indian UN representative in the Congo 1960–61 in succession to Andrew Cordier; displayed a greater sensitivity to Afro-Asian concerns over the Congo than his predecessor.

De Gaulle, Charles (1890–1970): Leader of the 'Free French' forces during Second World War and head of government 1944–46; president of France 1958–69; advocate of continued national sovereignty against any shift in international authority to an 'independent' UN.

Dobrynin, Anatoly (1919–2010): Veteran Soviet ambassador in Washington; in office through a succession of cold war crises; helped coordinate Soviet response to 1973 Middle East war with that of the US and cooperated in arranging a UN peacekeeping response.

Dulles, John Foster (1888–1959): Secretary of state during the (Republican) Eisenhower administration in the US during the 1950s; architect of the policy of 'containment' towards the Soviet Union.

Eden, Anthony (Earl of Avon) (1897–1977): British Conservative foreign secretary before and during Second World War; prime minister from 1955 to 1957 when he conspired with Israel and France to attack Egypt after Nasser's nationalisation of the Suez Canal in 1956; accepted the interposition of UNEF as a face-saving device to cover British withdrawal.

Eisenhower, Dwight D. (1890–1969): US Republican president 1953–61; in office during the most glacial period of the cold war; critical of Britain and France over their actions in the Suez crisis of 1956.

Ford, Gerald (1913–2006): US Republican president 1974–76; vice-president in Nixon administration; came to office after the fall of Nixon in the wake of the Watergate scandal.

Gemayal, Bashir (1947–82): President-elect of Lebanon whose assassination (for which Syrian agents were blamed) precipitated a catastrophic deterioration in Lebanon's civil conflict.

Gorbachev, Mikhail (1931–): Soviet president 1985–91; reformer who presided over the end of the cold war and the break-up of the Soviet Union.

Gromyko, Andrei (1909–89): Veteran Soviet diplomat and foreign minister; Soviet representative at Dumbarton Oaks conference in 1944; deputy foreign minister and UN representative 1946–52; Soviet foreign minister 1957–85.

Hammarskjöld, Dag (1905–61): Swedish second secretary general of the UN from 1953 until his death in Africa during the Congo crisis in 1961;

widely regarded as the founding father of UN peacekeeping following the establishment of UNEF in 1956.

Johnson, Lyndon B. (1908–73): US Democratic president 1963–69; elevated from the vice-presidency after the assassination of Kennedy and then elected in his own right; presided over deepening American involvement in Vietnam.

Kasavubu, Joseph (1910–69): First president of the Congo 1960–65; pro-western rival of prime minister Patrice Lumumba but ultimately dependant on army chief Joseph Mobutu who eventually ousted him from the presidency and took his place.

Kennedy, John F. (1917–63): US Democratic president from 1961 until his assassination in 1963; brought US policy on the Congo closer into line with the concerns of the Afro-Asian states in the UN; confronted the Soviet Union in the Cuban missile crisis of 1962.

Khrushchev, Nikita (1894–1971): Prominent in collective Soviet leadership after the death of Stalin in 1953 and then leader in his own right from 1956 until being deposed in 1964. Suspicious of western dominance in the UN and particularly hostile to Hammarskjöld during the Congo crisis; advocated a bloc-based *troika* to replace the office of secretary general.

Kim Il Sung (1912–94): Communist leader of North Korea from 1948; invaded the south in 1950 precipitating the Korean War; object of huge personality cult who maintained North Korea in international isolation throughout his decades in power.

Kissinger, Henry (1923–): American academic and politician; foreign policy adviser and then secretary of state during the Nixon and Ford administrations; oversaw the development of détente between the superpowers and 'co-opted' UN peacekeeping in its service in the Middle East in the 1970s.

Lie, Trygve (1896–1968): Norwegian first secretary general of the UN 1946–53. In office during the Korean War when his approach deepened Soviet suspicions of the UN's pro-western character.

Lumumba, Patrice (1925–61): First prime minister of the Congo after its independence from Belgium; requested UN intervention in 1960 though soon became disaffected with the UN's supposed western bias and became increasingly pro-Soviet in his pronouncements; deposed in September 1960 and then captured and murdered by his political enemies.

MacArthur, General Douglas (1880–1964): American commander in Asia during the Second World War; appointed to lead the 'UN' Unified Command in Korea in 1950; his increasingly independent and political behaviour caused concern both among the allies fighting in Korea and in Washington; dismissed by President Truman in 1951.

Makarios III, Archbishop (Michail Christodolou Mouskos) (1913–77): Greek Cypriot first president of independent Cyprus from 1960; his attempts to enhance the constitutional and political power of his own ethnic community in 1963–64 led to the creation of UNFICYP; attempted coup against him by pro-Greek rightists in 1974 led to Turkish invasion and *de facto* partition.

Meir, Golda (1898–1978): Israeli (Labour) prime minister 1969–74. In office during the war of 1973 and involved in the early stages of the subsequent US-brokered peace negotiations.

Mobutu, Joseph (Sese Seko) (1930–97): Commander of Congolese army after independence from Belgium; instrumental in ousting and subsequent murder of Lumumba; Presided over deeply corrupt but pro-western Congo (Zaire) from 1965 until 1997 when he was overthrown.

Molotov, Vyacheslav (1890–1986): Soviet foreign minister during the establishment and early development of the UN (1941–49, 1953–57); his close identification with Stalin caused him to fall from favour during the Khrushchev years.

Nasser, Gammal Abdel (1918–1970): Nationalist army officer who led Egypt from 1952 until his death in 1970; nationalised the Suez Canal in 1956 prefiguring the establishment of UNEF; leading figure in 1967 combined Arab attack on Israel (the 'Six Day War').

Nixon, Richard (1913–94): US Republican president 1969–74; although fundamentally conservative in foreign policy (as regards, for example, American policy in southeast Asia) he presided over the development of détente – including rapprochement with communist China – in tandem with his secretary of state Henry Kissinger; resigned after the Watergate scandal in 1974.

O'Brien, Conor Cruise (1917–2008): Irish diplomat, politician and writer; seconded from the Irish foreign service to act as UN representative in Katanga in 1961 where he ordered UN forces to take action against foreign military personnel supporting secession; the ensuing crisis led indirectly to the death of Hammarskjöld.

Pearson, Lester (1897–1972): Canadian foreign minister 1948–57 closely associated with Canada's 'middle power' role in the UN; his General Assembly initiative during the Suez crisis in 1956 was instrumental in the creation of UNEF; Nobel Peace Prize winner; prime minister of Canada 1963–68.

Pérez de Cuéllar, Javier (1920–): Peruvian secretary general of UN 1982–92; the end of his term of office saw the beginning of the UN's post-cold war phase of peacekeeping after the dormant period of the late 1970s and 1980s.

Prem Chand, Lt. Gen. Dewan (1947–2003): Indian soldier with extensive command responsibilities in UN operations including the Congo, Cyprus and Namibia.

Rabin, Yitzhak (1922–95): Israeli (Labour) prime minister from 1974 to 1977 and from 1992 until his murder by a Jewish extremist; negotiated with Henry Kissinger in 1974 over the formation of UNDOF in the Golan Heights and was involved in the Israel–Egypt talks which led eventually to the Camp David agreement.

Reagan, Ronald (1911–2004): US Republican president 1980–88; presided over the worst years of the 'second' cold war in the 1980s; his administration pursued a distinctly conservative foreign policy and was frequently hostile to the UN as an institution.

Roosevelt, Franklin D. (1882–1945): US (Democrat) president for three terms from 1933 until his death in 1945; his 'New Deal' policies helped alleviate the worst effects of the depression in the 1930s; took America into the Second World War and became the chief architect of the UN and a strong advocate of collective security; died on the eve of the San Francisco conference at which his efforts came to fruition.

Sadat, Anwar (1918–81): President of Egypt from 1970 until his assassination by opposition elements in the Egyptian army in 1981; leading actor in the Arab attack on Egypt in 1973 and then subsequently in the peace process which led to the Camp David agreement between Egypt and Israel in 1978.

Savimbi, Jonas (1934–2002): Leader of the UNITA rebel movement in Angola which fought to overthrow the MPLA government from the time of Angola's independence in 1975 until his own death at the hands of government forces in 2002.

Stalin, Joseph (1879–1953): Leader of the Soviet Union after the death of Lenin in 1923; over the following thirty years he was the architect of massive repression at home; led the Soviet Union to (a costly) victory in the Second World War; cooperated with Roosevelt and Churchill in the planning of the UN in 1944–45 to ensure that the USSR was not isolated in post-war international relations; gave encouragement to North Korea's invasion of the South in 1950.

Stettinius, Edward (1900–49): US Secretary of State under Truman; previously chairman and participant at the Dumbarton Oaks conference in 1944.

Stevenson, Adlai (1900–65): US representative at the UN under Kennedy and Johnson; associated with a distinctly 'liberal' approach to American UN policy; previously Democratic candidate in the presidential elections of 1952 and 1956.

Sukarno, Ahmed (1901–70): First president of Indonesia from 1945 to 1967; prominent internationally in the development of the Non-Aligned Movement while pursuing an aggressively nationalist foreign policy in the Asia-Pacific region; succeeded in annexing West New Guinea with the help of a UN transitional administration in 1962–63.

Syngman Rhee (1875–1965): First president of South Korea 1945–60; pro-western, right-wing nationalist; in office during the Korean War.

Thant, U (1909–74): Burmese secretary general of the UN who took over after the death of Hammarskjöld in September 1961 and remained in office until 1972; successfully managed the financial-constitutional (article 19) crisis of 1964; presided over the formation of UNFICYP and, controversially, the withdrawal of UNEF from Egypt before the Six Day War in 1967.

Truman, Harry S. (1884–1972): US (Democratic) president from 1945 to 1953; succeeded Roosevelt at key stage in the formation of the UN; in office during the Korean War.

Tshombe, Moise (1919–69): Leader of the Congo province of Katanga which attempted to secede (with foreign encouragement and help) from the new state; after UN-led extinction of Katangese secession, became prominent for a short time in Congolese national politics.

Waldheim, Kurt (1918–2007): Austrian secretary general of the UN 1972–82; in office during the formation of UNEF II and UNDOF in 1973–74 and of UNIFIL in 1978; his term coincided with the high point of superpower détente; later president of Austria despite controversy surrounding 'hidden' past in war-time German army.

Wilson, Woodrow (1856–1924): US Democratic president from 1912 until 1920; strong moral voice at the Versailles conference following the First World War; architect of the League of Nations and early advocate of collective security; vision not shared by US Congress which rejected US participation in the League.

Yeltsin, Boris (1931–2007): Russian president who succeeded Gorbachev at the end of 1991 at the break-up of the Soviet Union; cooperated with the west in the UN during the 1991 Gulf War; more hostile to western positions on the former Yugoslavia.

Glossary

38th parallel Line of latitude separating North and South Korea; the armistice line established following the Korean War.

Abyssinia Older name of present-day Ethiopia; invaded by Italy in 1935.

An Agenda for Peace 1992 report and recommendations by secretary general Boutros Boutros-Ghali on the challenges facing UN peace operations in the immediate post-cold war period.

ANC Congolese National Army (*Armée Nationale Congolese*) whose mutiny immediately following the country's independence in 1960 helped precipitate UN intervention.

Article 19 crisis General Assembly wrangle in 1964 following the Soviet Union's refusal to pay for peace operations and the resulting threat to its voting rights under article 19 of the UN Charter.

Atlantic Charter Anglo-American declaration of August 1941 setting out joint aspirations for the post-war international world including the creation of a new collective security system.

Balfour Declaration Affirmation in November 1917 by foreign secretary Lord Balfour that the British government was favourable to the establishment of a Jewish state in Palestine.

Bipolarity The configuration of the international system in two dominant, ideologically opposed blocs (or poles); characteristic of the cold war period.

Blackhawk Down 2001 film directed by Ridley Scott (starring Josh Hartnett and Ewan McGregor) presenting a partly fictionalised account of the 'Battle of Mogadishu' of October 1993 which led eventually to the end of UN operations in Somalia.

Camp David agreement Outcome of American-brokered talks between Israel and Egypt during 1978 and 1979 which formed the basis of a permanent peace between the two countries.

CIA United States Central Intelligence Agency.

CIS Commonwealth of Independent States formed from among the former federal republics of the Soviet Union which became independent states after its dissolution in 1991.

CNN effect The impact on public opinion of instant and graphic news coverage of foreign conflicts, which can create pressure on governments to intervene; named for the US-based Cable News Network.

Collective security The multilateral maintenance of international security (based on the United Nations or other international body) rather than by sectional actions on the part of individual states or competing military alliances.

Congo Club Group of UN officials chaired by secretary general Dag Hammarskjöld which planned and supervised the organisation's approach to the Congo crisis in 1960 and 1961; criticised by the Soviet Union and others for its supposed western bias.

Dayton Accord US-brokered agreement ending the Bosnian war following NATO's robust intervention in the form of Operation Deliberate Force in 1995.

Détente Description of the relatively cooperative superpower relationship during the late 1960s and 1970s based on their recognition of mutual interests in cooperating to manage conflict despite the background of continuing cold war.

Dual key Inter-agency arrangement in Bosnia between the United Nations and NATO which required both to agree before air operations could be mounted by NATO in support of the UN Protection Force in 1994–95.

Dumbarton Oaks Washington venue for the planning of the new United Nations by representatives of the major allied powers between August and October 1944.

Enforcement measures Military action designed to secure a predetermined outcome against an aggressor; contrasts with peacekeeping which seeks to manage conflicts rather than force a particular conclusion to them.

Enosis Aspiration of many Greek Cypriots for the formal political unification of Cyprus with Greece.

Fedayeen Irregular Arab anti-Israeli guerrilla forces.

Formosa Old name for Taiwan; island state formed by the Chinese Nationalists forced from the mainland by the Communists in 1949.

Host (state) consent Key principle of peacekeeping which asserts that the deployment of operations should only take place after the consent of all parties has been secured; the original focus on the consent of 'governments' became less relevant as peace operations were increasingly deployed in intra-state (civil) rather than inter-state (international) conflicts.

Humanitarian intervention Peace operations undertaken specifically with a humanitarian purpose; contrasted with traditional peacekeeping which was largely concerned with the management of conflict in the interests of international stability.

ICJ International Court of Justice (which sits in the Hague); one of the principal organs of the United Nations responsible for judgments in contentious cases between states and for the interpretation of the UN Charter.

I-FOR NATO Implementation Force deployed in Bosnia to implement the Dayton agreement of 1995.

Inter-governmentalism International organisation based on institutions within which states cooperate without surrendering significant parts of their national sovereignty; the UN is in most respects an inter-governmental organisation but the collective security articles of its Charter do involve some significant qualifications of sovereignty.

Interposition Traditional peacekeeping strategy involving the deployment of international forces as a physical buffer 'interposed' between hostile forces.

Intra-state Description of peace operations deployed in civil (political, ethnic, regional) conflicts within states rather than international conflicts between states.

League of Nations Global organisation formed after the First World War which was the precursor to the United Nations; became largely irrelevant in the larger currents of international relations after the mid-1930s and was formally wound up in 1946.

Mandate system League of Nations innovation whereby the colonies of the defeated powers in the First World War were 'mandated' to the victors not as acquisitions but as responsibilities to be prepared for self-determination; replaced by the UN Trusteeship system.

Maronite Christians Adherents of the Eastern Catholic Church in the Middle East; the Maronite community in Lebanon was traditionally dominant in the country's government but frequently challenged by Muslim aspirations.

MFO Multinational Force and Observers established formally in 1981 to oversee the Camp David agreement in the Sinai region between Israel and Egypt; effectively a successor to UNEF II whose mandate was terminated in 1979 after the withdrawal of Soviet support in the Security Council.

Middle powers The 'ideal' force contributors to peace operations: 'middle' in terms both of capacities and (at least during the cold war) of bloc loyalties; Sweden, Ireland, Canada and India were typical middle power peacekeepers.

Military observation Peace operations involving the monitoring and oversight of truces and ceasefires rather than large-scale force interposition.

MSC Military Staff Committee, composed of the chiefs of staff of the five permanent members of the Security Council responsible under article 47 of the UN Charter for control of military enforcement actions; never properly operational.

Mission creep Tendency for peace operations (and other military actions) to move beyond their original mandates – usually leading to deeper embroilment in a conflict – because of circumstances on the ground.

MNF US-led Multinational Force in the Beirut area of Lebanon established to deal with the upsurge of instability and violence in 1982 and 1983; operated simultaneously with but wholly independent of the UN Interim Force in southern Lebanon.

Multilateralism Commitment to collective, institutional responses to international challenges through the UN or other organisations (rather than unilateral action by individual states).

NATO North Atlantic Treaty Organization, established in 1949 as the leading element of the western alliance system in the cold war.

ONUC United Nations Operation in Congo (*Opération des Nations Unies au Congo*), deployed between July 1960 and June 1964.

Operation Deliberate Force US-led NATO enforcement operation in Bosnia against Serbian and Bosnian Serb forces in 1995; instrumental in creating conditions for the Dayton Accord.

Operation Desert Storm US-led military action in 1991 to eject Iraqi occupation forces from Kuwait; authorised by the UN Security Council under resolution 678.

Peace enforcement units Form of peace operation proposed by Boutros-Ghali in *An Agenda for Peace* (1992) which would involve limited enforcement action to ensure compliance with previously agreed settlement plans; never implemented.

Peacekeeping The traditional form of UN peace operation typically involving either military observation of ceasefires or interposition between hostile forces (or a mixture of both); based on the three key principles of consent, impartiality and use of force only in self-defence.

Plebiscite Popular vote (or referendum) often used to establish the political future of a designated territory (thus embodying the principle of self-determination).

PLO Palestine Liberation Organization formed in 1964; historically the voice of the Palestinian people ejected from their homeland by successive wars and Israeli occupations; a key actor in Lebanon during the conflicts of the 1970s.

Protocol of Sèvres Secret agreement between Britain, France and Israel to engineer the conditions for the Anglo-French invasion of Egypt following the nationalisation of the Suez Canal by President Nasser in 1956.

Six Day War Arab-Israeli war fought from 5–10 June 1967 beginning with an Egyptian attack and ending in Israeli victory.

Sovereignty Doctrine that the state (usually in the form of the government which represents it) internally holds ultimate power within its own borders and externally remains free from interference by other states and organisations in the international system.

Summary Study In full, 'The Summary Study of Experience Derived from the Establishment of the United Nations Emergency Force', produced by secretary general Dag Hammarskjöld in 1958, two years after the creation of the Suez force; the first systematic definition of UN peacekeeping.

Tehran Conference Meeting of allied leaders in November 1943 in the capital of Iran, at which early ideas for the creation of a post-war global organisation were discussed.

Troika proposal Soviet plan presented to the General Assembly in 1960 for the replacement of the office of UN secretary general by a triumvirate of western, eastern and Afro-Asian bloc representatives; the proposal failed to attract significant support.

Trusteeship UN successor to the League of Nations mandate system by which colonial territories of the defeated countries of both world wars were held 'in trust' by UN member states responsible for preparing them for self-determination; overseen by the Trusteeship Council, a principal organ of the United Nations.

UNAVEM The first United Nations Angola Verification Mission, formed in January 1989 to supervise the withdrawal of Cuban forces from Angola; mission ended successfully in May 1991.

UNAVEM II The second UN Angola Verification Mission, established in 1991 to oversee implementation of an agreement to end Angola's civil war; withdrawn in 1995 after the collapse of the peace process.

UNAVEM III A third UN Angola Verification Mission, created in 1995 and mandated to oversee a new peace process for Angola; withdrawn amidst general failure of the process in 1997.

UNDOF The UN Disengagement Observer Force deployed in the Golan Heights from June 1974 to monitor the ceasefire line between Israel and Syria following the 1973 war.

UNEF The United Nations Emergency Force, deployed after the Anglo-French invasion of Egypt in the Suez crisis of 1956; generally regarded as the first UN peace 'force'; UNEF was withdrawn at Egypt's insistence on the eve of the Six Day War in 1967.

UNEF II The second UN Emergency Force, deployed in Sinai between Israeli and Egyptian forces after the 1973 war; withdrawn in 1979 following Soviet refusal to renew its Security Council mandate.

UNFICYP The UN Force in Cyprus, established in March 1964 in response to inter-communal violence between Greek and Turkish Cypriots; one of the longest enduring UN peace operations.

UNGOMAP The UN Good Offices Mission in Afghanistan and Pakistan, formed in May 1988 following the withdrawal of Soviet forces from Afghanistan; mission ended in March 1990.

Unified Command US-dominated general staff overseeing the anti-communist (nominally 'UN') forces in the Korean War between 1950 and 1953.

UNIFIL The UN Interim Force in Lebanon, formed in March 1978 and deployed in the south of the country adjacent to the border with Israel.

UNIKOM The UN Iraq-Kuwait Observer Mission, established in April 1991 in the aftermath of Operation Desert Storm; mandated to monitor the security of the border between Kuwait and Iraq; withdrawn in 2003 following US-led invasion of Iraq.

UNIPOM The UN India-Pakistan Observer Mission; a relatively short-duration operation established in September 1965 following conflict between the two countries; withdrawn after six months.

UNITAF The (non-UN) American Unified Task Force in Somalia, which operated between December 1992 and May 1993.

Uniting for Peace Process introduced by a western bloc General Assembly resolution in 1950 by which discussion of security issues deadlocked in the Security Council could be transferred to the General Assembly (where there was a western majority and no veto).

Universality The principle of open and comprehensive membership of international organisations (a general characteristic of the United Nations).

UNMOGIP The UN Military Observer Group in India and Pakistan, established in 1949 after the end of the war between the two countries over the disputed territory of Kashmir.

UNOGIL The UN Observation Group in Lebanon, formed in June 1958 to monitor the Lebanese-Syrian border following complaints by the Lebanese government of Syrian infiltration; withdrawn after a six-month deployment.

UNOSOM The UN Operation in Somalia, established in April 1992 to oversee and protect the distribution of food aid; superseded in December 1992 by the US Unified Task Force and then re-established as UNOSOM II; finally withdrawn in March 1995.

UNPROFOR The United Nations Protection Force in the former Yugoslavia; deployed originally in Croatia in May 1992 and subsequently in Bosnia (and for a time in Macedonia); dissolved in December 1995 after Operation Deliberate Force in Bosnia.

UNSCOP The United Nations Special Committee on Palestine, formed in May 1947 to consider the future of territory after Britain announced its intention to relinquish its mandate over the territory.

UNSF The UN Security Force for West New Guinea (Irian Jaya), responsible for the territory's internal and external security during the period of the United Nations transitional administration pending the transfer to Indonesian sovereignty in 1963.

UNTAC The UN Transitional Authority in Cambodia, created in March 1992 to provide a temporary administration for Cambodia and to organise elections to determine its future government; mission ended in September 1993.

UNTAG The UN Transition Assistance Group for Namibia, formed in April 1989 to oversee elections and the independence of Namibia from a disputed South African Trusteeship; mission successfully completed in March 1990.

UNTEA The United Nations Temporary Executive Authority in West New Guinea (Irian Jaya), formed in October 1962 to provide a transitional administration for the territory after its removal from Dutch sovereignty pending its transfer to Indonesia in April 1963.

UNTSO The UN Truce Supervision Organization for Palestine, formed in June 1948 after the Arab-Israeli war which followed the declaration of the state of Israel; the first and longest enduring UN peace operation.

UNYOM The UN Yemen Observation Mission, established to monitor the border between Yemen and Saudi Arabia in July 1963 and to oversee the agreed disengagement of Egypt and Saudi Arabia from the Yemen civil war; mission completed in September 1964.

Veto The power held by each of the five permanent members in the Security Council individually to prevent action being taken on any non-procedural matter with which it might disagree regardless of the position of the majority.

Warsaw Pact East European Soviet bloc military alliance formed in 1955 to confront NATO; it was dissolved in 1991.

Yalta Conference Meeting of allied leaders at the Russian Black Sea resort in February 1945 where, among other post-war plans, the proposals which emerged from the Dumbarton Oaks discussions for the new United Nations were discussed at head of government level.

Yom Kippur War Arab-Israeli war of October 1973, named for the Jewish religious festival of the Day of Atonement.

Zionism Ideology promoting Jewish nationhood within a territorial state (Israel); movement founded in 1897 by Theodor Herzl.

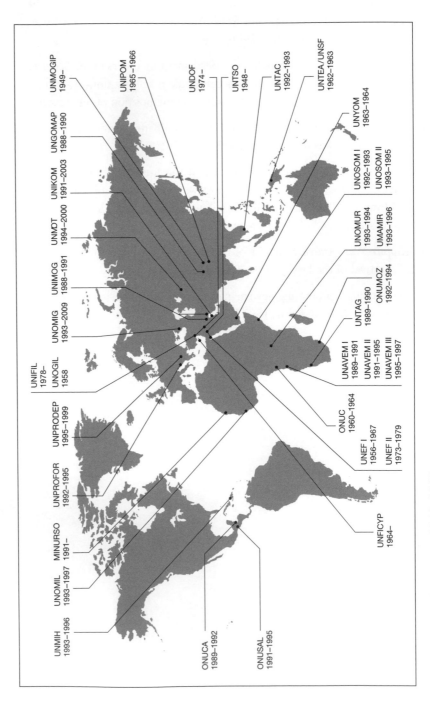

Map UN Peace Operations, 1948–1995

Part 1

BACKGROUND

1

The 'Failure' of the League of Nations and the Beginnings of the UN

U sually, historical comparisons between the **League of Nations** and its successor the United Nations emphasise the contrasts between the two organisations rather than their similarities. This tendency is understandable when viewed from the perspective of 1945 when the UN came into existence. The view of the League held almost universally at that time was one of weakness and failure. The League had not performed the function that it had been created for: the prevention of a second world war. Now, in the aftermath of that conflict a new organisation was being forged to succeed where its discredited predecessor had failed. This negative attitude towards the League was natural, but it was also driven by political calculation. In order to sell the idea that the League of Nations should actually *have* a successor to a sceptical, war-hardened world, the United Nations had to be presented as something new and historically unique. It could not be allowed to carry the taint of failure that too close an association with the League would have placed on it. Yet in reality the League of Nations provided the blueprint for the new institution. The organisation of the United Nations, its broad political structure and of course its fundamental raison d'être within the international system, were all essentially drawn from the template of the League.

League of Nations: Global organisation formed after the First World War which was the precursor to the United Nations; became largely irrelevant in the larger currents of international relations after the mid-1930s and was formally wound up in 1946.

A NEW WORLD ORDER?

The League of Nations, whatever its ultimate fate, had been a profoundly innovative, indeed radical, departure in international relations. This was a reality which only came to be properly acknowledged at the end of the century of the League's creation; for succeeding decades after its disappearance the League continued to be regarded in the popular memory as a by-word for empty rhetoric and diplomatic hypocrisy. Despite this, it eventually provided

Inter-governmentalism: International organisation based on institutions within which states cooperate without surrendering significant parts of their national sovereignty; the UN is in most respects an inter-governmental organisation but the collective security articles of its Charter do involve some significant qualifications of sovereignty.

the model not just for the United Nations but for almost all of the major **inter-governmental organisations** whose growth was to be such a prominent feature of twentieth-century international politics. The League's basic organisation, consisting of an 'executive' Council of the big powers and a 'parliamentary' Assembly of all its country members, both managed by an international civil service, was in essence a bold transposition of national constitutional arrangements to the international environment. Like many seminal ideas, of course, this approach to the organisation of international institutions has come with familiarity to be seen as something obvious and routine. But in the context of a post-First World War world where there was a natural tendency to look backwards to the pre-catastrophic certainties of the nineteenth century, the League had set out a truly novel manifesto for a new international politics. The fundamental logic of the League's structure, once the shock of the new had been absorbed, became so deeply embedded in the political consciousness that any successor organisation would naturally tend towards the same basic architecture.

The purposes of the League, or at any rate those envisioned by its American planners and their supporters, were also startlingly new. Responsibility for the security and defence of all member countries was, as far as possible, to be removed from those countries themselves. The fears and insecurities which had generated the arms races and aggressive alliances that evidently lay at the root of the catastrophe of 1914–18 would be alleviated by the construction of nothing less than a new world order. National security and therefore international security would now, the visionaries of the League proposed, become the collective responsibility of the world community working through the structures of its new global organisation. Again, this new **'multilateralism'** was both strikingly bold and somehow obvious, and the basic idea outlived the League itself.

Multilateralism: Commitment to collective, institutional responses to international challenges through the UN or other organisations (rather than unilateral ones by individual states).

MANAGING POST-WAR ADJUSTMENT

During its first decade the League of Nations made a hugely valuable contribution to the management of the post-war international system. Throughout the 1920s it provided mediation in border disputes at various times between such neighbours as Finland and Sweden, Yugoslavia and Albania, and Hungary and Czechoslovakia. It had also initiated what were in effect international peacekeeping operations.

One such force was deployed in the disputed Saar territory between France and Germany. In the aftermath of the war the predominantly German Saar was removed from Berlin's control and 'internationalised' pending a future act of self-determination. This arrangement was itself an achievement for the new international values represented by the League. Initially, France had intended simply to annex the heavily industrialised territory as both punishment and reparation for the damage inflicted on its own industry by Germany's war of aggression. Instead the French government was prevailed on to accept the economic benefits of the Saar but with the territory placed under a League of Nations administration until 1935. At that date permanent sovereignty over the Saar would be determined by a popular vote of its inhabitants. This was in effect the precursor to the UN's provision of temporary administrations in such disputed regions as West New Guinea in the 1960s and East Timor and Kosovo at the end of the century. Intriguingly, though, in the case of the Saar the 'final status' options included the future government of the territory by the League of Nations itself in perpetuity, a radical choice never offered subsequently by the UN. In the event, the 1935 plebiscite – policed by a peacekeeping force composed of British, Italian, Dutch and Swedish troops – resulted in an overwhelming vote for a return to German sovereignty [**Doc. 1, p. 116**]. Almost one in ten of those voting, however, would have preferred to remain 'citizens of the League'.

An international administration and security force also controlled Danzig (the modern-day Polish city of Gdansk) which was removed from German administration and declared a Free City, a status it maintained until it was forcibly reintegrated into Germany by the Nazis in 1939. Elsewhere the League or other multinational agencies supervised and policed with international forces **plebiscites** designed to settle fraught post-war border issues on the basis of national self-determination (Walters, 1960).

Plebiscite: Popular vote (or referendum) often used to establish the political future of a designated territory (thus embodying the principle of self-determination).

The League also brought a new moral sensibility to the question of colonialism when, instead of the colonies of the defeated powers in 1918 simply being transferred to the victors, they were made the responsibility of the League which '**mandated**' their administration and responsibility for their eventual self-determination to appropriate member states. This system was not without its difficulties, and in a number of cases led directly or indirectly to United Nations peace operations later in the century. This was the case in South West Africa (Namibia) which was mandated from Germany to South Africa, and in both Rwanda and Burundi which passed from German imperial rule to be mandated to Belgium. Nevertheless, the new system (inherited as 'Trusteeship' by the United Nations), marked a clear advance on the post-conflict values of the past.

Mandate system: League of Nations innovation whereby the colonies of the defeated powers in the First World War were 'mandated' to the victors not as acquisitions but as responsibilities to be prepared for self-determination; replaced by the UN Trusteeship system.

THE BREAKDOWN OF THE COLLECTIVE IDEA

Despite these bright prospects, a fatal fissure quickly opened at the heart of the new institutionalism. The United States – in the person of President

Woodrow Wilson – had driven the planning of the League as part of the Versailles Treaty negotiations. Ultimately, however, the US Congress refused to ratify American membership. As a result, responsibility for the direction of the new organisation passed from those whose vision had guided its construction to the more diplomatically conservative Europeans like Britain and France.

In time it became clear that the nature of international relations in the 1920s would be in sharp contrast with that of the following decade. By the early 1930s the international environment had begun to change. The 'post-traumatic' calm of the immediate post-war years now gave way to a new instability. Territorial and ideological revisionism on the part of states which for various reasons rejected the post-Versailles status quo challenged the principles of the League whose origins were inextricably tied to that settlement. It seemed that the 'successes' of the League in soothing the international system of the 1920s perhaps had more to do with the character of the system than the actions of the organisation. And, it must be said, the League itself, or at least its leading members, bore some responsibility for the emerging tensions within the system. Not only had the League of Nations been born of the Versailles treaty, which had become an object of hate for some and disappointment for others, but in its first years it had denied membership to a number of key powers, most importantly Germany and the Soviet Union. Their eventual admission could not eradicate their sense of exclusion from the system which the League sought to manage.

In this deteriorating climate the capacity of the League to translate collective security from theory into a practical tool of international relations was now put under severe test. It was a test that the organisation – or more correctly the dominant powers within it – ultimately failed. The League's **collective security** plans were outlined in article 10 of its Covenant, its basic constitutional document [**Doc. 2, p. 117**]. Joint measures were to be taken to preserve the territorial integrity of member states 'against external aggression'. Tellingly, however, the actual means by which this was to be done were left vague. The League Council had the responsibility to advise on methods to be employed when necessary. The strongest instrument of enforcement which members were supposedly required to apply on the 'direction' of the Council was economic sanctions. The Council might 'recommend' military action but members were under no obligation to comply, according to article 16 of the Covenant (Archer, 2001). On the rare occasions when economic sanctions were implemented by the League, many members simply declined to participate in them. In this way Italy's aggression against the African state of **Abyssinia** (Ethiopia) in 1935 went effectively unpunished. A range of sanctions were agreed belatedly, but they were disregarded by member states which for political or economic reasons did not wish to confront the Fascist regime in Rome (Armstrong, 1982).

Collective security: The multilateral maintenance of international security (based on the United Nations or other international body) rather than by sectional actions on the part of individual states or competing military alliances.

Abyssinia: Older name of present-day Ethiopia; invaded by Italy in 1935.

Earlier, in 1931, the League had been even more passive in the face of Japan's naked aggression against China in Manchuria. For the big European powers in the League Council this conflict in a remote part of Asia was simply not important enough in the calculation of their own national interests to justify any robust action.

In both these cases the central weakness in the concept of collective security in a world of sovereign states was exposed. However high-minded and idealistic the original conception of the League presented by Woodrow Wilson at Versailles, older and harsher realities governed the behaviour of the states which now dominated the institution (Williams, 2007). States like Britain and France had traditionally conducted their foreign policies on the basis of narrowly defined national interests. The calculation of these interests rarely went beyond considerations of the physical security of the state and its economic well-being (Bennett, 1994). In this sense the international system of the 1930s was, as international relations theorists would put it, highly 'realist' and 'state-centric'. The more generous vision of national interest as best safeguarded by a just and secure global system – the conception at the heart of collective security thinking – simply did not progress during the life of the League.

In the dangerous international conditions of the 1930s the League retreated from the ethical high ground it originally tried to occupy. The terrible fate of China at the hands of Japan featured hardly at all when the powers which made up the League Council made their separate calculations of national interests. Italy, being closer to the centre of a still predominantly European international system, was more problematic – but not much. As a result, in the second half of the 1930s as the world stumbled towards another general war the League became marginalised in global politics. National security remained, as it always had been, the responsibility of the individual state and its alliance partners. Once again a cycle of world conflict would precede a new attempt to reconstruct international security on a multilateral basis. As we have emphasised already, though, the new project did not begin from a *tabula rasa*. The model and the experience of the League was there to be drawn on, even if those utilising it for the new body were reluctant to acknowledge the fact (Northedge, 1985).

THE WAR-TIME ORIGINS OF THE UN

The concept of the United Nations developed by stages after the United States entered the war following the Japanese attack on Pearl Harbor in December 1941. Already, however, in the previous August, a meeting had

Atlantic Charter: Anglo-American declaration of August 1941 setting out joint aspirations for the post-war international system including the creation of a new collective security system.

taken place between President Franklin Roosevelt and the British prime minister Winston Churchill on board a warship off the Canadian coast. Here the idea of a collective security system for the future post-war world was resurrected. The **'Atlantic Charter'** which came out of this insisted that 'all nations of the world, for realistic as well as spiritual reasons must come to the abandonment of the use of force'. To this end it spoke of 'the establishment of a . . . permanent system of general security' [**Doc. 3, p. 118**]. By the beginning of 1942 the twenty-six anti-Axis powers had committed themselves to this declaration and themselves had begun to describe their military alliance as the 'United Nations'. During the remaining years of the war, ideas for the new peacetime organisation developed. They did so, of course, under difficult circumstances. The overriding priority for the allied states was the pursuit of victory. This was the obvious prerequisite for the implementation of any post-war blueprint. Too much speculation on the nature of the new international system would have been a misuse of political energies. Additionally, Roosevelt, who like his First World War predecessor Woodrow Wilson a quarter of a century earlier was at the forefront of thinking about the new institution, was anxious to avoid a repeat of the isolationist backlash at home which had kept America out of the League by focusing too much on its proposed successor.

Nevertheless, ideas began to emerge. Roosevelt's initial thoughts centred on the management of security by the big allied powers after the end of the war: the United States, Britain, the Soviet Union and, perhaps, China (Boyd, 1971). This would be made possible by the generalised disarmament of the other states in the international system which would entrust their national security to the collective. Churchill had a more sceptical European perspective on the feasibility of this plan. He was less confident that the necessary cooperation could be achieved and maintained among the big powers. From a more traditionalist perspective he was convinced that states would continue to define their national interests in the same narrow way that had undermined the League's attempts to implement the earlier plan for collective security. Certainly, the participation of the United States in the new arrangements would be a positive advance, but it would be unlikely to alter the basic approach to national foreign and defence policies ingrained in the attitudes of national leaders across the world. More positively, Churchill was also anxious to avoid the marginalisation of the smaller and middle-sized powers which was implicit in Roosevelt's proposals. The prime minister's evolving view was that a strong European dimension should be central to post-war Britain's external relations. As the two world wars had both begun in the centre of Europe, it was not perhaps blindly Eurocentric to seek global solutions in a new system of relationships there. He therefore favoured a new organisation with a predominantly regional rather than global structure. The new body should, ideally, be one in which loose worldwide arrangements acted as an umbrella for strong local inter-governmental institutions (Luard, 1982).

At the **Tehran Conference** in November 1943, when the tide of the war was clearly turning in the allies' favour, the Soviet Union was brought fully into the debate. Joseph Stalin was now presented with the American idea of the 'four policemen' (the major allied powers) acting as a global coalition able to deploy military **enforcement** powers at the head of a world assembly. The Soviet leader, like Churchill, was wary of the concentration of power in so few hands and initially shared the British preference for a strong regional dimension to any new security regime. However, Roosevelt warned Stalin that American public opinion, still touched by isolationist attitudes, might resist US involvement in security commitments determined by local states in other parts of the world. If post-war security was to be regionalised, there was no obvious reason why the United States should concern itself with anything other than the western hemisphere. While such a system might enhance Soviet power in eastern Europe, it would tend to limit it at the global level. In view of this, Stalin moved towards the more centralised conception of the Americans (Luard, 1982).

As in the case of the League, it was the Americans who provided the leadership in the construction of the new organisation and who pursued their conception in the face of the doubts of the other key actors. On both occasions this situation was no more than a reflection of the balance of power among the respective sets of allies. There was, of course, an irony in this: while the collective security project was designed to remove dangerous national power competition from international relations, it was reliant on the dominating national power of its architect.

It was therefore largely an American plan that was put forward for discussion when allied representatives met to deal with the specifics of the proposed post-war organisation in 1944. Meetings took place in between August and October at **Dumbarton Oaks**, an estate on the edge of Washington, DC. The key negotiators here were the Soviet and British ambassadors to the United States, Andrei Gromyko and Sir Alexander Cadogan, and the American assistant secretary of state, Edward Stettinius, who acted as chairman. Representatives of Nationalist China were also present, though they had a lesser role in the planning process. The objective of the Dumbarton Oaks talks was to reach a consensus among the four powers and then to present the wider anti-Axis alliance with an agreed blueprint for a new global organisation.

Agreement was quickly reached on the basic institutional form of the United Nations, largely because the outline model of the League was available to be exploited. There would be a Security Council of eleven members.

Tehran Conference: Meeting of allied leaders in November 1943 in the capital of Iran, at which early ideas for the creation of a post-war global organisation were discussed.

Enforcement measures: Military action designed to secure a predetermined outcome against an aggressor; contrasts with peacekeeping which seeks to manage conflicts rather than force a particular conclusion to them.

Dumbarton Oaks: Washington venue for the planning of the new United Nations by representatives of the major allied powers between August and October 1944.

(This would be increased to fifteen in the early 1960s to reflect the changing size and membership profile of the organisation.) The Council was to consist of the five big anti-Axis powers: the United States, the Soviet Union, Britain, China and France (now admitted as a 'fifth policeman'). These would be permanent members, each with the power of **veto** over Council decisions. In addition, six (later ten) non-permanent members without power of veto would be appointed on a rolling basis from the various regions of the world represented in the organisation. All member states of the United Nations would have a seat in its General Assembly. Both the Council and the Assembly would be serviced by a secretariat of international civil servants.

A nascent system of collective security was also approved at Dumbarton Oaks. In outline this envisaged that disputes between members would in the first instance be settled by processes of negotiation, mediation and conciliation. If these failed, the problem would become the responsibility of the Security Council which would propose its own settlement terms. If this also failed, then the Council could apply economic and other sanctions against the 'aggressor' with, in the last resort, recourse to military action. All members of the United Nations would be required to commit themselves legally to undertake such action on the instructions of the Security Council. The Council would itself be advised on the strategic and operational aspects of these measures by a **Military Staff Committee (MSC)** made up of senior military representatives of its permanent members (Russell, 1958; Yoder, 1997).

Despite these quite wide areas of agreement among the powers, significant points remained at issue after Dumbarton Oaks. Some of these were essentially technical. There was dispute over the extent of the commitments to be required of UN members and the nature of preparedness and earmarking of national forces for UN service. More ominously, a profoundly important issue remained unresolved: the voting system in both General Assembly and Security Council which, by extension, touched on the question of national representation.

In the case of the General Assembly the Soviet Union sought representation for all sixteen of the constituent republics of the USSR. This would obviously have been a misuse of the concept of 'sovereign equality' on which the UN was to be based – the principle that all independent states in the international system should have equal rights and powers. The Soviet Union itself and not its component parts was obviously the sovereign power. But the Soviet position was in some ways understandable. Although the world had yet to fall into the extremes of cold war **bipolarity** between capitalist west and communist east, the rudiments of this global cleavage had been present virtually since the Bolshevik revolution of 1917. It did not take any great prescience on the part of Stalin and his representatives at Dumbarton

Veto: The power held by each of the five permanent members in the Security Council individually to prevent action being taken on any non-procedural matter with which it might disagree regardless of the position of the majority.

MSC: Military Staff Committee, composed of the chiefs of staff of the five permanent members of the Security Council responsible under article 47 of the UN Charter for control of military enforcement actions; never properly operational.

Bipolarity: The configuration of the international system in two dominant, ideologically opposed blocs (or poles); characteristic of the cold war period.

Oaks to see east–west divisions as a major feature of the post-war inter-national system – and therefore of the new global organisation. The Soviet Union was at this time at an obvious disadvantage in terms of simple political arithmetic. The Dumbarton Oaks talks were held before the creation of the so-called 'people's democracies' of eastern Europe and therefore of a com-munist bloc. The process of European decolonisation which would change completely the composition of the United Nations was even further in the future. From the perspective of 1944–45 the USSR would obviously be ideologically isolated in the new organisation.

The idea of sovereign equality had a certain moral force in an international system where states were personified as strong and weak individuals. In a world based on collectively secured 'justice', the rights of the weak should obviously be as great as those of the strong. But the international system was in reality composed of sovereign states with hugely divergent sizes of population and territory. In this real world, sovereign equality could be seen as fundamentally inequitable and 'undemocratic'. Why should El Salvador (another founding member of the UN), say, have the same powers in the global polity as the incomparably larger and more populous Soviet Union?

Beyond the General Assembly there were divisions between the Soviet Union and the other big powers over the Security Council veto and the pre-rogatives of the five permanent members. There was no disagreement on the basic principle. The delegates at Dumbarton Oaks all agreed that the veto was a necessary mechanism. It was in fact an advance on the voting system operated at the League where unanimity was required before any action could be taken. The proposed UN veto was for the permanent members of the Security Council alone and would only be activated by a negative vote, not merely by abstention or absence. The difficulty which emerged at the talks was over restrictions on its use. The British and Americans argued that the veto should not be available to a permanent member when its own behaviour was the subject of discussion. Aware of its political vulnerability in an overwhelmingly western institution, the Soviet Union insisted that the veto should be an absolute right of the great powers in all Security Council business other than the purely procedural.

Agreement on both these issues eluded the ambassadors at Dumbarton Oaks. Subsequent attempts to settle them in the remaining months of 1944 were also unsuccessful. The search for an agreement now passed up to the allied foreign ministers and heads of government rather than their ambassa-dors in Washington. In February 1945 a summit meeting took place at **Yalta** on Russia's Black Sea coast. Soviet foreign minister Molotov gave some ground by accepting a restriction on the veto where 'peaceful settlement' rather than collective security 'enforcement' in issues affecting permanent members were under discussion. With rather more difficulty, a compromise

Yalta Conference: Meet-ing of allied leaders at the Russian Black Sea resort in February 1945 where, among other post-war plans, the proposals which emerged from the Dumbarton Oaks discus-sions for the new United Nations were discussed at head of government level.

was also reached on the issue of General Assembly representation. It was accepted that the Soviet Union could have two further seats for the republics of Ukraine and Byelorussia. Roosevelt agreed to this only reluctantly, having at one point threatened to demand separate representation for all of the (then) forty-eight states of the United States if Stalin did not give way (Yoder, 1997). These relatively small western concessions, though, were seen as a reasonable price for progress towards the inauguration of the new organisation.

This advance on the plans for the new organisation was reflected in the final communiqué of the Yalta meeting. Roosevelt, Stalin and Churchill pronounced that:

> We are resolved upon the earliest possible establishment with our allies of a general international organisation to maintain peace and security. We believe that this is essential, both to prevent aggression and to remove the political, economic, and social causes of war through the close and continuing collaboration of all peace-loving peoples.
>
> The foundations were laid at Dumbarton Oaks. On the important question of voting procedure, however, agreement was not there reached. The present Conference has been able to resolve this difficulty.
>
> We have agreed that a conference of United Nations should be called to meet at San Francisco in the United States on April 25, 1945, to prepare the charter of such an organisation, along the lines proposed in the informal conversations at Dumbarton Oaks.
>
> (Yalta Agreement)

In preparation for the San Francisco meeting the presumed permanent members of the new Security Council sent out invitations to fifty states who were then anti-Axis belligerents. This was a status acquired only very recently by some of these countries as the outcome of the war had become plain and the prizes that went with being on the winning side beckoned. This swelled the ranks of founding members, bolstering the ideal of **universality** of membership. The absence of such universality, it will be recalled, had been a major defect of the League system.

Universality: The principle of open and comprehensive membership of international organisations (a general characteristic of the United Nations).

Franklin Roosevelt died ten days before the opening of the San Francisco session but his successor, Harry Truman, immediately affirmed his own and America's commitment to the new organisation. This was greeted with relief among many who had feared a repeat of the isolationist spasm which ended American participation at a similar stage in the development of the League. In reality, however, the prevailing trend in American politics in 1944 and 1945 was if anything anti-isolationist. Roosevelt's Democratic administration had already worked to ensure a bipartisan approach with the Republicans in

Congress. Edward Stettinius, who had led the Dumbarton Oaks talks, had been elevated to the post of secretary of state. He now cooperated closely with the Republicans' principal foreign affairs adviser (and future secretary of state), John Foster Dulles, who accepted an invitation to participate in the San Francisco conference (Divine, 1974).

Driven on by the 'big five', whose authority was enhanced by their leadership of the huge military alliance poised on the verge of final victory in mid-1945, the San Francisco conference (held in the city's Opera House) confirmed the decisions taken at Dumbarton Oaks and Yalta. The structure of the institution, familiar in outline to most of the participants from their League experience, was accepted without dissent. Similarly, the basic constitution of the United Nations, its Charter, was adopted with only marginal and technical modifications. Having been ratified by the five governments of the permanent members, the Charter came into force and the United Nations became a political and legal reality on 24 October 1945.

Part 2

ANALYSIS

2

The United Nations and the Dilemmas of Collective Security

There was no ambiguity about the fundamental aims and intentions of the United Nations set out in the Charter. Its preamble committed the organisation to 'save succeeding generations from the scourge of war which twice in our lifetime has brought untold sorrow to mankind' and the first article which followed set out the more specific purposes involved in this. The United Nations was, according to article 1 of the Charter, to:

> maintain international peace and security, and to that end: to take effective collective measures for the prevention and removal of threats to the peace, and for the suppression of acts of aggression or other breaches of the peace, and to bring about by peaceful means, and in conformity with the principles of justice and international law, adjustment or settlement of international disputes or situations which might lead to a breach of the peace.
> (United Nations Charter, 1945)

The mechanism for this was to be a new comprehensive system of global security. The lesson which had been taken from the League experience appeared to be not that collective security was an unattainable ideal in a world of sovereign states, but rather that with the right legal and political structures it could be made to work. The legal-constitutional basis of the UN's collective security ambitions was to be found in Chapter VII of the Charter which dealt with 'Action with Respect to Threats to the Peace, Breaches of the Peace, and Acts of Aggression' [**Doc. 4(i), pp. 119–21**].

INTERNATIONAL SECURITY AND THE UN CHARTER

The plans laid out here were essentially those which had been agreed in outline at Dumbarton Oaks and which have already been briefly described.

Article 39, the first of the twelve articles of Chapter VII, gave the Security Council the responsibility of determining when a situation required collective security action and what form that action should take. It thus underlined from the outset the predominance of the Security Council in the process. The following three articles, 40, 41 and 42, set out an escalating series of measures available to the Council in enforcing its collective will. Article 40 dealt with 'provisional measures' on which the Council might insist before moving to enforcement action. The nature of these measures was not elucidated, but they were generally assumed to include demands for ceasefires and troop withdrawals. Article 41 dealt with more substantive but still non-military enforcement action of the type which had been tried unsuccessfully by the League. These were explicitly identified as economic sanctions, transport and communications boycotts and the interruption of diplomatic relations, though other steps might also be taken as long as they fell short of military action.

The military options were dealt with in article 42 which empowered the Security Council to take such action as necessary 'to restore international peace and security' using the 'air, sea or land forces of Members of the United Nations'. It is at this point that the similarities between the collective security concepts of the League and the United Nations begin to disappear. The divergence became even more obvious in article 43. This outlined the nature and extent of members' commitments. These made not only acceptance of, but active participation in, military measures a legal obligation on all Charter signatories when the Security Council should require it. On its call, UN members would be required to provide forces and facilities to enforce decisions against aggressor states. These forces were to be provided under the terms of prior agreements, but such arrangements would be essentially technical and could not be a means of evading participation.

The undertakings envisaged under article 43, if they had ever been properly implemented, would have been just one step short of the creation of a UN standing army. The idea of a permanent international force had been discussed early in the planning process (it had at one stage been proposed for the League as well). But there was general agreement among the big powers in 1944 and 1945 that such an arrangement would raise too many practical and political difficulties. Issues of financing, training and equipment as well as larger questions over national sovereignty would probably have been insurmountable. Under article 43 many of the advantages of a permanent force would have been gained with none of these disadvantages. The details of the Military Staff Committee which was to direct the enforcement of collective security (and which had first been suggested at Dumbarton Oaks) were contained in article 47. The MSC was to be composed of the chiefs of staff of the five permanent members and had the responsibility of advising the Council on military enforcement action. It would also direct any such operations. Perched at the politically fraught apex of the collective security machinery, the MSC quickly became redundant as the cold war set in and the relationship between the chiefs of staff of the polarised power blocs became anything but cooperative.

The final part of Chapter VII, article 51, was the only one which suggested any significant limitation on the power of the Security Council. It affirmed the 'inherent right of individual or collective self-defence'. The use of the term 'inherent' was significant in that it implied a natural order in which in the last resort states must have recourse to their own resources for their own defence. Despite the sweeping ambitions of the new organisation to extend collective security, the Charter stopped short of insisting on *replacing* individual (or alliance) security. Even here, though, the overall dominance of the Security Council was still implicit in the suggestion in article 51 that national self-defence would only be appropriate in situations where for practical reasons the United Nations could not provide the necessary collective security, and only for so long as this was the case.

Certain limits on Security Council 'absolutism' were implied in Chapter VIII of the Charter which also touched on collective security. Articles 52–54 dealt with 'Regional Arrangements' [**Doc. 4(ii), p. 121**]. Here there was a nod to the early position of Winston Churchill who, it will be recalled, favoured a more decentralised collective security system. The legitimacy of 'regional arrangements' (in other words regional alliances and inter-governmental organisations) was recognised by article 52 which acknowledged their potential role in the maintenance of security. Article 53, however, made it clear that such a role was ultimately dependent on the Security Council (Goodrich *et al.*, 1969). It was the Council which would, 'where appropriate, utilize such regional arrangements or agencies for enforcement action *under its authority*' (emphasis added). Lip service having been paid to local alliances and organisations, the over-arching authority of the Security Council was then reasserted (Russell, 1958). The regional dimension to the security functions of the UN would be little thought about during the cold war. Later, though, the issue would be revived as post-cold war peacekeeping demands threatened to outstrip the supply available from the centre and as increasingly assertive regional organisations sought legitimacy from the UN for their own actions.

The central importance bestowed by the Charter on the permanent members of the Security Council to the exclusion of other parts of the organisation, evident in Chapters VII and VIII, harks back to Roosevelt's war-time conception of the big powers as 'policemen'. The intention was to prevent the general institutional paralysis caused by the diffusion of authority in the League. In the UN the Security Council would decide whether a situation warranted action. It – and it alone – would then determine the measures necessary to deal with the situation up to and including the use of force. Any such force would be directed by the military commanders of the permanent members. If regional organisations were to have a role it would be one initiated and closely supervised by the Security Council.

While the United States saw the primacy of the Security Council as a precondition for the operation of successful collective security, the Soviet Union supported it for different reasons. Conscious as always of its potential weakness in a forum based on the one-member–one-vote principle of sovereign equality, Moscow sought to retain the most important powers of the organisation within the ambit of the veto [**Doc. 5, pp. 123–4**]. This coincidence of position on the part of the two emerging superpowers did not, however, alter an inescapable fact: that collective security was simply incompatible with the basic structure of international relations in a bipolar system.

Needless to say, the dominance of the Security Council, while acceptable to its permanent members, was not welcomed by all in the new organisation. At San Francisco, Australia and New Zealand argued for a larger role to be given to the General Assembly in security matters than the Dumbarton Oaks plan had envisaged. A proposal by New Zealand that the Assembly should approve any enforcement action planned by the Council was quickly rejected by the big powers, however. This would have threatened a repeat of the League's tendency to allow the decision-making process to run into the sands of vague and inconclusive debate. However, the proposal of Australia and New Zealand that the General Assembly should have broad rights of discussion and the power itself to refer issues to the Security Council was accepted and embodied in articles 10 and 11 of the Charter (Luard, 1982). It was also agreed that the General Assembly should receive annual reports from the Security Council, a procedure which gave the impression if not the reality of democratic accountability. Beyond these limited concessions to the General Assembly, the Security Council also agreed to a special prerogative for the secretary general. By the terms of article 99 of the Charter he could 'bring to the attention of the Security Council any matter which in his opinion may threaten the maintenance of international peace and security' (United Nations Charter, 1945). Although accepted as unexceptional by the big powers in 1945, this would have real significance to peacekeeping as the cold war deepened (Gordenker, 1967).

Viewed from the glacial bipolarity into which the post-war international system settled after 1945, the UN's emphasis on big power cooperation seemed wholly misplaced. How, it seemed reasonable to ask in the depths of the cold war, could there be any hope of a viable collective security system emerging from a divided Security Council whose decisions could be vetoed by any one of its permanent members? In an ideologically divided international system virtually all international crises would be seen through the opposing lenses of the two global poles of power. In such a situation there could be no objective evaluation of disputes, let alone agreement on the identity of aggressors. Tellingly, perhaps, nowhere in the Charter was the concept of 'aggression' defined or any guidance given as to how it might be applied to states in conflict situations. Without agreement on the basic terms, there could be no enforcement, and without enforcement, meaningful collective security was impossible.

In 1945, however, perceptions and predictions were determined by factors specific to the time. It is possible that the speed of the development of the east–west conflict after the end of the war led later observers to underestimate in hindsight the strength of the war-time impetus for cooperation among the allies. Having spent hard years locked in a struggle with a common enemy, it was a quite reasonable assumption at the immediate end of the fighting that the allies would maintain a unified sense of purpose in the post-war period. This certainly must have played a part in Roosevelt's early ideas of international security based on the disarmament of all but a small group of powerful 'policemen' states. Previous conflicts, after all, had produced effective post-war regulatory mechanisms among allies with little in common in their domestic politics. The European 'concert' system following the end of the Napoleonic Wars in 1815 was an example of this, where naturally competitive big powers like Britain, Austria and Prussia agreed to manage their differences in the higher interest of overall stability. More recently, it was at least arguable that, but for the withdrawal of the United States, the League might have proved a reasonably effective system of international security founded on the continuation of war-time relationships. It must be borne in mind too that the technical-strategic factors that eventually characterised the cold war – the mutual possession by the opposing blocks of nuclear weapons – did not exist while the Charter was being drafted. The bombing of Hiroshima and Nagasaki came four months after the San Francisco conference (and a full year after Dumbarton Oaks). The Soviet Union did not acquire any atomic weapons until 1949 and it was 1955 before both superpowers set out on their deterrent relationship based on roughly balanced nuclear capacities. In short, in 1945, while east–west tensions might be seen on the horizon, there was no reason to suppose that all international disputes would tend to merge into one conflict built around the unique military capability of two superpowers.

There was perhaps another, more immediate, element in the calculations which drove UN planners to build the organisation on cooperative foundations which could not be sustained in the long term. A major concern of the western allies during 1944 and 1945 was obviously the war against Japan in Asia and the Pacific. Although the advanced planning for the United Nations took place in the triumphalism surrounding an increasingly inevitable victory in Europe, the situation in the other theatre of war was much less settled. The United States was therefore anxious to persuade the Soviet Union (at this still pre-atomic point) to commit its forces in Asia (Boyd, 1971). Public exploration of the potential for future east–west conflict would certainly not have helped in this. The positive realities of war-time unity rather than negative predictions of possible post-war futures were therefore uppermost in the calculations of the White House and US state department.

It is also possible to approach the question from an entirely different direction. The apparently misplaced emphasis of the UN's architects on post-war cooperation could have signalled an awareness of the likelihood of future schisms rather than a wilful denial of them. The concentration of authority in the Security Council and the power of veto might be seen as an acknowledgement of likely big power division, not unity. The location of any significant security powers in the General Assembly where the Soviet Union would automatically be out-voted would merely ensure Moscow's departure from the whole system. Likewise, safeguarding the national interests of the five permanent members through the power of veto, far from weakening collective security, was the minimum price to be paid for even the slimmest chance of its ever being implemented.

THE ONSET OF THE COLD WAR AND THE END OF THE ILLUSION: KOREA

The flaws at the heart of the UN's collective security plans became more and more obvious as the cold war deepened. In some early crises in east–west relations, like that over Berlin in 1947–48, the UN had only a marginal role rather than the central position that the Charter seemed to promise. In general, the position of the organisation in the deteriorating conditions of the international system in the late 1940s was a difficult one. As international relations came to be determined by bipolar loyalties, the idea of a truly disinterested global body seemed increasingly untenable. Assured of the support of the large majority of the membership, the United States (underlining the fears of the Soviet Union) came increasingly to regard the UN as an arm of its foreign policy. 'The United Nations', wrote one of Truman's aides in 1948, 'is a God-given vehicle through which the United States can build up a community of powers . . . to resist Soviet aggression and maintain our historic interests' (Armstrong, 1982: 59). In such a climate, a critical reckoning for the new system could not be long delayed. This came in 1950 in Korea.

The western allies had committed themselves early in the Second World War to the independence of Korea. Japan had annexed Korea in 1910, though it had long had the role of informal colony of its powerful neighbour. At the end of hostilities the northern part of the Korean peninsula had been occupied by Soviet troops after Moscow's belated declaration of war against Japan in August 1945. In the meantime American forces had moved into the south. In key respects Korea was Asia's equivalent of post-war Germany: a country ideologically and geo-strategically divided as a result of the distribution of particular allied forces at the end of hostilities. In this situation the original objective of a unified, independent Korea would not be easily realised (Gaddis, 1997). In the five years following the Japanese surrender, both Moscow and Washington nurtured their own client regimes in their respective areas of influence in Korea. Each side supplied and trained the military forces of 'its' part of the partitioned nation. In the north the Communist Party under Kim Il Sung became dominant while in the south an election in May 1948 was won by the right-wing nationalist leader Syngman Rhee. To complicate matters, North and South claimed sovereignty over the other as the route to unification and were doing so in increasingly belligerent terms. A peaceful process of union between equal partners became simply impossible. The United Nations General Assembly, with its in-built western majority, recognised the regime in the South, though the Soviet veto in the Security Council prevented the formal admission of this 'Korea' to the organisation.

The first months of 1950 had seen increasing and increasingly serious incidents at the **38th parallel** (line of latitude) which marked the border dividing the country. Then, on 25 June, the UN was informed that a full-scale invasion of the South by the North was taking place (Whelan, 1990).

38th parallel: Line of latitude separating North and South Korea; the armistice line established following the Korean War.

The Security Council's initial discussion of the Korean crisis was held under unusual circumstances which would affect the UN's entire approach to the issue. The Soviet delegation was absent from the meeting, pursuing a boycott of the Security Council begun at the beginning of the year. The point at issue was the seating of **Formosa** (later known as Taiwan), whence the remnants of the Nationalist forces in China's civil war had fled after the final victory of the Communists in 1949. This off-shore fragment of 'Chinese' sovereignty, thanks to western domination of the General Assembly, maintained its status as sole legitimate representative of the country in the UN. The Soviet Union had no opportunity to veto this arrangement (as it could the admission of South Korea) because it was the Nationalists who had formed the government of China when the Charter was signed in 1945. It was this regime that had taken its seat as a permanent 'great power' member of the Security Council. Regardless of the subsequent defeat and forced exile of the Nationalists from mainland China, that was and remained the status

Formosa: Old name for Taiwan; island state formed by the Chinese Nationalists forced from the mainland by the Communists in 1949.

quo in the UN and any attempt to change it would have been vetoed by the United States. It was a status quo which persisted until the rapprochement between Washington and Beijing in 1971, at which point the United States changed its policy and the Nationalist delegation was unceremoniously excluded from the United Nations and replaced in the General Assembly and the Security Council by the Communist regime of the mainland. In June 1950, however, the absence of the Soviet delegation meant that the Security Council was in effect a wholly western entity and its decisions were not subject to Soviet veto (Hastings, 1988).

Whatever the short-term advantage the west might take of this situation, it carried a clear lesson about the futility of collective security in an ideologically polarised world. Exploiting their momentary advantage, the Americans tabled a Security Council resolution demanding the withdrawal of the northern forces back to the 38th parallel. The North, now embarked on an apparently unstoppable offensive, unsurprisingly showed no inclination to comply with this western appeal. A further Security Council resolution 'recommended' that UN members should assist South Korea against the northern invasion. In the meantime the United States responded unilaterally as well as multilaterally through the UN. The US Seventh Fleet was deployed between mainland China and Korea, and a series of naval bombardments and air strikes was mounted against the invading forces. On 30 June American troops from the garrison forces still in Japan were fully committed in support of the South Korean army. This move was justified by Washington under the terms of article 51 of the Charter which, as we have seen, permitted 'collective self-defence' outside of the collective security system of the Charter **[Doc. 4(i), pp. 119–21]**. Britain, Australia and New Zealand also signalled their intention to intervene.

The western powers continued to use the freedom of initiative in the Security Council given to them because of the Soviet absence. An Anglo-French resolution in July called on all anti-North Korean forces to put themselves behind a **'Unified Command'** which would fight under the UN flag. The United States was to provide the commander for this force who would 'report' to the Security Council. General Douglas MacArthur, a celebrated war-time commander and the senior American general in Asia at this time, was consequently appointed to lead a 'UN force'. By the end of the following year this would consist of contingents from seventeen states.

The deep flaws in this action as 'collective security' within the UN's original framework were immediately evident. The Unified Command was not established under the terms of article 43 of the Charter which placed military obligations on all Charter signatories. It was, instead, an American initiative legitimised by a Security Council resolution (Yoder, 1997). MacArthur remained an American officer answerable first of all to Washington and was

Unified Command: US-dominated general staff overseeing the anti-communist (nominally 'UN') forces in the Korean War between 1950 and 1953.

required only to 'inform' the Security Council of developments. The multilateral character of the undertaking was certainly not enhanced by the fact that MacArthur himself was clearly politically ambitious and an ideological anti-communist hawk. The composition of the force, moreover, was plainly western. It included nine of the thirteen members of the **North Atlantic Treaty Organization (NATO)**, the western military alliance which had been formed in 1949. In addition, three 'white dominions' of the Commonwealth – Canada, Australia and New Zealand – were included. The remaining participants were drawn from American allies in Asia and Latin America. Yet even these resolutely western states made up only a minority of the Unified Command; two-thirds of the force was American [**Doc. 6, p. 124**].

NATO: North Atlantic Treaty Organization, established in 1949 as the leading element of the western alliance system in the cold war.

This western alliance had a number of early successes. The North Korean advance seemed unstoppable throughout July and August and eventually reached the far south of the country. But in mid-September MacArthur launched a bold counter-attack by sea and air on Inchon, behind the North Korean line of advance close to the South Korean capital, Seoul. Taken by surprise and now deprived of the strategic initiative, the northern forces fell back and within a few weeks were close to the 38th parallel once again. But within this military success lay political danger for the west. Would the 'UN force' maintain its momentum by crossing into the North? From a supposedly impartial United Nations perspective this could hardly be acceptable. It would involve a UN counter-invasion of North Korea and would transform a limited enforcement action into a war of conquest. Against this, however, were ranged strategic and political considerations. From a strictly military viewpoint, it was argued, the initiative ought to be pursued and the offensive momentum of the Unified Command maintained. In the American view, of course, an occupation of the North by the 'UN' could prepare the way for the unification to which the organisation was committed on terms favourable to the west.

Circumstances in the Security Council had in the meantime changed significantly. In August 1950 the Soviet Union not only resumed its participation but became (by routine rotation) president of the Council. The free ride the west had enjoyed, with decision-making unencumbered by the prospect of veto, now shuddered to a halt. If the American-led force were to cross into the North it would not now do so with the cover of a new Security Council resolution. The crossing of the 38th parallel (to which MacArthur was enthusiastically committed) would have to be justified on the basis of existing Security Council mandates and the support of the pro-western (and veto-less) General Assembly. Consequently, a western-sponsored resolution in the Assembly was passed in October 1950 calling for the UN to establish stability 'throughout Korea'. This was taken by the US-led force as sufficient legitimisation for its northward offensive and it now followed its South

Korean allies into North Korea. Already, at the beginning of that month, Beijing had warned that an invasion of the north would be viewed by China as a threat to its own security. Excluded from the UN by the alliance between its nationalist enemies and their American allies, China had even less interest than the Soviet Union in the peculiarities of UN politics and regarded it simply as a foreign enemy. Now, as the western forces crossed the 38th parallel, a large force of Chinese 'volunteers' crossed the Yalu River which separates Manchuria from North Korea. Within weeks the fortunes of the war had been reversed once again and the western forces were in headlong retreat from the North before the advancing Chinese.

If the claim of the original military campaign to be a collective security action was weak, the American-led invasion of the North damaged it further. The renewed presence of the Soviet delegation in the Security Council drove home the fundamental inconsistencies between the US-led Unified Command and consensus-based UN action. If UN legitimisation of the war were to be maintained, it was now essential that the Security Council be moved from centre-stage. But while the General Assembly had established its right (in articles 10 and 11 of the Charter) to *discuss* issues of international security and to make recommendations to the Security Council, it had no power to authorise enforcement. America now sought to resolve this problem to its own benefit by subverting one of the fundamental principles at the heart of the original planning of the organisation. Power was now given to the General Assembly in direct contradiction to the collective security mechanisms so delicately constructed at Dumbarton Oaks and Yalta. In effect, the United States arranged to move the constitutional goal-posts to serve its military and political objectives. If the Charter gave the Soviet Union the power to block enforcement with its veto, the Charter must be circumvented. On 3 November 1950 the General Assembly passed the

Uniting for Peace: Process introduced by a western bloc General Assembly resolution in 1950, by which discussion of security issues deadlocked in the Security Council could be transferred to the General Assembly (where there was a western majority and no veto).

so-called **Uniting for Peace** resolution by a large majority (White, 1997). Effectively an informal amendment to the Charter which reversed its original intent, this permitted the transfer of decisions over security measures to the General Assembly when action by the Security Council was blocked by a veto [**Doc. 7, pp. 124–5**].

A draft Security Council resolution which called on China to withdraw from Korea which had been vetoed by the Soviet Union was now passed by the Assembly. Admittedly, the significance of this was somewhat blunted by the absence of any threat of military enforcement in the resolution. In reality the UN was not now in a position to make military threats or to carry them out. Events were taking their own course on the ground and the Security Council could do little to help or hinder them. Yet the circumstances from which the Uniting for Peace resolution emerged – and the institutional balance of power which ensured its adoption – were a further measure of the obstacles to effective collective security which were inherent in the international system of the early 1950s.

At the beginning of 1951 the military situation in Korea had switched yet again. The Chinese–North Korean forces which had once more swept into the South were checked and pushed back across the 38th parallel. Despite the availability of the Uniting for Peace process, the UN was now more cautious. MacArthur, whose actions and pronouncements had been causing growing unease among America's allies and in the White House itself, was summarily dismissed in April 1951 after making some loose and politically reckless comments about the possibility of using nuclear weapons against North Korea and China. Henceforward western interests were redefined and the war aim of enforced unification quietly dropped. In this way the UN was able to adopt a posture more appropriate to a global security organisation. It now appeared less compromised by the pursuit of western foreign policy objectives. After long and fraught negotiations, an armistice was signed in July 1953. No final settlement based on unification or any other arrangement was reached, however (Calvocoressi, 2008; Rees, 1967).

For the United Nations the Korean War simply provided the empirical proof of what its members and officials had already accepted: that collective security and cold war were incompatible. It also pointed up an inescapable secondary truth, which was that this situation could not be changed simply by the expedient of altering constitutional rules. The collective security system developed at Dumbarton Oaks and fine-tuned at Yalta was probably the best available at that historical conjuncture. If it could not work in its original form then a wholly different role would have to be found for the UN. Otherwise the organisation could have no positive impact on the maintenance of international security. The United Nations would face the prospect of following its predecessor into obscurity.

3

The (Re)discovery of Peacekeeping

While the Korean crisis may have tested the UN's will and capacity to implement its ambition for collective security by enforcement, the organisation had already deployed military personnel on a much more modest level to deal with the aftermath of two regional wars in the latter part of the 1940s. Military observers were used in Palestine between the new state of Israel and its Arab neighbours, and also in south Asia between the two states which emerged from the partitioning of the former jewel in the crown of the British empire: India and Pakistan. At the time, these were not characterised as '**peacekeeping**' operations because the activity had yet to be described in that way; they were simply ad hoc responses to particular crises. But their principal functions (monitoring ceasefires and facilitating peacemaking) and the methods by which these were carried out (the use of multinational forces with the consent of the antagonists) located them firmly within what was to become the established list of UN 'peace operations'.

Peacekeeping: The traditional form of UN peace operation typically involving either military observation of ceasefires or interposition between hostile forces (or a mixture of both); based on the three key principles of consent, impartiality and use of force only in self-defence.

Here as in so many aspects of the UN's formation and early activities, the experience of the League of Nations was of real, though generally unacknowledged, significance. In January 1948 the General Assembly's Palestine Commission, then struggling to construct a plan for the territory, produced a document pointing to the possibility of what would later fit the description of a peacekeeping operation. This paper was designed 'to show that immediately after the First World War and again in 1935 it was possible to create international forces with a view toward assisting international commissions to fulfil the functions assigned to them' [**Doc. 8, pp. 125–6**]. The document gave thumbnail sketches of the various allied powers and League of Nations undertakings (including that in the Saar territory). What might be described as a trans-institutional memory was evidently present in other words, and United Nations officials were clearly aware of the possibilities of military intervention in forms other than of coercive enforcement.

TRUCE SUPERVISION IN PALESTINE

The **United Nations Truce Supervision Organization (UNTSO)** in Palestine was established in June 1948 in the aftermath of fighting between Israel and the surrounding Arab states (sometimes referred to as the 'first' Arab-Israeli war). The territory of Palestine had become the responsibility of the League of Nations after the dissolution of the Ottoman empire at the end of the First World War. As an 'A' class mandate, the territory was assumed to be close to the necessary conditions for self-determination. While this might have been considered an advantage for all parties, Britain, the mandated power, faced unique problems in Palestine at the end of the Second World War. Although the vast majority of Palestine's population was Muslim Arab, it was also the location of a Jewish homeland, the creation of which Britain itself had committed to in the **Balfour Declaration** of 1917. The objective had been pursued in the inter-war years by an increasingly influential international **Zionist movement**. The situation changed fundamentally after 1945, however, when thousands of European Jews who had survived the Holocaust sought refuge in the biblical 'promised land' of Palestine. Continued British occupation along with the attempt of the colonial authorities to control the influx of Jewish migrants were met by a vicious terrorist campaign by Zionist extremists. Exhausted after the war and facing its own more direct colonial problems (most obviously at this time in India), Britain became increasingly anxious to find an escape from its mandate responsibilities and enlisted the UN to this end (Ovendale, 1989).

The intractable nature of relationships between the ethnic and religious communities in Palestine made an agreed negotiated solution impossible to achieve, however. Even consensus among allies was elusive. Britain found itself at odds with the United States which, in part for domestic political reasons, tended to favour the Jewish claims for a separate homeland. Britain, on the other hand, was concerned at the equity of such a partition for the Arab population. Interestingly, the crisis did not initially have any obvious cold war dimension. The Soviet Union's position was in fact close to that of the United States in favouring partition and the creation of a separate Jewish state. As the mainstream Zionist leadership at this time was predominantly left-wing, Moscow saw an opportunity to develop a new alliance in the Middle East. The USSR, however, remained deeply suspicious of any exercise of power or authority by the United Nations, aware as it was of its own weakness within what was still a predominantly western organisation.

A **UN Special Committee on Palestine (UNSCOP)** made urgent efforts during 1947 but failed to produce a viable plan for the territory. Britain, now despairing of its untenable position as the responsible power, announced its

UNTSO: The UN Truce Supervision Organization for Palestine, formed in June 1948 after the Arab-Israeli war which followed the declaration of the state of Israel; the first and longest enduring UN peace operation.

Balfour Declaration: Affirmation in November 1917 by foreign secretary Lord Balfour that the British government was favourable to the establishment of a Jewish state in Palestine.

Zionism: Ideology promoting Jewish nationhood within a territorial state (Israel); movement founded in 1897 by Theodor Herzl.

UNSCOP: The United Nations Special Committee on Palestine, formed in May 1947 to consider the future of Palestine after Britain announced its intention to relinquish its mandate over the territory.

intention to relinquish the mandate in May 1948 at which time responsibility would pass fully to the United Nations as the legal successor to the League of Nations. Fighting in Palestine escalated as the date approached. On 14 May 1948, on the very eve of the end of the mandate, the Jewish leadership declared the creation of the state of Israel and regional war erupted.

The Security Council responded with the appointment of a mediator, the Swedish diplomat Count Folke Bernadotte, who managed to negotiate a fragile ceasefire. Using the powers delegated to him by the Security Council, Bernadotte established the Truce Supervision Organization. This was composed initially of military personnel from his native Sweden along with contingents from the United States, Belgium and France. Although Bernadotte's authority was strengthened by a Security Council resolution threatening enforcement action under Chapter VII of the Charter, his impact on the chaotic conditions in the region was limited. Then, in September 1948 Bernadotte, along with a senior French member of UNTSO, was assassinated by Jewish extremists [**Doc. 9, pp. 126–7**]. Yet despite this setback, UNTSO grew both in numbers (to nearly 600 in its early days) and in the range of national contributors (Louis *et al.*, 1986). Uniquely during the cold war, both American and Soviet officers would eventually serve in it. As political conditions in the Middle East changed, the mandate of UNTSO was adjusted. The first UN peace operation, the Truce Supervision Organization was still in place in the second decade of the twenty-first century.

MILITARY OBSERVATION IN KASHMIR

The situation in Kashmir between India and Pakistan in the late 1940s was similar to that in Palestine. Both crises were rooted in issues of territorial division, emergent statehood and competing cultural and religious identities. Both, in short, were crises of decolonisation.

Dissolving the Indian empire confronted the post-war British Labour government with particular problems. The ethnic mix of British 'India' and the potential for conflict between religious groups led to the decision not just to decolonise but to do so simultaneously with a partitioning of the vast territory. The most significant international border which was created as a result was that between predominantly Hindu India to the south and Muslim Pakistan to the north. Inevitably, this process of division was imperfect in terms of the alignment between territorial statehood and ethnic-religious identity. In consequence, decolonisation and partition were accompanied by horrific levels of violence along some parts of the frontier as populations were 'adjusted' and exchanged.

The territory of Kashmir presented a unique set of difficulties in this regard. As well as the directly ruled provinces of British India, there were almost 600 so-called 'princely states' which had a considerable level of autonomy under their local feudal rulers – with the British authorities having a supervisory role. The status of these entities was fiercely argued over in the independence negotiations and it was determined that they should be absorbed into the new state in which they were located. Those in the frontier region were themselves to decide whether to go with India or with Pakistan. In effect, of course, this 'self-determination' was really the determination of the ruler himself. At the date of independence, 15 August 1947, the Hindu ruler of predominantly Muslim Kashmir had failed to make a choice. Soon, internal discontent in Kashmir brought an irregular, but government-supported, invasion by Muslims from Pakistan. In response, the ruler called on India for help and in due course opted to integrate Kashmir into India. A full-scale war ensued with India and Pakistan accusing each other of engineering the conflict and thus committing an act of aggression under the terms of the UN Charter.

The Security Council avoided any judgement on these claims: a necessary prerequisite for the deployment of a peacekeeping mission. Instead the UN helped to negotiate a ceasefire to take effect from 1 January 1949 and deployed monitors to supervise it. This **Military Observer Group in India and Pakistan (UNMOGIP)** was located on both sides of the ceasefire line between India and Pakistan. The major part of Kashmir, however, remained in India in line with its ruler's decision and despite its majority Muslim population. This continued to be a major point of friction between India and Pakistan over the coming decades and into the twenty-first century. Like its immediate predecessor, UNTSO in Palestine, UNMOGIP remains in place today, though it has been a much smaller undertaking, with a strength rarely exceeding a hundred observers at any time (Wainhouse *et al.*, 1966).

UNMOGIP: The UN Military Observer Group in India and Pakistan, established in 1949 after the end of the war between the two countries over the disputed territory of Kashmir.

The difficult relationship between India and Pakistan brought another UN intervention in 1965–66, this time to supervise the disengagement of forces following the outbreak of another round of large-scale fighting. This **United Nations India-Pakistan Observer Mission (UNIPOM)** operated in parallel with UNMOGIP and in coordination with it. This was located in another sensitive area of the border, that between what was then West Pakistan (a few years later to become the new state of Bangladesh) which was physically separated from the larger East Pakistan by Indian territory.

UNIPOM: The UN India-Pakistan Observer Mission; a relatively short-duration operation established in September 1965 following conflict between the two countries; withdrawn after six months.

Once again, the UN had intervened in a regional crisis at one remove from the centre of cold war competition but still with the potential to be being drawn into it if left unattended. Like UNTSO, the Observation Group in India and Pakistan and later UNIPOM were brought into being to deal with local crises which had much larger international implications. The Truce

Supervision Organization oversaw a crisis point in a broader confrontation between the states of the Middle East region as a whole. The Kashmir conflict, and then that over West Pakistan, had similar ramifications. As well as being located on the border between two powerful and mutually hostile regional states (both of which in due course would acquire nuclear weapons), these crises had their epicentre close to borders with the Soviet Union and China, both of which were prepared to project their power in the region. In this sense, therefore, the UN's commitment of forces, however modest, served a preventive peacekeeping role going far beyond the ethnic and religious conflicts on the ground.

Both Palestine and the India–Pakistan frontier illustrated the double purpose of UN peace missions at this time. The two dominating circum-stances in world politics in the second half of the twentieth century were the superpower polarisation of the cold war on one hand and the fundamental reordering of the international system brought about by decolonisation on the other. Frequently they became tangled with each other and it was the principal function of UN military intervention between the 1940s and the end of the 1980s to manage the consequences of this and ameliorate the threats to international peace that they generated.

THE UN'S FIRST PEACEKEEPING 'FORCE': SUEZ

In April 1953 the UN's first secretary general, the Norwegian Trygve Lie, was succeeded by another Scandinavian, the Swedish diplomat Dag Hammarskjöld. Initially at least, Hammarskjöld seemed to bring a more neutral and 'institution-oriented' approach to his office than his predecessor. Although originally a politician of the centre left, accusations from the Soviet bloc of Lie's pro-western sympathies had mounted during his six years in office (Archer, 2001). His position was not helped by his oversight of the UN's 'pro-western' role in Korea. In contrast, Hammarskjöld's loyalty appeared to be to the organisation first rather than to any national or bloc interests within it. Hammarskjöld's task was to develop the UN in the difficult post-Korea phase as an impartial instrument of what he described as 'preventive diplomacy'.

Interposition: Traditional peacekeeping strategy involving the deployment of international forces as a physical buffer 'inter-posed' between hostile forces.

The first aim of the organisation in this view should be to intervene actively in conflicts or potential conflicts *before* the question of a collective security response arose. His evident political detachment, combined with a cerebral approach to the problems of international politics, provided an initial impetus to the emergence of **'interposition'** (or 'buffer') peacekeeping as an alternative to the enforcement of collective security originally envisaged in Chapter VII of the Charter. In hindsight, of course, it is easy to see this function as a natural extension of the type of **military observation** in which the UN had already been involved in Palestine and Kashmir. The second necessary element in the epiphany – or more correctly evolution – of the peacekeeping project was an actual crisis in which theory could be catalysed into practice. This presented itself in 1956 with the conflict surrounding Egypt's nationalisation of the Suez Canal and the military reaction which it provoked from Britain, France and Israel.

Military observation: Peace operations involving the monitoring and oversight of truces and ceasefires rather than large-scale force interposition.

After the end of the 1948 war in the Middle East, the fundamental conflicts of the region were still unresolved. Throughout the early 1950s tensions between Israel and its neighbours remained high. The Armistice Agreement which had followed the end of the first Arab-Israeli war had become more and more fragile. Egypt, despite Security Council protests, denied Israeli shipping access to the Suez Canal. It also took no steps to prevent Arab guerrilla (*fedayeen*) incursions across its frontiers with Israel in the Sinai desert and the Gaza Strip. By the beginning of 1956 the situation, particularly on the Israeli-Egyptian border, had become so bad that Hammarskjöld himself spent several weeks in the region at the request of the Security Council, actively engaged in his preventive diplomacy. He did not, however, meet with any obvious success in this.

Fedayeen: Irregular Arab anti-Israeli guerrilla forces.

Quite apart from its relations with Israel, Egypt faced other difficulties, both domestic and diplomatic, which affected its international behaviour. Under the presidency of Gammal Abdel Nasser who had taken power in 1954 following an earlier military coup against the monarchy, Egypt pursued a distinctly nationalistic set of political objectives which had interrelated internal and external aspects. Domestically, Nasser sought to modernise and industrialise what he and his supporters regarded as a backward-looking and tradition-bound country which in the past had too readily accepted external interference. Internationally, he put himself forward as the natural leader of the Arab movement as a whole, in particular the coalition of states confronting Israel. The long-term objective of his regional foreign policy was the forging of a progressive, secular pan-Arab alliance which could form the basis of a 'united Arab republic'.

One large-scale project in particular formed a central part of his development project for Egypt and for the projection of his modernising vision throughout the Arab world. This was the creation of the colossal Aswan Dam on the Nile, which was designed to provide irrigation and hydroelectric power for the entire Nile delta where the mass of the Egyptian population was concentrated. The Aswan project was originally to be funded by an international consortium led by the United States and involving the World Bank. In July 1956, however, Washington suddenly announced its withdrawal from the scheme after becoming concerned at Nasser's political and military flirtation with the Soviet Union (Thomas, 1967). At the diplomatic level this was simply a marker of his determination to pull Egypt away from its earlier close relationship with the 'imperialist' west. It was also, however, a function of a developing arms race in the region. France had secretly agreed in 1954 to supply Israel with fighter jets. In response Egypt had also tried to buy advanced weapons from the west and, having been rebuffed, turned to the Soviet bloc.

The decision of the administration of President Eisenhower (which had succeeded that of Harry Truman in the presidential elections of 1952) to withhold support from the Aswan scheme was a reprisal for this (Louis and Owen, 1989). Eisenhower's secretary of state, John Foster Dulles, was the driving force of the west's policy of 'containment' at this time. According to this, any threat of an expansion of Soviet influence into new areas such as the Arab world had to be robustly resisted. Faced with the loss of a central component of his modernisation programme and resentful at the west's apparent exploitation of the project in pursuit of cold war ends, Nasser now made a characteristically dramatic gesture: the Suez Canal was nationalised. The Canal had originally been a French enterprise but a few years after its opening in 1869 Britain had bought a share in it and henceforward it had been the responsibility of a private Anglo-French company. It had, however, been designated an 'international waterway' open to the shipping of all nations by a treaty of 1888. The nationalisation served a number of purposes for Nasser. It was 'pay-back' against the west for what was seen in Cairo as a breach of faith. It underlined the nationalist credentials of his regime by reclaiming 'national' territory and could be represented as a bold assertion of Afro-Asian rights by one of the emerging third world's natural leaders. Finally, the revenues from the Canal might go some way to providing an alternative source of funding for the Aswan project (Kyle, 1991).

Egypt was careful to emphasise its acceptance of the 1888 agreement and its obligation to keep the Canal open to international (if not Israeli) shipping. Initially therefore it seemed as though the west might simply absorb the impact of the nationalisation. Dulles, although far from relaxed on international issues touching on the cold war, was nevertheless aware of the importance of the growing Afro-Asian bloc in international politics and sought to establish agreements on the management of the Canal while appearing to accept the fact of its change of ownership. The policy of containment might reasonably involve rebuking those states who would be Moscow's friends, but over-reaction could be counterproductive if it provoked a backlash from the postcolonial world as a whole. The crisis appeared to be receding therefore when, on 29 October 1956, Israel launched an attack on the Canal Zone. The Israeli assault, it later emerged, was part of a broader conspiracy hatched by

Britain and France following the Canal's nationalisation, acting independently of their American ally, which was not informed of the scheme. The second phase of the plan involved an ultimatum from London and Paris to 'both sides' in the fighting demanding their withdrawal from the Canal and their agreement to its 'protection' by an Anglo-French force. The fact of a formal agreement to this plan of action between Britain, France and Israel was an open secret from the outset, but it was not officially confirmed until 2006 when the UK National Archives released details of the so-called **'protocol of Sèvres'** signed by the three countries in October 1956. The ultimatum, as its authors were well aware, would be wholly unacceptable to Nasser (Shlaim, 1997). Consequently, on 31 October, the RAF began bombing Egyptian positions in the Canal Zone and troop landings followed some days later. Egypt had, in the meantime, robbed the invasion of its supposed purpose by scuttling ships to block the Canal.

Protocol of Sèvres: Secret agreement between Britain, France and Israel to engineer the conditions for the Anglo-French invasion of Egypt following the nationalisation of the Suez Canal by President Nasser in 1956.

Washington, when it became aware of the covert background to the crisis, immediately saw through the Anglo-French pretence and reacted with considerable anger. A Security Council meeting was immediately convened at America's request. Beyond its ire at being so comprehensively disregarded by its NATO allies, US indignation also derived from sound cold war calculations (Vadney, 1998). The Anglo-French adventure had exposed a basic contradiction between two cultural-historical strands in the western alliance: that between 'democrats' and 'imperialists'. The post-colonial spasm of the Suez invasion was, in American eyes, a disastrous blunder in a bipolar competition which was increasingly focused on winning the favour and support of the emerging ex-colonial world. More immediately, the Suez crisis dominated international attention at precisely the same time as Soviet tanks were crushing a popular anti-communist uprising in Hungary. What should have been an open goal for the west in the cold war propaganda game was thus turned into an own goal *by* the west. Additionally, Eisenhower resented the sense of diplomatic confusion and bungling brought by the crisis to his own (ultimately successful) campaign for re-election which was underway at the time (Verrier, 1981). In all, Suez was probably the worst intra-alliance crisis faced by the west in the five decades of the cold war.

When the Security Council met on 30 October an American draft resolution was tabled which called for an Israeli withdrawal. In a clear reference to Britain and France – which had not at that point been involved in military action – it also called on other UN members to refrain from interference in the conflict. This provoked Britain's first-ever Security Council veto, deployed to block a resolution of the United States, its own alliance leader. The irony of this took on a further dimension when, as a result of this veto, the Uniting for Peace procedure was brought into operation. This, it will be recalled, was the western manoeuvre during the Korean War which in effect moved the goalposts of the Charter rules by permitting the transfer of issues deadlocked by a veto from the Council to the Assembly. The assumption had been that this would operate to the advantage of the west against the Soviet bloc. Now it was invoked by communist but non-aligned Yugoslavia (then a non-permanent Security Council member) with support and American acquiescence in order to outflank this veto by a western power. Despite the oddness of the bedfellows involved in the process, it was a development which was probably in the interest of the western bloc as a whole. In the more diffuse setting of the General Assembly the divisions between the European and American wings of the alliance were less obvious than in the starker forum of the Council. At all events, it was in the Assembly, meeting in its first-ever Emergency Special Session in the opening three days of November 1956, that the outline of the UN's first peacekeeping force began to emerge.

The key actor at this stage was not in fact Dag Hammarskjöld but the Canadian foreign minister Lester Pearson. Pearson was deeply involved in the institutional diplomacy of the UN, in many respects setting the standard for Canada's historically close and enduring relationship with the organisation. (He had in fact been a candidate to become the first secretary general in 1945 before being rejected by Moscow as being too pro-western.) Beyond Canada's special position in the organisation, however, was the fact that it was the other North American member of the North Atlantic Alliance. It therefore had a special interest in any situation that opened a breach between Washington and the leading European members of NATO [**Doc. 10, p. 128**]. The United States, while remaining in the background, strongly encouraged these moves towards a UN-based solution. On 4 November the General Assembly passed a Canadian resolution proposing the creation of a **United Nations Emergency Force (UNEF)** to be deployed in the Canal Zone initially as a buffer between Egyptian and invading forces and then to remain as a restraining presence on the Egyptian-Israeli border area.

UNEF: The United Nations Emergency Force, deployed after the Anglo-French invasion of Egypt in the Suez crisis of 1956; generally regarded as the first UN peace 'force'; UNEF was withdrawn at Egypt's insistence on the eve of the Six Day War in 1967.

At this point Hammarskjöld brought his organisational skills to bear, quickly providing a preliminary plan for the force. Pointing up for the first time what would become a fundamental principle of cold war peacekeeping, he suggested that UNEF should not include contingents from any of the permanent members of the Security Council (Urquhart, 1973). This would have the effect of immunising the situation against infection by the larger international conflict of the cold war. His suggestion that the force commander should be the current UNTSO chief of staff, the Canadian General E.L.M. Burns – who was of course already in the region, familiar with local conditions and readily available – was therefore based on both practicality and principle (Burns and Heathcote, 1963). On 5 November the General Assembly formally authorised the establishment of the force.

A more detailed plan was presented by Hammarskjöld to the Assembly on 7 November, by which time British and French forces had occupied the strategic town of Port Said on the Canal. Further basic principles were laid down in this blueprint which would endure in peacekeeping practice long beyond the UNEF itself. The force would not be used to coerce the host state. On the contrary, Egypt's consent to the intervention of UNEF and its continuing acceptance of its presence would be a fundamental condition of the operation. UNEF would be temporary, existing only as long as was necessary to achieve the objective of the mutual disengagement of opposing forces and the stabilisation of the general situation. It would have no role in altering the political or military conditions of the region. Nor would it have any internal power in the territories in which it operated (UNEF would be located only along agreed ceasefire lines). The costs of the operation would be borne by the states contributing forces and by a special fund rather than from the regular UN budget. (The departure from this approach in later operations would prove to be extremely controversial, as we will see.) In short, it was emphatically not a collective security operation mounted formally by the UN under the terms of Chapter VII of the Charter and designed to impose and enforce a particular outcome (Pearson, 1973; Comay, 1976).

The Soviet Union, while happy to exploit the embarrassment of the NATO allies (and presumably relishing the use of the west's own Uniting for Peace procedure against it), nevertheless was concerned that the basic principle of Security Council primacy should not be compromised by the precedent of UNEF. This resistance to any diffusion of security powers beyond the Council remained a major factor in eastern bloc attitudes to peace operations throughout the cold war. Within a few years it would cause a major crisis for the organisation during the Congo venture. But in 1956 over Suez, with a powerful Afro-Asian momentum behind the proposal for the force in the General Assembly, Moscow did not demur. Britain and France would have preferred a UN operation in which their own forces had a prominent role. This would have supported the particular interpretation of UNEF they wished to advance: that the UN force was completing a necessary job they themselves had begun. But both Hammarskjöld's proposal for a force free of great power involvement and the principle of Egyptian consent completely ruled this out. Neither London nor Paris was disposed to argue the point. The intensity of the international condemnation of their attack on Egypt had taken them by surprise. Moreover, in Britain at least, the adventure had been hugely divisive domestically in a way that no foreign or defence policy issue would be again until the invasion of Iraq in 2003. The crisis led directly to the resignation of the prime minister, Anthony Eden, just a few months later in January 1957 and split the governing Conservative party. The arrangement on offer from the United Nations provided Britain and France with as good a face-saving formula as they could reasonably hope for. Even if the decision-making process had remained within the Security Council rather than being assumed by the General Assembly, it is unlikely that they would have used their veto against the deployment of the force.

For his part, Nasser was quick to appreciate, and then exploit, the power that the 'host state consent' principle offered to him (Luard, 1989). He had considerable leeway to shape both the functions and the composition of the force. UNEF's primary task, therefore, was understood to be the supervision of an Anglo-French-Israeli withdrawal. The nationalities of the contributing forces were also influenced by Cairo. In all there were twenty-four offers of contingents of which ten were initially accepted by Hammarskjöld. These all came from middle-range powers: Brazil, Canada, Colombia, Denmark, Finland, India, Indonesia, Norway, Sweden and Yugoslavia.

Meanwhile, Nasser's evident (if conditional) cooperation with the UN contrasted sharply with the grudging reaction of Israel. There, the government of prime minister David Ben-Gurion refused UNEF consent to operate on the Israeli side of the joint border (Verrier, 1981). The Suez affair of 1956 represented a further stage in a continuous deterioration in Israel's relations with the UN and its military interventions which had begun in the 1940s. This would continue for the next half century and beyond.

The first elements of UNEF arrived in the Canal Zone on 15 November 1956, barely two weeks after the crisis erupted, and within three months had reached its maximum operational strength of 6000. The British and French invading forces had finally withdrawn just before Christmas 1956. The process of Israeli disengagement was slower but gradually progress was made here too.

UNEF remained in place until May 1967 when Egypt, exercising its right to withdraw its consent to the force's presence, brought the operation to an end (Harbottle, 1971). Arab-Israeli tension had once again been increasing and the protagonists were preparing for what was to be the **Six Day War**. UNEF had in fact been running down for some time prior to 1967 as its main objectives were successively achieved. Secretary general U Thant's compliance with the Egyptian instruction to withdraw the force nevertheless generated much controversy [**Doc. 11, pp. 129–30**]. It was clear at the time that UNEF was being removed as a preliminary to the Egyptian attack on Israel that triggered the 1967 war. To end a peace operation at such a time was seen by some as a betrayal of the entire peacekeeping project. In reality, though, the secretary general had no real option but to respect the fundamental principle of host state consent to the presence of the peace force. Later, he revealed that Israel had rejected his plea to change its original position and allow UNEF to be deployed temporarily on its side of the border to permit a UN presence to remain. Both sides in the Six Day War, therefore, appeared resigned to and prepared for the conflict.

Six Day War: Arab-Israeli war fought from 5–10 June 1967 beginning with an Egyptian attack and ending in Israeli victory.

In virtually all respects this first 'Hammarskjöldian' peacekeeping operation had been successful. It had performed the tasks assigned to it by the secretary general via the General Assembly – for this was the real order of command, whatever the formal distribution of authority among UN organs might have suggested. It had done so by relying on interposition and moral authority rather than the use of force. Crucially, the operation had been free of entanglement in any significant east–west conflict. The Middle East in the late 1950s and early 1960s had not fully emerged as the major arena of bipolar conflict it became in subsequent years. In many ways, therefore, UNEF was the model for the UN's peacekeeping function in the cold war. It dampened and contained conflict in an area in which the superpowers did not (then) perceive core national interests to be engaged. The purpose of the operation in cold war terms was to maintain this situation as far as possible.

4

Cold War Peacekeeping Conceptualised

Before moving on to explore later crises and the UN operations mounted to deal with them during the cold war years, it is important to set out more fully the concept of peacekeeping which was elaborated by Dag Hammarskjöld in the 1950s. One way of approaching this is to place the basic propositions of peacekeeping against those of the collective security planned for the United Nations at Dumbarton Oaks and Yalta in 1944 and 1945. The first point to make in this respect is that the legal basis of peacekeeping has none of the clarity of collective security which, as we have seen, was fully set out in Chapter VII of the Charter. The word 'peacekeeping' does not appear in the UN Charter. As it began essentially as a series of *ad hoc* responses to particular crises, its fundamental characteristics and 'rules' have had to be elaborated *post facto* on the basis of experience.

For those determined to find a legal 'location' for UN peace operations, Chapter VI of the Charter which deals with the 'Pacific Settlement of Disputes' is often the starting point [**Doc. 4.(iii), pp. 121–2**]. Article 34 gives the Security Council authority to 'investigate' any situation of 'international friction' while article 36 allows it to 'recommend appropriate procedures or methods of adjustment'. But nowhere is the basic philosophy of peacekeeping or its defining mechanisms touched on. Quite simply, preventive diplomacy and peacekeeping had not been envisaged when the Charter was being drafted. They emerged only when the machinery which had been placed at the centre of the UN's security aspirations was seen to be inoperable in a polarised world. Hammarskjöld acknowledged this paralysis of collective security and made the conceptual leap which permitted the UN to reinvent a viable military role for itself within the constraints of bipolarity. He himself reportedly called peacekeeping a 'Chapter 6½ activity' based on the pacific terms of Chapter VI but with the military elements of Chapter VII also present. In October 1958 he drew on the accumulated experience of two years of the Suez force to provide the General Assembly with a conceptualisation of the activity.

HAMMARSKJÖLD'S SUMMARY STUDY AND THE 'RULES' OF PEACEKEEPING

The '**Summary Study**' built on Hammarskjöld's initial reports in 1956 when the nature and character of the Suez operation was first evolving. It was as close as he was to come to providing a systematic outline of the basic peace-keeping project [**Doc. 12, pp. 130–2**]. While acknowledging that the Suez operation had a number of unique features which would not necessarily be replicated in future emergencies, he sought to identify 'certain basic principles and rules which would provide an adaptable framework for later operations which might be found necessary'. His practical purpose in this was to encourage the development of a framework of stand-by arrangements which UN planners and potential contributing states could work within.

Peacekeeping, he maintained, was not 'the type of force envisaged under Chapter VII of the Charter'. There was, therefore, no legal obligation on either the host state or potential force contributors to comply with UN plans. Host state consent must be obtained. In other words, a peace operation could not be forced on a country. National **sovereignty** remained paramount in relation to any arrangements that the UN might put in place. The United Nations itself was, after all, an inter-governmental organisation based on the principle of sovereign equality. As we have seen, when U Thant, Hammarskjöld's successor as secretary general, immediately complied with Egypt's requirement that UNEF should be withdrawn in May 1967, his decision was controversial. How could the United Nations agree to walk away, in effect facilitating the outbreak of a major international war? But this was to disregard a central tenet of peacekeeping which stood in contrast to the type of coercive collective security envisaged in Chapter VII of the Charter. Egypt had sovereignty over its territory, and the presence of a UN peace operation did not affect this basic reality. The principle of host state consent went much further than abstract notion, however. Practically, states would hardly be persuaded to agree to the presence of UN military personnel in the first place if they had no means of requiring their departure when circumstances changed. The position of states contributing personnel to peace operations was at least as important. It was one thing to volunteer contingents to operate in locations where they would be accepted, even welcomed, by the local power. But sending forces to impose a contested occupation would be an entirely different military and political prospect, one which few states would contemplate.

The principle of **host consent** was one which would be tested in future years, however. It was only properly applicable where a relatively secure state existed. In operations where the host state was itself fragile and vulnerable to collapse during the course of the mission, the situation was obviously much

Summary Study: In full, 'The Summary Study of Experience Derived from the Establishment of the United Nations Emergency Force', produced by secretary general Dag Hammarskjöld in 1958, two years after the creation of the Suez force; the first systematic definition of UN peacekeeping.

Sovereignty: Doctrine that the state (usually in the form of the government which represents it) internally holds ultimate power within its own borders and externally remains free from interference by other states and organisations in the international system.

Host (state) consent: Key principle of peacekeeping which asserts that the deployment of operations should only take place after the consent of all parties has been secured; the original focus on the consent of 'governments' became less relevant as peace operations were increasingly deployed in **intra-state** (civil) rather than inter-state (international) conflicts.

Intra-state: Description of peace operations deployed in civil (political, ethnic, regional) conflicts within states rather than international conflicts between states.

more complicated. In the future, both during and after the cold war, when the United Nations found itself involved in 'intra-state' rather than relatively straightforward inter-state conflicts, the whole issue of consent might be irresolvable. Who was to give consent, with what legitimacy and on what basis? In the 'clean' circumstances of the Middle East and even Kashmir, however, where the hostile parties were responsible established states, it was a relatively easy rule to apply.

Host state consent, Hammarskjöld insisted, should not amount to 'host state interference', however. States should have no absolute right, for example, to dictate the composition of peace forces deployed on their territory. There could be no power of veto over contributing states. Some sensitivity towards the host state's preferences might be necessary, but it was preferable that the United Nations itself should adopt general principles on the type of states which should be considered appropriate as contributors to peace operations. The Summary Study proposed that as a general rule contributions should not come from the permanent members of the Security Council nor from any other state which 'might be considered as possibly having a special interest in the situation which has called for the operation'. As we have seen, UNEF was composed of contingents from what could be described as

Middle powers: The 'ideal' force contributors to peace operations: 'middle' in terms both of capacities and (at least during the cold war) of bloc loyalties; Sweden, Ireland, Canada and India were typical middle power peacekeepers.

'middle powers' (Rosner, 1963).

Henceforward the middle power peacekeeper became a familiar player on the UN stage. 'Middle' had two connotations in the context of UN peace operations during the cold war. First it related to capability. Clearly, peace-keeping contingents had to be sufficiently well trained and equipped to carry out their mandate. But an 'excess' of military capacity on the part of a contributor could raise perceptions of threat among the protagonists in a crisis. The trick, according to Lester Pearson, was to be 'big enough to discharge with effect the responsibilities we undertake (and) not big enough for others to fear us' (Fabian, 1973: 94). The second sense of 'middle' grows out of this. The peacekeeping participant state ought to occupy as nearly as possible an ideological mid-point between the cold war blocs. This would minimise the danger, real or perceived, of exposing a crisis to the bacterium of the bipolar conflict. In fact, relatively few peacekeepers were 'neutral' in the strict, international legal sense. Only Sweden and Finland in the initial composition of UNEF and Ireland and Austria in several later operations were neutral in a formal constitutional sense. But other states, despite being formally aligned with cold war blocs, had a sufficiently respected inter-national standing to permit their participation. In this way, Canada, Denmark and Norway – although members of NATO – were acceptable in UNEF and then in several subsequent operations.

Beyond the identity of contributors, a number of operational benchmarks established by UNEF should also, in Hammarskjöld's view, be adopted as general principles. One of these was freedom of movement for the peace-keeping force within the agreed operational area. This had been a central component of the UN's status of forces agreement with Egypt. The presence of a UN force which was restricted in its operational mobility would, literally, be worse than useless. It would be unable to carry out its mandate, but its presence would still offer a veil of respectability to the actions of those constraining it.

At the same time, Hammarskjöld insisted, UN forces must not attempt to exercise authority either in competition with the host state or in joint operations with it. Such a situation would expose the UN to the danger of involvement in internal politics (which was expressly prohibited by the Charter). In this UNEF was a poor guide to future practice. In the specific circumstances of the Suez crisis, non-involvement was easily maintained. This would not be the case in future undertakings, however, and the issue of the peacekeepers' impact on local political developments would become a major problem for the conduct of a range of UN peace operations. It was to present itself in a particularly vivid and complex form in the UN's next major commitment, that in the Congo in the early 1960s (and, indeed, in the same country when UN forces returned there at the turn of the century).

This touched on another central problem of the peacekeeping concept which was broached in the Summary Study: the use of force by the UN. Hammarskjöld took it as 'understood' that peacekeeping operations 'could never include combat activity'. Contributing forces would, however, have the basic right of self-defence. It was essential that the circumstances under which this right might be exercised should be strictly defined, however, if its interpretation was not to 'blur the distinction between (peacekeeping) operations . . . and combat operations, which would require a decision under Chapter VII of the Charter'. Here too the experience of Suez was not to prove a reliable guide to the future experience of peace operations. Once again it would be the impending Congo operation which would expose the fragility of Hammarskjöld's design.

Finally, the Summary Study touched on a non-operational area of peace operations which nevertheless would be extremely controversial in the future: how they were to be paid for. Could peacekeeping – an activity not thought about when the UN was established and not clearly located within the Charter – be considered a 'routine' cost of the organisation and therefore be supported by the regular budget? For Hammarskjöld it clearly should be. As they were activities 'based on decisions of the General Assembly or Security Council', the cost of peace operations 'should be allocated in accord-ance with the normal scale of contributions'. In short, they should be an obligatory expense for all UN members. This was a point of controversy even in 1956 when UNEF was created with the general agreement of the major powers in the UN. The Soviet Union, in line with its long-standing approach to the distribution of power in the UN, argued that only the Security Council could impose costs on members. UNEF, as a product of the Uniting for Peace procedure, was a General Assembly undertaking. From a different perspective, some Arab states took the position that the behaviour of Britain, France and Israel, had 'caused' the expense of UNEF. On the principle that the aggressor should pay, the argument ran, they should be responsible for the costs of the operation. These were, though, relatively mild opening exchanges in what would develop into a full-scale crisis over authorisation and financing in later years (Bloomfield *et al.*, 1964; Higgins, 1969).

Distilling the lessons Hammarskjöld took from Suez for his Summary Study, it is possible to arrive at an irreducible trio of essential characteristics of what we might describe as 'traditional' or 'classical' peacekeeping. These have acquired an iconic status to the extent that they are sometimes described as the 'holy trinity' of peacekeeping (Bellamy and Williams, 2010: 174). They are: first, the requirement of consent; second, the principle of non-intervention in the politics of the crisis; and third, restriction on the use of force to direct self-defence.

Hammarskjöld was anxious to capitalise on the experience of Suez in order to establish the broader concept of peacekeeping and 'market' it within the UN system and beyond. But in doing so he risked building too great a superstructure on the fairly shallow foundations of the single and in some ways unrepresentative Suez experience. UNEF was born of an unusual consensus between the superpowers (even allowing for Soviet misgivings over its

Table 4.1 Key Contrasts Between Chapter VII Collective Security and Peacekeeping

	Collective Security by Enforcement	*Peacekeeping*
Trigger for UN action	Identification of aggression	Identification of a crisis
Contributing forces	Chosen and led by permanent Security Council members	Middle and small powers
Basis of participation	Legal obligation (Charter article 43)	Voluntary
Control	Security Council	Security Council or General Assembly
Relationship with protagonists	Imposed	Consensual (Host consent)
Methods	Coercive military action	Interposition and observation
Objective	Secure pre-determined outcome	Create conditions for political settlement

General Assembly authorisation). The operation had clearly defined and achievable objectives which did not drift amidst changing circumstances. The protagonists on both sides were content to accept UN intervention as providing, respectively, vindication (Egypt) or a respectable cover for disengagement (Britain and France). And, importantly, these actors were all sovereign states, well established within international society. They therefore provided reliable partners for the UN, being conscious of their international standing and the importance of protecting their national prestige. Operationally UNEF was contained within a clearly demarked zone (around the Canal) with a firmly defined purpose. It could not, therefore, easily stray into the internal affairs of the host state. At no stage did UNEF have to approach the difficult dividing line between self-defence and combat because it did not face situations where even self-defence was a consideration.

No subsequent peacekeeping operation would demonstrate these text-book characteristics. It was Hammarskjöld's error, though perhaps without benefit of hindsight an understandable one, to assume that they would. Most member states of the UN seemed content to accept the secretary general's assumptions. In consequence a potentially dangerous 'just leave it to Dag' mentality began to take hold which would complicate the ensuing and very challenging developments in peace operations (Zacher, 1969).

ARAB NATIONALISM AND THE INTERNATIONAL SYSTEM: LEBANON AND YEMEN

In the meantime, as the success of UNEF entered international political and public consciousness, high expectations of the UN became the norm. This perception was then consolidated by two further UN operations mounted in the Arab world in the late 1950s and 1960s.

The first of these was in Lebanon, deployed just as Hammarskjöld was elaborating the Summary Study. In the first half of 1958 a crisis developed in the internal politics of Lebanon which had clear international implications. It grew from a sharp deterioration of inter-ethnic relations in Lebanon's volatile patchwork of religions and cultures. The general atmosphere in the Middle East was especially unsettled at this time. In February 1958 the 'unification' of Egypt and Syria in the United Arab Republic (UAR) had been declared. This was seen in the region as the first step in the realisation of Nasser's pan-Arab vision. In response, the conservative pro-western monarchies of Jordan and Iraq themselves joined together in a federation, thus polarising the Arab Middle East. Lebanon, with its peculiar ethnic and religious texture and Maronite Christian-dominated government, remained to some extent detached from what could be seen as an intra-Muslim divide, though its natural affinities were with Jordan and Iraq. The Lebanese president, Camille Chamoun, was deeply worried at the apparent threat of a radical nationalist Muslim hegemony throughout the Middle East. Internal disorder in Lebanon in the form of protests by local Muslims was blamed by Chamoun on neighbouring Syria. In reality, much of the agitation was in protest at his own attempt to revise Lebanon's constitution to enable him to have a second term in office. The Lebanese army, as well as being quite inadequate in comparison to that of Syria, was also divided, with Muslim soldiers liable to support their co-religionists rather than the Christian-dominated government they supposedly served.

With an eye to mobilising western support for his regime, Chamoun claimed that the disturbances posed a threat to Lebanon's pro-western, anti-Arab nationalist position. In May 1958 he therefore sought the assistance of the still western-dominated UN to protect Lebanon from infiltration and what he claimed was a threat of a Syrian invasion which would expand the UAR by force of arms (Kedourie, 1992). The support of the Eisenhower administration in the United States, which seemed at the time to equate the rise of Arab nationalism with a regional communist threat, could be taken for granted. Unsurprisingly, but alarmingly, the Security Council split on the issue along cold war lines. The United States, Britain and France (the latter having held the League of Nations mandate for Lebanon after the First World War) were strongly sympathetic to Chamoun's case. The Soviet Union, for its part, gave total support to the counter-claims of the UAR. The danger of a Soviet veto in the Security Council therefore led Chamoun to dilute his original demand for a full-scale UN force to protect his borders. Instead, acting on a Swedish initiative, the Council agreed to the deployment of a military observer mission, the **Observation Group in Lebanon (UNOGIL)**.

UNOGIL: The UN Observation Group in Lebanon, formed in June 1958 to monitor the Lebanese-Syrian border following complaints by the Lebanese government of Syrian infiltration; withdrawn after a six-month deployment.

UNOGIL's activities went through two distinct phases in the seven months of its deployment between June and December 1958. During the first of these the UN military observers scoured the mountainous border area between eastern Lebanon and Syria in search of evidence of infiltration. Meanwhile, local faction fighting continued, bringing Hammarskjöld himself to the country to help broker a ceasefire. In the first week in July UNOGIL reported that it could find no evidence of systematic infiltration which, to the anger of the government, implied that the country's troubles were home-grown. This view was inadvertently confirmed when, after Chamoun announced that he would not after all seek a second term as president, the violence quickly subsided.

In the meantime, however, a new and dangerous regional element had entered the Lebanese equation, inaugurating a second phase of UNOGIL activity. In mid-July 1958 the Iraqi monarchy, which had formed the anti-Nasserist federation with Jordan the previous February in response to the creation of the UAR, was itself overthrown in a violent coup by radical nationalists. Western fears about pan-Arab militancy which had been encouraged by the formation of the UAR now deepened. The Lebanese government felt itself to be in the path of an irresistible wave of pan-Arab militancy. The Arab Middle East had become polarised in a way that reflected the larger cold war balance. Lebanon and Jordan now constituted the pro-western element in the regional system, with Egypt, Syria and Iraq, if not actively pro-Soviet, then certainly much closer to Moscow in their collective diplomacy than to Washington.

The cold war dimension was confirmed when, at Chamoun's request, a 14,000-strong force of United States marines was landed at Beirut. By this point King Hussein of Jordan had already asked for and received a British military presence (reflecting a close relationship forged in the First World War and subsequently consolidated by Britain's League of Nations mandate). Both the US and Britain claimed legal justification of their action by reference to article 51 of the UN Charter which, it will be recalled, guaranteed the right of self-defence in the context of collective security. This was the proposition used to justify American support for South Korea in 1950 and which would much later be thrown into the legal controversy surrounding the American-led invasion of Iraq in 2003. The scene was set for an east–west confrontation in the United Nations, with even a number of normally pro-western countries expressing doubts about the legality of the Anglo-American position (Higgins, 1969). UNOGIL had, after all, just reported that the political agitation in Lebanon was fundamentally domestic in origin and not the result of any physical infiltration from outside which would justify the claim of self-defence.

After several weeks of wrangling in the Security Council (and more widely in the General Assembly), during which ideas of a UNEF-style force for Lebanon and a UN military observer operation for Jordan were discussed and rejected, it was agreed simply to greatly increase the size of UNOGIL and extend its geographical range of operations. To this end, by November 1958 there were some 600 UN military personnel in Lebanon. In fact, the regional situation had been improving for some time before this. The new regime in Iraq, after an initial spasm of violence, had sought to integrate itself in the international system with declarations of its acceptance of the UN Charter and the pursuit of good relations with the west. In Lebanon itself political stability improved dramatically when the widely respected army chief, General Chehab, succeeded Chamoun as head of state in August. The US marine force was withdrawn at the end of October, leaving UNOGIL as the sole external military presence. This ended in December. UNOGIL had been deployed for a period of only months, but they were months of intense pressure during which at times the stability of the entire Middle East region weighed on the UN presence.

The danger of international conflict in the Lebanon in 1958 had been overstated by Chamoun for his own internal political reasons. But it was characteristic of the climate of the time that the United States was ready to take it seriously enough to engage in military action. In this environment the value of even an observation mission by the UN was clear. UNOGIL's prior presence appeared to constrain United States action after it had landed its forces. It helped to ensure that these American troops remained concentrated near their beachheads rather than being deployed to flashpoints where they might have provoked more problems than they solved. The UN presence also provided a cover for the withdrawal of the American forces – just as UNEF had for those of Britain and France in Suez (though in rather different circumstances) (James, 1990). UNOGIL appeared to represent, two years into the life of UNEF, another victory for preventive diplomacy and the peacekeeping method.

Five years on from the Lebanon operation a similar crisis in another part of the region brought a further UN military mission. In the Yemen a conflict between modernising Arab nationalism and a conservative royalist (and western-backed) regime led to civil war. As in Lebanon, the government in power appealed to the UN, claiming cross-border interference in internal politics. Here too the Security Council responded with military observers in a situation where local factionalism threatened to spill over into the broader arena of the cold war.

In September 1962 the Yemeni monarchy was overthrown by republican army officers influenced by the example of Egypt in the early 1950s when Nasser and his co-conspirators had removed the corrupt monarchical regime in Cairo. Like Egypt, Yemen occupied a sensitive geopolitical position with implications for the strategies of the big global actors. The country lies at the southern point of the Arab peninsula with Saudi Arabia to the north. In the early 1960s Britain still held the southern part of Yemen and its port, Aden. Britain's interests here were primarily strategic. Aden was in a sense an extension of the Suez Canal in that it was located on the Arabian coast at the point where the Red Sea enters the Indian Ocean – the outlet for shipping passing through the Canal to Asian destinations. The rest of Yemen had passed from Ottoman control to that of traditional rulers after the First World War. Unlike other former Turkish possessions in the Middle East it had not been subject to a League of Nations mandate.

The 1962 revolution, whose purpose was to replace this dynastic rule with a progressive republic, did not have a decisive outcome, however. The new republican regime was resisted by tribally loyal royalists in the country's

Plate 1 Dag Hammarskjöld, the United Nations' second secretary general (1953–61), pioneer of the organisation's use of peace operations.
UN Photo Gallery No. 60998. UN Photo/JO.

Plate 2   United Nations Truce Supervision Observers in the Middle East.
UN Photo Gallery No. 137794. UN Photo/Yutaka Nagata.

UNITED NATIONS EMERGENCY FORCE

FORCE D'URGENCE DES NATIONS UNIES

قوة الطوارى للامم المتحدة

חיל אלום לשעת חרום

No. ‗‗‗‗‗‗‗ رقم، .No

This is to certify that the bearer, whose signature appears hereon, is a member of the United Nations Emergency Force.

Le soussigné certifie que le porteur de la présente carte, dont la signature figure ci-après, est membre de la Force d'urgence des Nations Unies.

Plate 3 UNEF (Suez Canal) Identity Card.
UN Photo Gallery No. 141086. UN Photo.

Plate 4 The Congo – United Nations jet fighters (from the Swedish air force) used against secessionist forces in Katanga. UN Photo Gallery No. 72365. UN Photo.

Plate 5 Cyprus – United Nations post in the buffer zone between Greek and Turkish Cypriot Sectors. UN Photo Gallery No. 428506. UN Photo/Eskinder Debebe.

Plate 6 The Security Council votes on resolution 678 in November 1990 authorising military action (Operation Desert Storm) to remove Iraqi occupation forces from Kuwait.

UN Photo Gallery No. 31700. UN Photo/Milton Grant.

Plate 7 Aftermath of Israeli landmine explosion in the Sinai Desert in 1974 in which two Finnish peacekeepers died.
UN Photo Gallery No. 312326. UN Photo/Yutaka Nagata.

Plate 8 Voter registration by UNTAG for Namibia's 1989 independence poll.
UN Photo Gallery No. 144137. UN Photo/Milton Grant.

vast inhospitable hinterland. In the ensuing civil war the monarchist forces looked to Saudi Arabia as their natural ally while, unsurprisingly, the republican regime aligned itself closely with Nasser's Egypt, which sent armed forces in support.

An agreement between the sides was reached in April 1963 with encouragement of the United Nations. By the terms of this, the dangerous international dimension to the conflict would be removed. Egyptian forces supporting the republican regime would withdraw while, simultaneously, cross-border support for the monarchists from Saudi Arabia would cease. To ensure this happened, the UN, following an initiative from Jordan (which had itself been enmeshed in the crisis of 1958 in which UNOGIL was involved), would provide military observers. This was the **Yemen Observation Mission (UNYOM)**. Over its fourteen-month deployment from July 1963, UNYOM's strength rarely went above 200. While the cessation of Saudi cross-border support for the monarchist forces was verified by the UN observers, Egypt proved reluctant to end its military presence as agreed. This probably followed an initial political miscalculation by Nasser who had believed that without Saudi support resistance to the republican regime would simply disintegrate. Not for the first or last time, the modernising assumptions of the northern Arabs had led them to misread the social and political circumstances of southern Arabia.

From the broader global perspective, however, the UN presence fulfilled its purpose in the context of the cold war. There was a high degree of agreement between Washington and Moscow on the UN mission and its mandate. The United States, now with John F. Kennedy in the White House, was much more flexible in its approach to the Middle East and the phenomenon of Arab nationalism than it had been in the Eisenhower years. There would be no question, for example, of US troops becoming involved in Yemen as they had previously in Lebanon. The Soviet Union was also uncharacteristically accommodating towards the peacekeeping intervention. This was probably due to Egypt's ready acceptance of the UN plan; Moscow was not likely to cut across the preferences of what it increasingly regarded as a key Middle East ally.

The level of superpower cooperation was all the more remarkable when the larger international context of the early 1960s is taken into account. It contrasted with the respective attitudes of Washington and Moscow to the peacekeeping endeavours of the United Nations elsewhere in the world at the time. In particular, the large-scale intervention in the former Belgian Congo which had begun in 1960 was proving to be a critical juncture in the narrative of UN peace operations.

UNYOM: The UN Yemen Observation Mission, established to monitor the border between Yemen and Saudi Arabia in July 1963 and to oversee the agreed disengagement of Egypt and Saudi Arabia from the Yemen civil war; mission completed in September 1964.

5

The Peacekeeping Model Challenged: From the Congo to Cyprus

ONUC: United Nations Operation in Congo (*Opération des Nations Unies au Congo*), deployed between July 1960 and June 1964.

Between the two Middle East observer missions in Lebanon and Yemen, Hammarskjöld's model of UN peace operations (as set out in the Summary Study) had been tested to destruction. The UN force in the Congo ('**ONUC**'), from the acronym of its French initials, *Opération des Nations Unies au Congo*) operated between July 1960 and May 1964. Almost from the outset it was drawn into the politics of the cold war in a way that inverted the supposed purpose of peacekeeping. The major objective of peace operations at this time was to help smother local 'brushfires' before they spread to other countries in the region and, ultimately, to the polarised international system where they might aggravate the tensions between east and west. Reversing this, the involvement of the United Nations in the Congo seemed to draw the cold war into the conflict rather than sealing it off from the wider world. The Congo would create a crisis for the United Nations itself as an institution and on the way would bring the death of Dag Hammarskjöld.

POST-COLONIAL TEST: THE CONGO MORASS

On 30 June 1960 Belgium withdrew from its vast Congo colony (renamed Zaire in 1966 before reverting to the title Democratic Republic of Congo in 1997). The independence of this huge, ethnically diverse territory came suddenly and without any proper preparation by the decolonising power. In January 1960 following disturbances during the previous months, Belgium announced its intention to withdraw and to transfer power to an independent African government within six months. Apprehensive of the political and security dangers likely to be involved in a protracted preparatory phase and uncertain of its capacity to manage them, Belgium had reacted with something like panic to the first stirrings of African nationalism. The consequences for the newly independent state of this rushed and ill-planned process seemed to have no significant part in the calculations of the Belgian government. With no more than a handful of university graduates and no doctors, lawyers or trained military officers, the emergent state was courting disaster from the moment of its creation.

It was not wholly unexpected when, within two weeks of independence, the Congo's prime minister, Patrice Lumumba, and its president, Joseph Kasavubu, sought UN help to deal with a major crisis for the new state. The recently formed national army, the *Armée Nationale Congolese* (**ANC**) had mutinied against its European officers and a chaotic spasm of murder, rape and looting had followed. In response, Belgium troops, already garrisoned in the country as part of the independence agreement, were ordered by Brussels to protect the remaining European population. This was seen by the Congolese government as an act of neo-colonial aggression.

ANC: Congolese National Army (*Armée Nationale Congolese*) whose mutiny immediately following the country's independence in 1960 helped precipitate UN intervention.

Meantime, exploiting the chaos in Leopoldville (later Kinshasa) the national capital, the leader of the mineral-rich southern province of Katanga, Moise Tshombe, declared his own 'independence' from the Congo. This attempted secession had been, in the view of the central government, connived at by Belgium and France who had subverted Congolese politics in an attempt to safeguard their neo-colonial commercial and industrial interests in the province. From the outset it should have been clear that UN involvement in the Congo would be much more complex and dangerous than it had been in Suez, the UN's only previous experience of peace 'forces' as opposed to military observer operations.

There were multiple problems to be confronted by the UN force initially. First, the withdrawal of Belgian forces had to be arranged. This was the substantive reason for the Congolese government's complaint to the UN. It also provided the 'international' dimension to the crisis, which was a legal prerequisite for United Nations involvement. But this was relatively straightforward compared to the other challenges. Public order had to be restored; the ANC had to be properly trained and inculcated with military discipline to prevent a repetition of the crisis. Finally, the new state had to be reunified and separatism discouraged.

The inappropriateness of Hammarskjöld's Suez-based peacekeeping concept in such a situation should have been evident right at the beginning. The holy trinity of operational imperatives simply had no place in the complexities of what became an intra-state rather than truly international crisis. 'Host state consent' had hardly any meaning where control of the state was uncertain and contested. And, clearly, the issue of the self-defence of the UN force and how it was to be distinguished from active combat would be thrown wide open if the UN was to be responsible for the imposition of order. Most delicately, perhaps, the principle of non-interference in local politics was simply unsustainable if the UN was to act on behalf of the central government against regional secession. Finally, although the crisis in the Congo was essentially a domestic one, it had international implications which were potentially profound. Lurking behind the post-colonial machinations of the Europeans was the danger that the crisis would be re-shaped into a broader east–west confrontation (Hoskyns, 1965).

The issue was brought to the Council by Hammarskjöld himself, invoking for the first time in the organisation's history the power given to the secretary general under article 99 of the Charter. He initially sought Security Council authorisation for an operation which would cover the withdrawal of Belgian forces from the Congo. At this point the aims of the intervention were still familiar enough. The process should have been similar to that of UNEF in its 'replacement' of the Anglo-French invaders of Suez, and to a lesser extent of UNOGIL in its constraint of American action in Lebanon. Profound complications would not be long in coming, however. But these were largely unforeseen and on 14 July 1960 Tunisia, which was one of the non-permanent members of the Security Council at the time, produced an enabling resolution which established a force to provide 'assistance' to the Congolese government. The resolution also called for a withdrawal of Belgian forces, though it stopped short of direct criticism of Brussels [**Doc. 13(i), pp. 132–3**]. In an early sign of future divisions, both France and Britain abstained in the vote, though they did not veto it. ONUC would outstrip in size and ambition any UN project undertaken hitherto. It would involve major contributions from seventeen states with lesser participation by another nineteen. At its peak its strength would reach almost 20,000.

Hammarskjöld embraced the challenge of the Congo with enthusiasm. It was, in some respects, a natural extension of the peacekeeping project as it had been pursued in the 1950s, but updated to meet the shifting challenge of the 1960s. In the 1950s the problems of South Asia, the Middle East and Arab nationalism had dominated peacekeeping efforts. Now, at the beginning of the 1960s, the process of decolonisation and the problems this raised of integrating new states into the international system had shifted its geographical location. The new international challenges would come from the emergence of independent black Africa. Yet the 'international' justifications for the UN's intervention in the Congo were not, at the outset, especially strong. Certainly, Leopoldville's initial request related to 'Belgian aggression' against a new, independent state, but this was a symptom and not the cause of the fundamental problem.

The danger of cold war internationalisation which was to develop later was not obvious in mid-1960. Lumumba had first approached both the United States and the Soviet Union for bilateral help before being directed by each of them to the United Nations (Abi-Saab, 1978). Hammarskjöld's perception of the 'international' in the Congo probably derived from his general view of the UN's responsibility for the management of the international state system as a whole. In 1960 the strains on this system came, as we have said, from its rapid expansion through the process of decolonisation. The pressures on the new international entities produced from this should therefore be a major focus of UN attention. This inclusive definition of what was properly 'international' allowed the circumvention of the basic Charter principle – set out in article 2(7) – of non-intervention 'in matters which are essentially within the domestic jurisdiction of any state' (United Nations Charter, 1945).

From the outset, Hammarskjöld's wider view of ONUC's purposes cut across the more immediate and local perspectives of Patrice Lumumba. The Congolese prime minister, understandably enough, insisted that the UN's primary role should be to bolster the authority of his government in Leopoldville. This, after all, had been the basis of his original approach to the UN. These differing perceptions led quickly to conflict between Leopoldville and New York (Higgins, 1980).

Beyond this clash of views there were political constraints on the capacity of ONUC to deliver what Lumumba wanted. Belgium was reluctant to withdraw its forces before the internal situation in the Congo had stabilised. It was inconceivable that the Security Council, subject to western veto, would vote to take any strong measures against a member of the western alliance. Britain and France had already abstained on the original vote to establish ONUC and would hardly have supported any direct confrontation between the UN and Belgian forces. Yet in pursuing the restoration of order which would bring a Belgian withdrawal, UN forces were engaged in the disarming of the Congo's own national army. If this were not bad enough, relations between the UN and Leopoldville were damaged further by the secession of Katanga. Encouraged by Belgian officers in its paramilitary 'gendarmerie' and by locally based western diplomats, Katanga's defiance of the central government continued unchallenged by ONUC in the first months of its operations. To move against Katanga, Hammarskjöld insisted, would go beyond the 'peacekeeping' mandate and take the UN into the area of 'enforcement' (Lash, 1962). In Lumumba's and his supporters' view this amounted to a betrayal of the UN's original promise [**Doc. 14, pp. 134–5**]. Beyond the Congo itself this perception of ONUC as an instrument of 'imperialism' was increasingly held in other third world states. The situation was beginning to strike an opportunistic chord with the Soviet leadership.

This potentially disastrous situation worsened dramatically at the beginning of September 1960 when the central government fell into constitutional chaos. A long-standing and barely suppressed rivalry between Lumumba and President Kasavubu had been aggravated by the former's increasingly anti-western rhetoric. Kasavubu, more amenable to western blandishments, decided to dismiss his prime minister. Lumumba responded in kind by 'dismissing' the president. Caught in the middle, ONUC was made aware of the extent to which it had unintentionally become a major actor in the Congo's internal politics. Two fatal operational decisions were now taken by Andrew Cordier, Hammarskjöld's representative in Leopoldville. He ordered the closure of all airfields in the country and shut down the capital's radio station. The effect of these moves was to favour Lumumba's enemies. By grounding air traffic the UN prevented the arrival in the capital of troops loyal to the prime minister from his power base in Orientale province. By closing the radio station Lumumba was denied his only means of mass communication. Kasavubu meanwhile was able to broadcast from Brazzaville, the capital of the former French Congo where France still had influence, just across the Congo river (Abi-Saab, 1978).

The extent to which these steps were intentionally aimed against Lumumba cannot be judged. But Cordier was an American and indeed almost all of Hammarskjöld's key representatives in the Congo at this time were westerners. The so-called '**Congo Club**' of advisers the secretary general gathered round him in New York similarly had no communist bloc members (Luard, 1989). It is possible to see this as revealing a core truth about the whole concept of UN peace operations during the cold war. Peacekeeping was grounded in essentially western cultural assumptions, regardless of the 'impartiality' that was supposed to define its operational approach. The peacekeeping idea itself had no obvious place in Soviet views of international relations and their management at this time. In the case of Suez, UN intervention had little direct impact on the east–west contest; in fact it brought the bonus for the USSR of embarrassment within the western camp. Consequently, Moscow was content to go along with the process. The Congo situation was quite different, though. As the crisis developed it took on ideological and diplomatic dimensions which touched directly on the central cold war conflict. Obviously, therefore, the Soviet Union began to take a close critical interest in what was being done in the Security Council's name (Khruschev, 1974). With the best will in the world, the western managers of peacekeeping with no countervailing non-western views available would always be at risk of bringing their own cultural and ideological assumptions, however unconsciously, to their operational decisions.

Cordier was replaced after the airport and radio station affair as the secretary general's representative (supposedly in a routine changeover) by an Indian national, Rajeshwar Dayal, who brought a greater third world sensibility to the post (Dayal, 1976). But the Soviet Union used the issue to attack what it claimed was pro-western bias in the upper echelons of ONUC. In the Security Council in mid-September 1960 the Soviet representative

Congo Club: Group of UN officials chaired by secretary general Dag Hammarskjöld which planned and supervised the organisation's approach to the Congo crisis in 1960 and 1961; criticised by the Soviet Union and others for its supposed western bias.

denounced the failure of the operation to confront 'imperialism' in the Congo and pointed to the preponderance of western personnel at its head. The impression of a UN machine working against radical third world aspirations (here personified by Patrice Lumumba) was becoming widespread among the increasingly important Afro-Asian bloc in the UN. The always thin fiction of non-interference by the UN in the Congo's politics became even more threadbare with the waning of Lumumba's power. The Soviet Union, disregarding the complexities of the secretary general's own position, claimed to hold him personally responsible for what it alleged was a western conspiracy in the Congo. To a degree this was an inevitable consequence of the 'leave it to Dag' culture which had grown out of the Suez operation and which Hammarskjöld himself had, however unwittingly, tended to encourage. His close personal identification with the development of peacekeeping and his efforts to provide it with a general philosophy could now be turned against him. Hammarskjöld was particularly exposed over the Congo because the operation had its genesis in the use of his personal powers under article 99 of the Charter. Whatever the real limits of his own control over the politics of either the UN or the Congo, therefore, he would be a prime target for the side which felt itself to be the loser from the UN intervention.

On 23 September 1960 the Soviet leader Nikita Khrushchev himself addressed the General Assembly on ONUC's shortcomings and the controversial nature of its political direction. After denouncing the failure of the UN to deal with the secession of Katanga and excoriating its supposed anti-Lumumba manoeuvres earlier in the month, Khrushchev laid a proposal for radical reform before the Assembly [**Doc. 15. pp. 135–7**]. The office of secretary general concentrated too much power in the hands of one individual, he argued, and therefore should be abolished. 'There are neutral nations', he said, 'but no neutral men' (Luard, 1989: 204). Hammarskjöld's Swedish nationality did not make Hammarskjöld himself 'neutral'. The office should, therefore, be replaced by a **'troika'** (or triumvirate) composed of representatives of three distinct groups of states: western, communist and Afro-Asian. This would ensure that neither of the cold war blocs (though he clearly had in mind the west) could exploit the power of the office. Such a reform would ensure a truly internationalised United Nations. It would also, of course, dispense with the concept of an institutional bureaucracy loyal to the institution rather than the national origins of its personnel. The tradition of the international civil servant which had developed in the League of Nations would thus be abandoned. In other words, the troika system would have formalised the bipolar structure of the cold war international system into a permanent feature of the UN's architecture.

In the event, there was little support for the proposal. The opposition of the west was automatic, of course, but crucially, few third world countries

Troika proposal: Soviet plan presented to the General Assembly in 1960 for the replacement of the office of UN secretary general by a triumvirate of western, eastern and Afro-Asian bloc representatives; the proposal failed to attract significant support.

seemed to be enthused by the idea. Whatever their misgivings over the direction of the Congo operation, the Afro-Asians, unlike the Soviets, nevertheless saw in Hammarskjöld a figure committed to the UN as an institution rather than either of the two cold war blocs which sought to dominate it. Hammarskjöld himself was able to exploit this feeling in his own defence when he replied to Khrushchev's proposals (Urquhart, 1973). The Soviet leader, sensing the mood, quietly dropped them. With a bitter ideological dispute developing at this time between Moscow and Beijing (the incipient 'Sino-Soviet split') the mood of the Afro-Asian bloc was of great concern to the Soviet leadership. No initiative which might have brought Moscow into political conflict with the post-colonial world at the UN was worth pursuing.

Yet important issues were undoubtedly raised by the troika affair and it revealed some significant truths about the nature of the United Nations at this dangerous point in the cold war. First, the plain fact was that the senior and most sensitive strata of the UN secretariat were indeed populated disproportionately by western officials. The balance of bureaucratic power – and therefore control of much day-to-day decision-making not just for peacekeeping but across the range of the organisation's activities – was implicitly in anti-Soviet hands. The extent to which the officials involved really represented western bloc interests was obviously debatable. But Soviet suspicions, fuelled by a Marxist sense of the individual as agent of class or sectional or bloc interests (thus 'no neutral men') were understandable. Second, it was now evident that peace operations which were designed to prevent cold war involvement in peripheral areas of east–west competition could actually exacerbate that competition by themselves becoming political controversies. As Ernest Lefever put it, the UN 'did not . . . keep the cold war out of the Congo. On the contrary, it further politicised the crisis and ensured that the cold war would be fought in that chaotic arena' (Lefever, 1967: 207). Paradoxically, cold war competition now posed a threat to the idea of peacekeeping – which had itself developed to manage that competition. Thus the Congo illustrated something not evident over Suez: that dangerous situations can deteriorate despite *or even because of* UN intervention. The Congo of September 1960 was not the Congo of July 1960. The political environment altered fundamentally over that short period and the danger of cold war involvement had increased dramatically in consequence. Once committed, however, ONUC had no option but to adapt as best it could to rapidly changing circumstances.

Meanwhile, as the troika issue was argued out in New York, in the Congo itself it was unclear who exactly constituted the central government. Both Kasavubu and Lumumba sought legitimacy by sending their own separate delegations to the General Assembly, which initially declined to accept either. Confusion deepened in mid-September when the ANC commander, Colonel

Joseph Mobutu, announced an army coup and proceeded to expel Soviet and other eastern bloc diplomats from Leopoldville. Moscow was not alone in scenting western connivance in this conveniently anti-Soviet turn of events amidst the chaos, and Afro-Asian concern over the drift of events increased. For Hammarskjöld the immediate danger was that Lumumba would be provoked into inviting a direct Soviet intervention. A suspiciously rapid rapprochement between Mobutu and Kasavubu forced Lumumba onto the defensive, however. He had now, somewhat humiliatingly, to place himself under UN protection as his Congolese enemies moved against him (Hoskyns, 1965).

In November 1960 the General Assembly, with encouragement from the western bloc, finally accepted the credentials of the Kasavubu delegation [Doc. 16, pp. 137–8]. This effectively legitimised the Mobutu–Kasavubu regime in Leopoldville. It also marked a reversal of the UN's previous commitment to seek conciliation between Kasavubu and Lumumba. This apparent victory for western interests was not in fact welcomed by Hammarskjöld but he could not avoid being identified with the whole process (Urquhart, 1973). The decision to accept the anti-Lumumba faction as the official representatives of the country at the United Nations triggered a sequence of events in the Congo which would make Hammarskjöld's position – and that of ONUC on the ground – even more difficult. Responding to the defeat in New York, Lumumba slipped away from his UN protectors in Leopoldville. His aim was to reach his Orientale power base where he hoped to rally sufficient support to mount an armed challenge to the new regime. He was captured by Mobutu's ANC *en route*. A few weeks later the central government, which was now firmly under Mobutu's control, handed him over to Tshombe's administration in Katanga. There Lumumba was quickly and brutally murdered, an outcome which had probably been pre-arranged between Mobutu and Tshombe.

The consequences for ONUC were immediate. The shortcomings in its protection arrangements for Lumumba had been bad enough, but its failure to prevent his transfer to Katanga and subsequent murder seemed to suggest at the minimum a culpable negligence. Although no convincing suggestion of UN complicity in Lumumba's fate was ever made, later revelations pointed to direct Belgian involvement. Other persistent and credible reports suggested that the United States **Central Intelligence Agency (CIA)** was deeply involved in the affair through their influence over Mobutu (Crockatt, 1996).

CIA: United States Central Intelligence Agency.

The impact on the UN operation was immediate as Afro-Asian states dissociated themselves from ONUC. Indonesia, the UAR and Morocco withdrew their contingents in protest and others threatened to follow suit. The UAR and Guinea also formally recognised a rival 'central government' declared by Lumumba's supporters in Stanleyville (later renamed Kisangani), capital of Orientale province (Luard, 1989). The Soviet Union once again demanded Hammarskjöld's resignation.

As a direct consequence of Lumumba's death and the political and diplomatic events that followed, the Security Council authorised a new, more robust mandate for ONUC. On 21 February 1961 it was authorised to use force if necessary to prevent civil war **[Doc. 13(ii), p. 133]**. This of course represented an abandonment of the basic Hammarskjöldian principle, one of the holy trinity, that peacekeepers should use force only in self-defence and only then with great circumspection. The new mandate meant that ONUC now had an enforcement function, albeit a negative one, in the requirement placed on it to prevent civil war by military means. This was the first sign in UN peace operations of a phenomenon which would much later be described as **'mission creep'** and which would afflict many future interventions. Despite misgivings on Hammarskjöld's part, the new mandate did at least improve ONUC's international credibility. Meanwhile, the superpower relationship within which the UN was required to operate had also changed for the better. In January 1961 President John F. Kennedy moved into the White House, bringing with him a greater sensitivity to African and other third world feelings than that demonstrated by the Eisenhower administration (Weissman, 1974; Mahoney, 1983).

Mission creep: Tendency for peace operations (and other military actions) to move beyond their original mandates – usually leading to deeper embroilment in a conflict – because of circumstances on the ground.

In the Congo itself, regardless of the international anger provoked by Lumumba's murder, his removal permitted the consolidation of the Mobutu–Kasavubu government in Leopoldville. This brought some stability to the situation at the centre and as a result ONUC could now give greater attention to the issue of Katanga. Henceforward Katanga would dominate the UN's operations in the Congo. While the rest of the country had been struggling through the successive crises of army mutiny, foreign intervention and violent political factionalism, secessionist Katanga had been left largely alone by the UN (though ONUC troops remained stationed there). The UN's position in relation to Katanga therefore remained opaque during the first year of ONUC's deployment in the Congo. Katanga's claims to independence had been justified by its apologists abroad by the contrast between the chaos elsewhere in the Congo and Katanga's evident prosperity, efficient administration and political tranquillity (James, 1990). Its fundamental reliance on external support from both European and white-ruled African countries was apparent to anyone who chose to look, however. Yet even when free to devote attention and resources to the problem, and now armed with a supposedly more effective mandate after February 1961, it was still unclear whether ONUC was specifically authorised to end its secession by force. Could such a course of action reasonably be interpreted as 'preventing civil war'? As far as Katanga's supporters were concerned, it had already successfully separated from the Congo and was a distinct sovereign entity with no connection to the Congo's domestic problems. The Security Council itself could not possibly agree on this, with France and to a lesser extent Britain fundamentally sympathetic to

Katanga; the question therefore was never resolved. The continuing ambiguity led to the next major crisis – and to the death of Dag Hammarskjöld.

The secretary general himself seemed not to favour the more robust interpretations of the UN's mandate in regard to Katanga which would have led to its forcible reintegration in the Congo. By mid-1961 he had been relieved of much of the Soviet and radical Afro-Asian pressure which had surrounded the troika debates and the murder of Lumumba. He now sought to pull ONUC as far as possible back towards a 'peacekeeping' role within his own conception of the term. Certainly the cold war dimension to the Congo question became less marked as both Moscow and Washington were now committed to a unified Congo. But the absence of obvious superpower conflict could not of itself create conditions for Suez-style interposition peacekeeping. The internal situation in the Congo remained highly volatile, with no agreed political consensus among the factions. There was, therefore, no peace for ONUC to keep. Even with the worst cold war tensions muted, the UN's position remained complex and dangerous. Throughout the first half of 1961 the Katangese regime defied all UN attempts to negotiate its reintegration into the Congo. Its heavily armed gendarmerie, led by European officers and backed by foreign mercenaries, was in reality more of an army than a police force. Tshombe and his European advisers were unmoved by pressure from the UN.

In August 1961, with growing tension between local UN personnel and the Katangese forces in the provincial capital Elisabethville (later Lubumbashi), a major crisis erupted. Hammarskjöld's local representative, the young Irish diplomat Conor Cruise O'Brien, determined to cut through the separatist regime's temporising and provocations, ordered ONUC forces to arrest and expel foreign military personnel [**Doc. 16, pp. 137–8**]. The ill-planned operation was unsuccessful and turned into another humiliation for the UN in Katanga. Buoyed by this evident victory over ONUC, Tshombe became even more obdurate. In response, O'Brien, now with support from ONUC headquarters in Leopoldville, ordered a second, more forceful operation in Elisabethville a few weeks later. In the flush of the initial success of this second venture, O'Brien foolishly announced the end of Katanga's secession. There was an immediate international reaction. This was not what the United Nations member states had assumed to be happening in the Congo. The ambiguity of the February Security Council resolution had not been clarified in a way that would permit the UN to end the secession of Katanga by force. The western members of the Security Council in particular were angry at not having been consulted. Two quite different versions of events now emerged. O'Brien, with some backing from UN officials in Leopoldville, claimed that Hammarskjöld had given prior approval to the operation. The secretary general, through his aides in New York, insisted to the contrary that the operation had been conceived and organised locally without his knowledge. It would not, they insisted, have been approved had they been consulted (Hoskyns, 1965; Urquhart, 1973).

In the face of a deeply hostile diplomatic reaction in the west and with the secretary general himself apparently disassociating himself from the actions of his local representatives, the anti-secessionist operation petered out despite its strong initial momentum. The net effect had merely been to increase tensions in Katanga still further. For Hammarskjöld personally the crisis must have brought a huge intensification of the stress he had been working under virtually from the start of the Congo operation [**Doc. 17, pp. 138–9**]. He now flew to the Congo in an attempt to rescue the situation. After consultations in Leopoldville, he arranged to meet Tshombe in neighbouring Northern Rhodesia whence the Katangese leader had fled beyond the reach of ONUC when the latest operation began. On the evening of 17 September 1961 Hammarskjöld was killed with all on board when his plane crashed near the town of Ndola *en route* to this meeting.

Hammarskjöld's death did not bring any immediate change to the character of the UN operation in the Congo. His replacement, however, was the UN's first non-European secretary general, the Burmese diplomat U Thant, whose Afro-Asian identity was to prove significant in the future. (Thant took over automatically as acting secretary general on Hammarskjöld's death but was later confirmed in office in his own right.) The furore over ONUC's moves against Katanga in August and September 1961 had been generated by western powers. But in reality the situation was already more nuanced in terms of the competing interests and positions taken than it had been in the first stage of the UN's operations in Congo when the main division was a cold war, east–west one. The sharpest edges of this had been blunted by mid-1961, as we have seen. The cleavage now was, loosely, one between the west European 'imperialists' (France, Belgium and Britain) on the pro-Katanga side and the Afro-Asian world on the other. The United States, although angered at the lack of consultation over ONUC's military operations in Katanga in August and September, was now ranged against its European allies on this 'colonial' issue in a way reminiscent of the line-up of forces over the Suez crisis in 1956. The pro-Katanga westerners were now confronted by the increasingly cohesive 'non-aligned' bloc which objected not to military action by the UN against Katanga but its ineffectiveness. As with Suez, the United States was keenly aware of the broader value of keeping on the right diplomatic side of this important international grouping. The new secretary general's third world origins now went further in easing the pressure of the Afro-Asians on the UN.

In the aftermath of the August–September crisis and Hammarskjöld's death, a new Security Council resolution was adopted in November 1961 which again changed ONUC's mandate. The UN now committed itself to an even more forceful approach than that of the February resolution. ONUC was instructed to take 'vigorous action' including the use of force to end Katangese secession [**Doc. 13(iii), pp. 133–4**]. Following this overt commitment to enforcement, the UN's intervention in the Congo moved towards its endgame. There was no immediate military campaign against Katanga and in the short term this may have emboldened the foreign mercenaries who had sustained its secession and were now used to half-hearted advances followed by abject retreats by ONUC. If so, this was a fatal miscalculation. Having absorbed routine provocations and petty humiliation over most of 1962, the UN military in Katanga, now reinforced with a large and effective Indian component, moved decisively to defeat and expel foreign military personnel and take control of what quickly became once again the Congolese province of Katanga. The Congo was thus reunified under a central administration in Leopoldville.

The confusing and apparently capricious cross-currents of Congolese politics now saw Tshombe appointed prime minister of the unified state. Real power, however, lay with Mobutu who finally formalised his authority when he displaced Kasavubu as head of state in 1965. In the meantime, ONUC had withdrawn from the Congo in June 1964. Mobutu remained in power for more than three decades, being ousted only in 1997 shortly before his death. His regime, over the birth of which the United Nations had presided, was one of the most inefficient and corrupt in the world (Ikambana, 2008). The longevity of this kleptocracy was due in no small part to Mobutu's continuing loyalty to western interests, a loyalty first demonstrated in the critical months of 1960. But just as Mobutu had ruled by virtue of the cold war, the end of it brought his rapid downfall. No longer an asset to western interests, by the mid-1990s he had become an embarrassment and was overthrown by internal enemies supported by neighbouring states, notably Rwanda and Uganda, which themselves had scores to settle with his regime. In the chaotic aftermath of his fall the Congo, which in truth had never fully established itself as a viable state after the turmoil of its beginnings, again descended into civil war and humanitarian disaster (Reyntjens, 2009). Again too, a large-scale United Nations operation was mounted to manage the consequences.

THE UN IN WEST NEW GUINEA: PEACE WITHOUT HONOUR?

Regardless of the strains placed on UN peacekeeping by the Congo experience, the basic concept of military interposition proved robust enough to survive. In the 1960s observer and buffer operations based on the precepts which emerged from Suez continued to be established in various parts of the world. Typically, these operations were designed to help contain crises on the periphery of superpower interests. That is to say, they involved conflicts which, while capable of entangling the polarised blocs, were marginal to the central ideological and geographical balance of the cold war. They were not potential flashpoints in the same category as, say, Berlin, Hungary or Cuba. In these areas of core interest the superpowers closely guarded their own direct control and rejected any other external involvement. UN intervention was acceptable, even desirable, to the superpowers where (as in the Middle East or the Congo) cold war alignments were present but in an indirect form.

One such commitment was in West New Guinea. Although this was an undertaking of great scope and represented in its form and objectives a real innovation for the United Nations, it has been somewhat overlooked by scholars and analysts. One reason for this was probably its geographical remoteness from the centres of global power. It took place, moreover, entirely within the period of the Congo operation where understandably world attention tended to be focused. But it is possible that another reason for the relative lack of attention given to the UN's involvement in West New Guinea is the morally questionable outcome of the process. Interestingly, the secretary general who oversaw the UN intervention, U Thant, gives only very cursory attention to West New Guinea in his published memoirs in contrast to the discussion he devotes to the Congo and to the later operation in Cyprus (Thant, 1978). There is an understandable assumption that UN peace operations are by their nature ethical in execution and moral in their objectives. If operations fail, they do so despite their underlying good intentions. When they succeed, it is proof of the fundamental decency of the international community. It is, however, possible that in pursuit of what is seen as the greater goal of international stability, justice and equity are not served well at the local level. Arguably, West New Guinea is one such case.

Historically, West New Guinea (or Irian Jaya as it was known in Indonesia) formed the easternmost part of the Dutch East Indies. Geographically it is in the South Pacific rather than Southeast Asia, forming the western half of the island of New Guinea (the eastern portion being Papua New Guinea). This location, and the issues of ethnicity that went with it, lay at the root of the conflict over the territory in the early 1960s. Dutch colonial administration had continued after the Netherlands had withdrawn from the rest of its huge imperial archipelago which became independent Indonesia after the Second World War. The Melanesian people of the physically wild and diverse territory of West New Guinea had little in common culturally with Indonesia and they showed little enthusiasm for exchanging the paternalistic colonialism of the Dutch for a potentially more dictatorial and exploitative rule from

Jakarta. The radical nationalist regime of President Sukarno in Indonesia was, however, determined to complete the territorial transfer from the Dutch by taking control of the territory.

The Netherlands, while generally benign in its rule of the territory, had done little to develop its people or its natural resources and this compromised the moral case the Dutch made for holding West New Guinea back from Indonesia. Perhaps more importantly, throughout the 1950s and 1960s the spirit of decolonisation pervaded the United Nations. An anti-imperialist orthodoxy was established which the cold war blocs could not lightly transgress as they sought to garner third world support to their side. This was in evidence over Suez in 1956 and had been strongly reinforced by the Congo experience. Sukarno's Indonesia was a leading voice in the emerging Non-Aligned Movement and could rely on considerable (though not total) Afro-Asian backing for its claims. Although the United States and its allies were wary of the Jakarta regime and its close relations with Moscow, they did not relish a confrontation in which the Netherlands, a NATO member, could be portrayed as an intransigent imperialist pitched against Indonesia's anti-colonial mission. Taking the obvious message from this diplomatic reality – and with its forces harried by Indonesian attacks in the territory – the Dutch eventually negotiated a withdrawal agreement with American and UN encouragement in 1962 (Higgins, 1970).

In the international circumstances of the time the United Nations was the obvious body to manage the implementation of this agreement. The ensuing operation had two components. The first was the familiar one of military observation. A mission was assembled to supervise the disengagement of Dutch security forces and the Indonesian commandos who had infiltrated the territory. The second part of the UN undertaking was more novel and ambitious. The **United Nations Temporary Executive Authority (UNTEA)** took over the government of the territory from the Dutch as an intermediate stage in the transfer of power to Indonesia. It was, moreover, a UN government with its own army, the **United Nations Security Force (UNSF)**. The observers were drawn from the increasingly familiar list of middle powers including India, Ireland and Sweden. The main body of the Security Force was provided by Pakistan alone, however.

A significant feature of the West New Guinea intervention, one which set it apart from most previous and subsequent UN operations during the cold war, was that it was initiated by the secretary general acting on his own initiative and then authorised and overseen by the General Assembly. The Security Council did not feature in the establishment or management of the operation. While UNEF in Suez was also, ultimately, a General Assembly operation, it became so only after transfer from the Security Council under the Uniting for Peace process. In the case of West New Guinea, U Thant

UNTEA: The United Nations Temporary Executive Authority in West New Guinea (Irian Jaya), formed in October 1962 to provide a transitional administration for the territory after its removal from Dutch sovereignty pending its transfer to Indonesia in April 1963.

UNSF: The UN Security Force for West New Guinea (Irian Jaya), responsible for the territory's internal and external security during the period of the United Nations transitional administration pending the territory's transfer to Indonesian sovereignty in 1963.

personally organised the initial military observer operation and then passed the issue to the General Assembly to have the larger process legitimised (Higgins, 1970).

This approach to peace operations would seem almost designed to bring down the wrath of the Soviet Union, the more so given the very recent conflict over the Congo force. For Moscow, only the Security Council could authorise the use of military personnel by the UN (under Chapter VII of the Charter). Only by restricting this power to the Council could the Soviet Union hope to control events, if necessary by the use of its veto. Otherwise it would be marginalised by the automatic western majority in the General Assembly (still a reality at this stage, though gradually eroding due to the influx of new post-colonial states into the UN). Yet the Soviet representative supported the enabling resolution in the General Assembly when it was passed in September 1962. No explanation of this vote was provided by the delegation but a number of possible factors can be inferred. For one thing, U Thant was not Dag Hammarskjöld. Much of the Soviet anger over the conduct of the Congo operation up until his death in September 1961 had been focused on Hammarskjöld personally. Thant, as an Afro-Asian, could not be so easily denounced as a western stooge. Beyond this, the final objective of the UN's intervention was the transfer of West New Guinea from European colonial rule to Indonesia, whose leader Sukarno was regarded in Moscow as a diplomatic ally. Finally, the costs of the operation, a point of great political importance for the Soviet Union, would not be borne by the UN as an institution but shared equally between the governments of the Netherlands and Indonesia. Unlike the Congo, therefore, the intervention in West New Guinea was free of any direct cold war entanglement.

This is not to say, however, that the operation was universally welcomed in the UN. France, another opponent of 'slippage' of authority from the Security Council to the General Assembly, abstained, along with most of its former African colonies (Higgins, 1970). To a degree this simply reflected continuing French influence on the post-colonial regimes in Francophone Africa. But there was another, more ethical, dimension to some of these votes by the new African states. The process did not involve genuine self-determination for the people of West New Guinea. They were simply to be transferred from one state jurisdiction to another. While this dissenting position probably reflected the true feelings of several western states, in the prevailing anti-imperialist climate of the time it was one which could be safely adopted publicly only by other post-colonial states.

Passed by a large majority, however, including all the eastern bloc members, the General Assembly plan was put in place. UN administration began in October 1962 and lasted until April of the following year when Indonesia took over the territory from UNTEA. Judged strictly against its mandate the undertaking was wholly successful. The two-stage transfer of power took place in a secure and stable environment. Indonesia achieved all of its objectives while the Dutch were spared the humiliation of handing the territory over directly to its rival, instead merely ceding control to the United Nations. More broadly, a complex issue of late imperial relationships was fully insulated from cold war politics.

The wider morality of the affair was altogether muddier, however. The UN was instrumental in delivering a largely reluctant people to the undemocratic rule of an alien and distant capital. An 'act of free choice' to be administered by Indonesia as part of the settlement was, as widely expected, a mere sham when it took place in 1969 (Chesterman, 2004). Subsequently the history of Irian Jaya was one of Indonesian colonisation, domination and repression against a background of sporadic ethnic rebellion. The operation in West New Guinea was a corrective to the view that the UN's peacekeeping ventures would always occupy a moral high ground above considerations of *realpolitik*. The outcome of the operation may have served to save diplomatic faces and, of course, the larger purpose of the safe management of the cold war system. It had, though, little to do with advancing democracy and self-determination (Saltford, 2002).

PEACEKEEPING WITHIN THE COLD WAR FAMILY: CYPRUS

The UN's next major engagement after the Congo was to be of much greater duration than anything else begun during the 1960s. Although unforeseen at the time of its establishment, the UN's peacekeeping commitment in Cyprus would continue through cold war, détente, return to cold war again and then into the twenty-first century with no clear prospect of its conclusion.

The Security Council established the **United Nations Force in Cyprus (UNFICYP)** in March 1964 after the outbreak of fighting between the island's Greek and Turkish communities. The immediate cause of the conflict was an attempt in late 1963 on the part of the Greek Cypriot president, Archbishop Makarios, to alter the constitution of Cyprus in a way that would reduce the influence of the Turkish Cypriot minority. The constitution, part of the 1960 agreement leading to Cyprus's independence from Britain, had been carefully constructed to safeguard the rights of the minority. The Turkish Cypriot community had been unenthusiastic about the independence which the Greek Cypriots had pursued politically and through acts of violence over a number of years. The agreement had been designed to maintain the integrity of the state against two contending challenges. One of these was the

UNFICYP: The UN Force in Cyprus, established in March 1964 in response to inter-communal violence between Greek and Turkish Cypriots; one of the longest enduring UN peace operations.

Enosis: Aspiration of many Greek Cypriots for the formal political unification of Cyprus with Greece.

union with Greece (**enosis**) aspired to by the more militant Greek Cypriots. The other was the partition of Cyprus into two ethnically based statelets favoured by many in the Turkish community. The price paid for a constitution acceptable to both communities was a political system which proved difficult to operate in practice. But it was so delicately balanced between the interests of the two mutually suspicious communities that any interference with its provisions was bound to lead to inter-communal conflict (Calvocoressi, 2008).

Initially Britain (which along with Greece and Turkey was a 'guarantor power' of the constitution) took the lead in restoring order in the disturbances that broke out in early 1964 by using army units which it maintained on the island under the independence agreement. The 'sovereign bases' where these troops were located were of strategic importance to Britain's larger Mediterranean and Middle East interests, and their security amidst the communal conflict was an additional cause for British concern. Such a role was not sustainable for the former colonial power, however, particularly as Britain was seen by the Greek Cypriots after their protracted independence struggle as being biased in favour of the Turkish community. Therefore the British government sought to widen the responsibility for keeping the peace by internationalising it. Attention turned first of all to the possibility of a NATO force (Verrier, 1981). This appeared to make sense as all three guarantor powers were members of the alliance and were willing to participate in such a force. The idea also won the support of the United States, although the Soviet Union was strongly opposed. Crucially, however, Cyprus was not itself in NATO (it was in fact a prominent member of the Non-Aligned Movement) and Makarios rejected the idea of such an intervention. He was suspicious of what he saw as an American and British preference for the Turkish community which he feared might be expressed in the conduct of a NATO force. The yet wider internationalisation of the situation through United Nations involvement was much more attractive to him. In consequence the Cyprus problem was passed to the Security Council in February 1964 and UNFICYP was created the following month. This time the Soviet Union, which with France was unenthusiastic about this latest extension of the peacekeeping project, abstained on the enabling resolution, though neither used their veto (Higgins, 1981).

The Soviet objection to the establishment of a peace operation for Cyprus was not based on previous concerns about the location of authority in the UN; UNFICYP was, after all, a Security Council-legitimised undertaking, unlike the operations in Suez and West New Guinea. But the crisis in Cyprus was, ostensibly, a purely domestic one between two Cypriot communities. As such it was not properly speaking 'international' and therefore the UN should be prevented by its own Charter from involvement. The Congo crisis may have developed rapidly into an internal conflict, but it had at least begun as an international issue (between the new Congo and its former colonial master, Belgium) and it was on this basis that the UN intervention had been authorised. To an extent, of course, this interpretation of the Cyprus conflict was disingenuous. While it may have been between two Cypriot factions, each was backed by a major regional power and the danger of this 'brushfire' setting light to the eastern Mediterranean in the form of a war between Greece and Turkey was a real one. But there were no obvious cold war implications. Indeed, successful peacekeeping in Cyprus would protect the internal cohesion of the NATO alliance, an outcome which was hardly in the interests of the Soviet Union. Cyprus's own desire for the UN force, however, ruled out a Soviet veto (just as Indonesian interests in UN intervention in West New Guinea had stayed the Soviet hand in that case). But the absence of full Security Council consensus pointed to a difficult future for the management of the Cyprus undertaking. Specifically, the continuing dispute over the financial basis of peacekeeping – whether it should be considered a legitimate regular UN expense – would soon grow into a major crisis for the organisation.

In the meantime, secretary general U Thant faced immediate problems in putting the force together. In a departure from Hammarskjöld's original scheme for middle power peacekeeping, a permanent member of the Security Council was to make a large operational contribution. Britain continued to provide its forces for the peacekeeping duties they had taken on when the crisis first blew up, but now under the UN flag. Other contributors were not so readily forthcoming. The experience of the Congo had understandably made governments wary of committing forces for UN duty and, at least at the outset, the Cyprus problem appeared to threaten considerable physical risks for the peacekeepers [**Doc. 18, pp. 139–41**]. Eventually, a group of the now traditional middle powers composed of Canada, Denmark, Finland, Ireland and Sweden was persuaded to contribute contingents. Moreover, in the uncertain financial circumstances of the operation the contributing states agreed to pay for their own involvement in the first instance pending reimbursement from the UN in the unspecified future.

The pre-deployment apprehensions about the dangers likely to be faced by the peacekeepers in Cyprus soon proved unfounded (Stegenga, 1968). UNFICYP quickly adopted the now standard interposition role between the two communities. Crucially, each of these accepted the neutrality of UNFICYP and its moral authority. It soon became clear, however, that the commitment was likely to be a long-term one as the parallel process of peacemaking by successive UN special representatives failed to make significant headway. During the first ten years of the operation periodic outbreaks of violence (most notably at the end of 1967) were dealt with pragmatically by

UNFICYP. While unable to resolve underlying conflicts, the peacekeepers were reasonably effective at containing their worst consequences (Harbottle, 1970).

Despite these sporadic difficulties, the situation remained largely static for a decade. However, this stability was dramatically interrupted in July 1974 when there was a confused coup attempt by Greek Cypriot extremists against their own government. The aim of this was to bring about *enosis* with the right-wing military regime then in power in Greece. Close to collapse at that time, the Athens junta sought to play the familiar trick of boosting domestic support by the pursuit of a national adventure abroad. Eight years later a similar regime in Argentina attempted the same ploy over the Falklands. In both cases the debacle that followed accelerated the end of military rule rather than prolonging it.

The scheme in Cyprus involved the overthrow of the Makarios government and its replacement by a right-wing nationalist junta which would simply impose *enosis* with the encouragement of the military in Athens. Disaster followed in the form of an immediate and devastating response from Turkey. Ruled itself by a nationalistic government at this time, it launched a full-scale invasion of the island to protect the minority community and snuff out any prospect of *enosis*. Initially pausing after occupying a relatively small part of the predominantly Turkish area of northern Cyprus, the Turkish army resumed its advance in mid-August. The result was the effective partition of the island and the southwards displacement of about 200,000 Greek Cypriot refugees.

Clearly, the capacity of a lightly armed peacekeeping force to intervene forcefully to prevent a military onslaught was limited even if, and it was unthinkable, the national contributors to UNFICYP were to agree to it. But the contributing states did respond positively to secretary general Kurt Waldheim's requests for more troops and UNFICYP quickly doubled in size. The mere physical presence of UNFICYP was probably instrumental in preventing the Turkish force from occupying the Cypriot capital, Nicosia, and in persuading it to remain in the northern half of the island. The invaders did try to occupy the capital's international airport, but on orders from headquarters in New York the UN force commander General Prem Chand of India withstood Turkish threats and maintained his positions there. Ultimately, the international consequences of engaging UN peacekeepers (and each of their national governments, some of which were fellow NATO members) were too great for Turkey to contemplate. This was a clear vindication for the principle of moral presence rather than physical force which underpinned the traditional Hammarskjöldian model of peacekeeping (James, 1989).

Nevertheless, the invasion had created an inescapable 'fact on the ground'. Following the outflow of the Cypriot inhabitants from the Turkish occupied north of the island, conditions were in place for the creation of the so-called Turkish Republic of Northern Cyprus under the protection of 25,000 Turkish troops. This political entity failed to win diplomatic recognition by any state other than Turkey itself. The Greek Cypriot part of the island, once again under constitutional government after the return of Archbishop Makarios, now effectively became the state of Cyprus as far as the international community was concerned. This outcome acquired an air of political permanence as peacemaking efforts made no significant progress throughout the rest of the 1970s and the 1980s. In the early post-cold war optimism about a new international order, the United States attempted to pursue a definitive solution to the Cyprus problem, but this did not survive early setbacks of the type that UN negotiators had been doggedly confronting since 1964.

There was, in truth, no real American national interest involved to sustain its peacemaking efforts. The passing of the cold war drained the situation of much of its importance for the west as concerns over alliance cohesion became much less urgent. In this sense UNFICYP illustrates a general risk for peacekeeping operations. A lack of impetus towards an overall settlement on the part of the big powers meant that the peace operation became more or less permanent and 'institutionalised'. In such an environment peacekeeping can develop into part of the problem rather than a tool for its solution. The interposition of the UN between the two *de facto* Cypriot states and the local stability this ensured had the effect of consolidating the post-1974 political *status quo*. It did nothing to encourage the building of a consensus for a long-term settlement mutually acceptable to the two communities.

THE LEGALITY OF PEACE OPERATIONS: THE ARTICLE 19 CRISIS

While UNFICYP carried out its operations on the ground, the Cyprus operation was at the centre of a major institutional crisis in New York. Divisions within the Security Council on the question of the political authorisation of peacekeeping had, as we have seen, been evident since the time of Suez. The means by which peace operations were financed became a major front in this conflict. If all peace operations were regarded as regular costs of the United Nations and therefore levied on all member states as part of their assessed annual contributions, then peacekeeping would have become an official and formal UN activity. This was not acceptable to Moscow because it had not agreed to any such arrangement when it accepted the terms of the UN Charter. Only activities with a clear legal standing – and therefore clear rules for their control – were acceptable to Moscow. The issue was, in short, about

Article 19 crisis: General Assembly wrangle in 1964 following the Soviet Union's refusal to pay for peace operations and the resulting threat to its voting rights under article 19 of the UN Charter.

power, prerogatives and interpretations of the Charter. Its roots could be traced back to the Soviet preoccupation during the planning of the UN in 1945 with the unequal balance of power between east and west in the organisation. From the beginning, the Soviet Union insisted on the primacy of the Security Council – where it could exercise a veto on decisions – whereas in the General Assembly, in the early days of the organisation at least, it would almost certainly be outvoted. Peacekeeping, because it was unforeseen by the founders of the organisation, had no clear identity in the Charter and so no agreed structures of authorisation.

While the Soviet Union was thus extremely cautious about the range and management of peace operations, it did not wish to see them ended. UN military interventions could, it had become plain, serve Soviet interests or at least those of its clients and potential allies. UN involvement in Suez had, after all, publicly exposed embarrassing transatlantic divisions in the western alliance. Indonesia and Egypt, both regarded as friends by Moscow, had sought to benefit from the UN interventions in West New Guinea and Yemen respectively. But, against this, the early course of the Congo operation had heightened Soviet fears that UN military intervention could be used by the west against the interests of its foreign policy. The finance question therefore became a cipher for the more fundamental political issue of the authorisation and control of operations.

Prior to Suez, the costs for UNTSO had been covered, without controversy, from the UN's ordinary budget as a 'regular expense' of the organisation. Similarly, the cost of UNOGIL in Lebanon was met from the UN's normal assessments on all members states. Hammarskjöld himself had taken the position in his Summary Study of the lessons of UNEF that the costs of all peacekeeping operations should be considered regular expenses of the UN and should therefore be payable by the whole membership. Initially, the Soviet objection to the financing of UNEF on this basis was not in itself a major problem. Voluntary contributions from the United States and Britain meant that the operation, which was in any case relatively inexpensive, was maintained without forcing any challenge to the Soviet position. But while UNEF cost about 20 million dollars annually in the early 1960s, ONUC devoured 120 million dollars in 1962 alone (Padelford, 1962; Stoessinger et al., 1964).

Part of the financial crisis which emerged with ONUC and came to a head over UNFICYP lay simply in the inability of many of the new, less developed members to meet their assessed commitments. But the main factor was the refusal of key states to pay up and the impossibility of others covering these defaults by additional voluntary contributions (as had happened over Suez). The grounds of the Soviet objection to compulsory payments for UNEF – its establishment by the General Assembly rather than the Security

Council – did not apply to ONUC, which was authorised by Security Council resolution. Moscow however rejected the right of the General Assembly to apportion costs as it had been doing under article 17(2) of the Charter. Instead, it insisted, this responsibility lay with the Security Council under article 48(1) [**Docs. 4(iv) and 4(i), pp. 121 and 122–3**].

The Soviets took the same rhetorical position on the Congo that they had over Suez: the cost of the operation should be met by the 'imperialists' who had caused the problem which necessitated UN intervention (Belgium in the case of the Congo). In addition to this, the Soviet Union argued that despite having been authorised by the Security Council, ONUC had been left far too much to the personal control of the secretary general (in the person of Dag Hammarskjöld). This view was obviously influenced by the conflicts surrounding the conduct and objectives of ONUC in 1960 and 1961. Concern over constitutional principle and the creation of undesirable precedents was combined with resentment at the damage being done to Soviet foreign policy interests. To drive the point home, Moscow began to withhold its assessed contributions to UNTSO in Palestine as well as to ONUC.

The Soviet Union was not alone in its rejection of funding by compulsory assessment. Its views were shared to some extent by France. Ironically, the French position also derived in part from resentment about the course of the UN operation in the Congo. But while Moscow denounced ONUC over the fall and death of Lumumba, Paris, from the opposite political bank, objected to the UN's threats to Katangese secession. Beyond this, the French also had objections in principle to compulsory support for peacekeeping (Luard, 1989). Under the nationalistic presidency of Charles de Gaulle, France was unhappy with the basic idea of multilateral military intervention by the UN or any other agency. In the French view, power in the international system should be distributed among sovereign states alone. Such authority as the United Nations might have, should extend no further than the performance of tasks delegated to it by member states in pursuit of their own interests. For the UN to require all members to pay for its military operations ran directly counter to this worldview.

By 1961 the UN's financial situation was already chaotic. Defaults in members' payments had caused a shortfall of 40 per cent in ONUC's 1960 budget. In December 1961 the General Assembly voted, over strong Soviet objections, to refer the issue to the **International Court of Justice (ICJ)** for a judgment on the legal position of states in default. The question put for adjudication was whether peacekeeping costs should be imposed by the General Assembly as 'expenses of the Organization' under article 17(2). Or, were such costs 'extra-ordinary' expenses and as such not recoverable on a compulsory basis by the General Assembly? The advisory opinion of the ICJ ('advisory' because the Court was not permitted to make definitive

ICJ: International Court of Justice (which sits in the Hague); one of the principal organs of the United Nations responsible for judgments in contentious cases between states and for the interpretation of the UN Charter.

pronouncements on the UN Charter) was issued the following July. The Court backed the western (and Hammarskjöld's) position that peacekeeping was indeed a regular expense of the UN and therefore could be apportioned by the General Assembly on all members [**Doc. 19, pp. 141–2**].

There was little likelihood that this advisory opinion from an international court (which was seen by Moscow as biased towards the west by virtue of the nationalities of its senior judges) would change Soviet policy. But sleeping dogs were no longer to be left lying. The United States, armed with the ICJ judgment and scenting some cold war points to be scored, now raised the question of sanctions against those with outstanding debts for peacekeeping. Under article 19 of the Charter, members of the General Assembly in default of their duly assessed payments could in certain circumstances be denied voting rights [**Doc. 4(iv), pp. 122–3**]. The Soviet Union responded to the implicit threat by announcing that any attempt to apply such sanctions against it would lead to its withdrawal from the General Assembly.

Once again, peacekeeping, which had been conceived as a means of immunising areas of world politics from cold war involvement, was itself threatening instead to cause a crisis of superpower rivalry within the UN. Full-scale confrontation was ultimately avoided as each side weighed the political odds of various courses of action. Just as the Soviet Union had quietly shelved its proposal in 1960 for a troika to replace the office of secretary general when it became clear that crucial Afro-Asian opinion in the Assembly was against it, now the United States recognised that it had over-estimated the Assembly's indignation at the Soviet position on the finance issue. In order to avoid the crunch towards which the invocation of article 19 was propelling the Assembly, the membership as a whole colluded during the 1964–65 session in conducting their meetings on a 'discussion-only' basis. In this way all votes and therefore any question of voting rights could be avoided.

While the immediate threat to the organisation had been averted in this way, the underlying problem of the financing and authorisation of peace-keeping remained. The Cyprus operation had now to be conducted on a precarious, hand-to-mouth basis which tested to the limit the goodwill and commitment of the contributing states (Thant, 1978). Tectonic shifts in the nature of the superpower relationship were on the horizon of world politics, however. Within a few years the global setting in which peace operations were mounted by the UN were to change fundamentally. The transformation would not be permanent, but throughout the 1970s the United Nations took on a very different role in the management of east–west relations, particularly in the Middle East.

6

Superpower Détente and Peace Operations in the Middle East

The end of the cold war has come generally to be dated from the collapse of communism in the Soviet Union and eastern Europe in the late 1980s and early 1990s. Yet this perspective obscures an earlier view which saw the cold war as having been supplanted by **'détente'** around the late-1960s. Détente was then displaced by a 'second' cold war dating from the end of the 1970s. The phase of détente between the two periods of cold war had various roots. It was in part an acknowledgement by the two blocs (particularly in the aftermath of the Cuban missile crisis) of their 'mutually assured destruction' if they allowed rivalry to slip out of control. But along with this there was a growing awareness from the 1960s onwards of the mutual benefits to be gained by the superpowers from accepting at least some level of economic and technological interdependency. These developments led to a consensus between the United States and the Soviet Union that international conflicts should, where possible, be mutually resolved rather than exploited by each side for its own ends (Bell, 1977; Garthoff, 1985).

This thinking was, of course, very much in line with the original rationale of the peacekeeping project itself. Peripheral disputes – or 'brushfires' – had to be smothered before they engulfed the superpowers themselves (Litwak, 1986). Détente thus brought a much closer marriage between the superpowers' perceptions of their own interests and the peacekeeping idea. A fundamental shift in the balance of forces within the UN itself also contributed to the new attitude. Throughout the 1960s membership of the United Nations had expanded rapidly with the admission of ever more newly independent states as a consequence of the dissolution of the European empires. By the end of the decade what had hitherto been an automatic western majority in the General Assembly had long gone. Now the national delegations to the UN, drawn in the majority from what was now called the third world, were for the most part non-aligned, though with a tendency towards anti-imperialist postures which were implicitly hostile to the west.

Détente: Description of the relatively cooperative superpower relationship during the late 1960s and 1970s based on their recognition of mutual interests in cooperating to manage conflict despite the background of continuing cold war.

The Soviet Union's deep seated suspicions about the UN therefore diminished as the organisation could no longer be exploited by the west as an anti-communist forum. However superficial and short-lived détente would eventually prove, in the 1970s it seemed to herald a historic shift in the nature of global relations (Ashton, 1989). As such it created a unique phase in the narrative of UN peacekeeping.

ISRAEL, EGYPT, SYRIA AND THE 1973 WAR

The principal area in which this 'détente peacekeeping' took place was the Middle East, a region which had moved relentlessly towards the centre of superpower rivalry from the 1950s. The Soviet Union's backing for the Arab states in their conflict with Israel became increasingly open and unqualified throughout the 1960s. Israel in turn had become ever more dependent on the diplomatic and military support of the United States and the western allies. As the region came to preoccupy the superpowers in the 1960s, so the space for UN involvement contracted. As a region of core national interest to both the United States and the Soviet Union, third parties could be permitted no significant role. No UN operation was mounted in the aftermath of the Six Day War of 1967, for example. Consequently no new United Nations presence replaced UNEF which, as we have seen, had been withdrawn on the eve of the war when Egypt as the host state withdrew its consent to the peacekeepers' presence. The Six Day War ended in victory for Israel and, by extension, western interests. Although the Security Council did call for the withdrawal of Israeli forces from Arab territory occupied in the fighting (in its famous resolution 242 in November 1967), no measures, whether of enforcement or peacekeeping, were proposed to ensure its compliance (Ovendale, 1992).

By the next round of the Middle East conflict in 1973, however, the international environment had changed. Beyond some dangerous points when the superpowers seemed to be reverting to a default position of mutual distrust and hostility, the impetus of détente asserted itself and brought an unprecedented level of cooperation between the United States and the Soviet Union in the management of the post-conflict situation.

Yom Kippur War: Arab-Israeli war of October 1973, named for the Jewish religious festival of the Day of Atonement.

On 6 October 1973, during the Jewish festival of **Yom Kippur** (and the Muslim one of Ramadan), Egypt, now led by Nasser's successor, Anwar Sadat, along with Syria launched a surprise attack on Israel. The Egyptians advanced from the west through Sinai and Syria from the east across the Golan Heights. Initial Arab gains were reversed, however, when the momentum of surprise faded and Israel's formidable armoured divisions began to push the attacking forces back on both fronts. The United States and the Soviet Union, taken genuinely by surprise and after an initial period of indecision, began to supply their respective clients in the region. Soon, though, having taken stock of the situation and their own potentially fatal responses to it, the larger importance of détente began to make itself felt in both Washington and Moscow. The superpowers' approach to the crisis was now to act together to manage the conflict rather than openly to pursue victory for their rival *protégés*. To this end, on 19 October the Soviet leader Leonid Brezhnev invited US President Richard Nixon's secretary of state Henry Kissinger to travel immediately to Moscow in order to work out the basis for a ceasefire (Isaacson, 1992). This was quickly achieved and on 21 October, Israel, Egypt and Syria were effectively 'informed' by the superpowers that they should no longer be fighting. The next day a unanimous Security Council resolution confirmed the ceasefire and called for its implementation within twelve hours. With the tide of the war running in its favour after initial losses, Israel was reluctant to comply and continued its encirclement of the Egyptian Third Army on the western side of the Suez Canal. There was now a momentary crisis in superpower cooperation when the Soviet Union moved nuclear weapons into the region and the US responded by putting its own nuclear capacity on high alert. In this challenge to détente it seemed that east–west relations might be returning to the dangerous state of the early 1960s. This flashback to pre-détente cold war conditions seemed to concentrate minds, however, and Israel was now strongly pressed to fall into line (Crockatt, 1996).

The second **United Nations Emergency Force (UNEF II)** was the first peace operation to be established by the UN since the Cyprus force in 1964. Authorised by the Security Council on 25 October, it was quickly deployed between the Egyptian and Israeli lines in Sinai. Although the detailed planning was undertaken at UN headquarters in New York, UNEF II was in a real sense an American-Soviet initiative. The key players in its genesis were Henry Kissinger and the Soviet foreign minister, Andrei Gromyko **[Docs. 20 and 21, pp. 142–3 and 143–4]**. The role of the UN secretary general, at this time the Austrian Kurt Waldheim who had succeeded U Thant in 1972, was to a degree a secondary one. The entire process, from the first Soviet move to the authorisation of an interposition peacekeeping force, had taken less than a week.

The significance of this could be interpreted in different ways, depending on the perspective of the observer. It could be seen as a leap forward for the UN and an illustration of what it could achieve in the absence of superpower rivalry. Alternatively it could be taken as a depressing sign of the subordination of the world organisation to superpower interests. In the view of one writer of the more pessimistic perspective, 'the United Nations in

UNEF II: The second UN Emergency Force, deployed in Sinai between Israeli and Egyptian forces after the 1973 war; withdrawn in 1979 following Soviet refusal to renew its Security Council mandate.

general and the Security Council in particular were pushed further along the road to the point where they became mere elements – however essential – in superpower strategy' (Verrier, 1981: 106).

UNEF II was initially formed by troops from UNFICYP hurriedly brought across the Mediterranean from Cyprus. This, as Kurt Waldheim acknowledged, was a risky strategy (Waldheim, 1985). The situation in Cyprus was deteriorating at this time in a protracted crisis which would eventually end with the Turkish invasion the following summer (as mentioned earlier, pp. 68–9). But the alternative would have been to create a new peace operation from scratch, a process that would have been expected to take several weeks. By simply transferring units from Cyprus (on hastily arranged British transport aircraft) the UN was able to deploy a force of 600 experienced Austrian, Swedish and Finnish peacekeepers within 24 hours. The force eventually grew to a strength of 7000.

The mandate establishing UNEF II made explicit what was already implicit in peacekeeping practice: it excluded the participation of the permanent members of the Security Council. But the composition of the force did depart in one key respect from the norm of contingents drawn from familiar middle power states. For the first time a **Warsaw Pact** country – Poland – contributed troops to a UN peacekeeping operation, though in a support role and not on the front-line. A further symptom of the impact of détente followed shortly after with the incorporation of Soviet officers in UNTSO to balance exactly the number of their American counterparts (the United States having had a small presence in UNTSO since its formation in 1948). And there was to be no major conflict over the financing of UNEF II. The supremacy of the Security Council (or at least its two key members) in the establishment and control of the operation meant that the Soviet Union accepted that costs could be levied on all UN members. The deployment of the force was carried through efficiently. Both Egypt and Israel (with more reservations) had little option but to cooperate with an intervention which, although having the imprimatur of the United Nations, was in many respects a special project of their respective international patrons.

The involvement of UN peacekeepers on Israel's other front in the 1973 war, where it faced Syria on the Golan Heights, was not so easily brought about. Although Syrian forces had regained some of the territory lost to Israel in the 1967 war in the first shock of the 1973 fighting, they were eventually pushed back beyond even the previous line. Initially, therefore, the regime of President Hafiz al-Assad in Damascus was not readily receptive to United Nations intervention as it feared a consolidation of the new Israeli gains. Sporadic fighting, mainly in the form of artillery duels, continued across the ceasefire lines in the Golan Heights for several months after the main fighting ended. Kissinger, fearing the consequences for US–Soviet relations

Warsaw Pact: East European Soviet bloc military alliance formed in 1955 to confront NATO; it was dissolved in 1991.

of continued Syrian alienation, set about a protracted process of shuttle diplomacy between President Assad and the Israeli prime ministers Golda Meir and (from April 1974) Yitzhak Rabin. By the terms of the agreement which emerged in May 1974, Israel was to withdraw more or less to its post-1967 positions and a **United Nations Disengagement Observer Force (UNDOF)** placed between the two sides.

The Security Council, conforming to recent practice, entered the process only after the superpowers themselves had carried through the substantive negotiations. Accordingly, on 31 May, a Security Council resolution was quickly passed authorising the establishment of the new force. Initially this was composed of contingents from Austria and Iran. Even a few years later such an arrangement would have been unthinkable for Israel, but at this time Iran was still under the rule of the pro-western Shah. Again, the UN was to some degree just an executive wing of superpower diplomacy (or, perhaps more correctly in this instance, American diplomacy acquiesced to by the Soviet Union). The UN's institutional role in this was to manage the practical implementation of *faits accomplis* arranged by the senior negotiators of the two cold war superpowers.

The unusual designation of UNDOF as an 'observer force' represented a compromise between different views of the nature of the operation on the parts of Syria and Israel. Syria, concerned that the operation would be located on its territory, sought to minimise the impression of a substantial 'occupation force'. Damascus therefore favoured a military observer mission on the lines of UNTSO or UNOGIL, which would involve no real or symbolic challenge to its territorial sovereignty. Israel, on the other hand, was sceptical of the depth of Syria's commitment to any long-term agreement. It therefore suspended its usual posture of antipathy to UN peacekeeping operations (with the added impetus of American diplomatic pressure) and sought the interposition of a large and well-equipped force on the Syrian side of the disputed frontier line. This, the Israeli government believed, would give the Syrians pause for thought. The possible gains for Syria of a surprise attack in the Golan would have to be seen against the diplomatic consequences of engaging (or, more likely, pushing aside) a major UN presence. UNDOF, therefore, maintained a strength of just over 1000 – considerably less than Israel would have wished, but much more than Syria had envisaged (Kissinger, 1982).

Slow to be established, and hedged around with misgivings when it finally was, UNDOF turned out to be the longer-lasting of the two post-1973 war operations. This, of course, was no special mark of success in a peacekeeping operation. It was mainly a reflection of the speed and effectiveness of Israel's peacemaking with Egypt which led to the winding up of UNEF II within six years. Certainly, UNDOF had an important part to play in regional

UNDOF: The UN Disengagement Observer Force deployed in the Golan Heights from June 1974 to monitor the ceasefire line between Israel and Syria following the 1973 war.

stability, especially in its earlier phase when it was responsible for the temporary occupation of territory from which Israel had agreed to withdraw pending its return to Syrian sovereignty. But this precarious role of agent between hostile post-belligerents was quite different from the more radical conciliation process in which UNEF II was participating further to the west (Comay, 1976).

UNEF II remained in operation until 1979 when, in a curious way a victim of the success of the peace process of which it had been part, its mandate was terminated at the insistence of the Soviet Union. In January 1974, again following a hurried sequence of shuttle diplomacy by Henry Kissinger, a comprehensive disengagement agreement was signed between Israel and Egypt. In contrast to the limited scope of the Israeli-Syrian disengagement which would be agreed the following May, the plan was far-reaching and pointed the way to a fundamental political settlement. Israeli forces withdrew eastwards across the Suez Canal to a point about twelve miles from the waterway. Egypt reoccupied the territory up to the Canal and six miles beyond on the eastern side. Beyond this a zone of similar width was left to be occupied by the UN, and to the east of this was an Israeli-held strip. Both sides accepted limits on the weaponry they could place in their respective zones on either side of the buffer provided by UNEF II. A subsequent phase, agreed later in 1974, widened the UN's area of responsibility and pushed the Israeli lines further back to the east. As well as the presence of UN troops on the ground, the supervision of the agreement was to involve United States Air Force reconnaissance. The process was not without its difficulties from time to time but it was ultimately successful. There can be little doubt that this was due largely to the close involvement of the superpowers. The principal impetus came from the United States which was, of course, Israel's *de facto* ally and with which Sadat's Egypt had an ambivalent relationship. But Soviet cooperation, at least in this first phase of the Egyptian-Israeli peacemaking process, illustrated the nature of the superpower relationship at this time, however short-lived it was to prove (James, 1990).

American initiative, Soviet concurrence and UN interposition brought an unprecedented stability to the diplomatic and military interface between Egypt and Israel and this deepened over subsequent years. The conditions were thus created for the negotiation of a comprehensive peace agreement. The external impetus was almost wholly American, however. In 1978, with strong encouragement from the then US president, Jimmy Carter, a treaty was agreed between Israel and Egypt at the presidential retreat at Camp David. The signing ceremony involving Anwar Sadat and the Israeli prime minister Menachim Begin took place in March 1979 under the benign supervision of President Carter. The Soviet Union was not represented, however.

The continuation of UNEF II into the new phase of peace implementation had been an underlying assumption throughout the Camp David negotiations. A central part of the agreement involved the withdrawal of Israeli forces from the Sinai and then continuing military monitoring of the area. But the UN had played a very marginal role in what was essentially an American foreign policy project ending with the **Camp David agreement**. This simultaneous marginalisation of UN authority with the assumption that its peacekeeping resources could be taken for granted was a viable policy only for as long as both superpowers were in agreement and acting together in the Security Council and beyond. The unilateral management of the Egyptian-Israeli rapprochement by the United States meant that this was no longer the case. Soviet acquiescence was withdrawn as the broader diplomatic implications of the agreement began to emerge. The completion of the Camp David process – unthinkable only five or so years earlier – had a major impact on Middle Eastern politics and, inevitably, on superpower relations. By making peace with Israel, Egypt had placed itself beyond the pale of acceptable behaviour in much of the Arab region where the very notion of a peace agreement with the historic enemy was rejected (Pipes, 1981; Quandt, 1986).

The Soviet Union now faced a dilemma. Although Moscow was closely associated with the earlier peacekeeping process in Sinai and had accepted the establishment and deployment of UNEF II without any significant reservations, it had done so while maintaining its ties with the Arab world as a whole. The isolation of Egypt from this world was now a major diplomatic complication for Moscow. As long as UNEF II acted as a traditional interposition presence between Egypt and Israel, the superpowers could give their mutual support to it in the spirit of détente and without compromising their existing ties with other regional states. Now, however, the success of US diplomacy in removing the Egyptian-Israeli dimension from the broader Middle East conflict threatened this arrangement. The role of UNEF II, if it was to continue in place, would now change from that of buffer between Arab and Israeli to that of facilitator of a western-driven, 'anti-Arab' accommodation. This was too great a step for Moscow to take. Détente, as its primary architect Henry Kissinger himself later wrote, 'defined not friendship but a strategy for a relationship between adversaries' (Kissinger, 1982: 600). The Camp David settlement was in effect a victory for the west, and the Soviet Union now raised its adversarial cold war colours once again. It would not, it made clear in the Security Council, agree to the transformation of UNEF II into the handmaiden of the Camp David process. Dependent as it was on regular Security Council renewals of its mandate, the operation could not be maintained, and accordingly UNEF II ceased to exist in July 1979.

Camp David agreement: Outcome of American-brokered talks between Israel and Egypt during 1978 and 1979 which formed the basis of a permanent peace between the two countries.

In truth, the broader fabric of détente was already unravelling at this time anyway. The sequence of communist victories throughout Southeast Asia in the later 1970s as well as new areas of ideological conflict, particularly in Africa, had steadily been exposing its limits. Soviet disaffection over Camp David was both a symptom of the decline of détente and a further cause of its deterioration. This shift in the Washington–Moscow relationship back to more competitive terms was in evidence elsewhere in the Middle East in the late 1970s, where another venture into détente peacekeeping was running into difficulty (Garthoff, 1985).

LEBANON IN THE TWILIGHT OF DÉTENTE

Lebanon, it will be recalled, was first the subject of UN military involvement in 1958 when UNOGIL provided a sedative presence through a nervous period of domestic, regional and, potentially at least, global tensions. Despite the successful outcome of UNOGIL the local instabilities which had brought the operation into being were deep and endemic. Lebanon's apparent prosperity in comparison to its Arab neighbours (it was sometimes called the Switzerland of the Middle East) and the apparent cosmopolitanism of its urban elite overlay deep socio-political fissures. Complex and interrelated factors of geographical location, diverse ethnic composition and government instability meant that the Lebanon's very existence as a state was precarious. Long-standing problems of Muslim–Christian relations (and indeed intra-Muslim and intra-Christian sectarian conflicts) were exacerbated by the creation of Israel in 1948 and the sequence of Arab-Israeli wars that followed over the next quarter century. Lebanon became a major destination for Palestinian refugees both directly from their dispossessed homes after the wars of 1948 and 1967 and in 1970 from Jordan which expelled its own population of Palestinian exiles. By the mid-1970s much of the southern part of Lebanon as well as areas of the capital, Beirut, were inhabited by Palestinians who now made up about 20 per cent of the country's population. Concentrated in semi-permanent camps with few amenities but no shortage of weapons,

PLO: Palestine Liberation Organization formed in 1964; historically the voice of the Palestinian people ejected from their homeland by successive wars and Israeli occupations; a key actor in Lebanon during the conflicts of the 1970s.

the loyalty of this Palestinian diaspora to the central government in Beirut was minimal. Its allegiance was primarily to the **Palestine Liberation Organization (PLO)**, at this time the main armed opposition to Israel in the Middle East and throughout the world. With southern Lebanon sharing a border with northern Israel, this was obviously an extremely worrying situation for the Israeli leadership.

In 1975 a long-threatening civil war erupted between an alliance of Palestinians and left-wing Lebanese Muslims on one side and rightist

Maronite Christian militias on the other. The rickety foundations of the Lebanese state and the inherent weakness of central authority in the country were quickly exposed. In the absence of any internal force of stabilisation, a dangerous international situation soon developed. To the south, Israel was naturally sympathetic to the anti-Palestinian Christians, while to the east Syria was faced by a political and strategic dilemma. Although the sympathies of the Syrian people naturally lay with the Palestinian-Muslim alliance, the government in Damascus had a prior concern with regional stability. The consequences for this of the collapse of the Lebanese state and its replacement by aggressive and well-armed competing factions would be grave. It would be an obvious provocation to Israel for Syria to invade and impose its own pro-Muslim solution throughout Lebanon. Whatever the thaw between Egypt and Israel, relations with Syria, over the Golan Heights and more generally, were extremely bad. The Syrians therefore intervened in 1976 not in support of the Palestinians but ostensibly to prop up the (Christian-dominated) government in Beirut. Israel accepted this involvement on condition that the Syrians did not press too close to the Israeli border in the south. The effect of this was to keep the forces of a long-standing enemy away from Israeli territory, certainly. But it also meant that the Palestinian-dominated south remained unregulated by the Syrian presence, which was restricted to the north. Cross-border attacks on Israel from southern Lebanon increased in frequency and destructiveness until, in March 1978, the Israeli army moved across the border in force (Calvocoressi, 2008).

With the Egyptian-Israeli peace negotiations moving towards a conclusion at this time, the United States was determined to stabilise the situation in southern Lebanon before it could threaten the process. Its shock-waves could not be allowed to undermine the delicate architecture of diplomacy leading towards Camp David. As in 1973, Washington sought a solution to its diplomatic difficulties through a UN peace operation. Now, however, with Moscow ill-disposed to the peacemaking effort between Egypt and Israel and with détente as a whole under increasing stress, the Soviet Union could not be co-opted into the process as easily as it had been five years earlier. The operation in Lebanon was therefore established in the twilight of détente and its fortunes would reflect this opaque beginning.

The **United Nations Interim Force in Lebanon (UNIFIL)** was authorised by the Security Council during a sequence of meetings on 19 March 1978 at the strong urging of the United States. The Soviet delegation abstained on the enabling resolutions, though it did not go so far as to veto them. UNIFIL's area of operation was in the south of Lebanon, from the southern bank of the Litani river to the Israeli border. It was established, in the words of the mandating resolution 'for the purpose of confirming the withdrawal of Israeli forces, restoring international peace and security and

Maronite Christians: Adherents of the Eastern Catholic Church in the Middle East; the Maronite community in Lebanon was traditionally dominant in the country's government but frequently challenged by Muslim aspirations.

UNIFIL: The UN Interim Force in Lebanon, formed in March 1978 and deployed in the south of the country adjacent to the border with Israel.

assisting the government of Lebanon in ensuring the return of its effective authority in the area' (Security Council resolution 425, 19 March 1978). In other words, it was to oversee an Israeli withdrawal from Lebanon and then itself to fill the territorial and security vacuum this would create. This was an extremely burdensome task, but its other responsibility – helping the Beirut government to regain its authority in the south – was even more challenging. This 'authority' had been difficult to discern even before the Israeli invasion and it was impossible to see how UNIFIL could undertake this. Nevertheless, secretary general Waldheim succeeded in putting the initial force together in a relatively short, though frenetic, period of planning [**Doc. 22, pp. 144–5**].

Confronted in the Security Council by Soviet objections to the plan, the Americans were also faced with Israeli grievances. Israel after its uncharacteristic support for the interposition of a United Nations force in the Golan Heights in 1974, now reverted to its more familiar stance of grudging and uncooperative acquiescence. The United States, the Israeli government felt, should have shown more understanding of its difficulties over Lebanon before engineering a UN intervention.

The absence of outright Soviet opposition meant that controversy was avoided over the operation's financing. But while the principle of General Assembly apportionment as a regular expense was accepted, the reality was that the Soviet Union initially, and then later the United States as well, were slow to pay up (James, 1990). Fundamentally, the recognition of mutual superpower self-interest that had driven arrangements over Sinai and the Golan Heights earlier in the decade was now gone. The international setting of the Lebanon operation had greater similarities to the Cyprus force than it had to either UNEF II or UNDOF. UNIFIL was seen by the Soviet Union as a western response to a problem of western international relations – those between the United States and Israel. In a similar way, UNFICYP in Cyprus sought to resolve the western problem of internal NATO strains between Greece and Turkey.

Differences between the superpower were also reflected in the refusal of any Warsaw Pact states to contribute to UNIFIL. This represented a retreat from the limited advances of 1973 when Polish personnel were deployed with UNEF II and Soviet observers joined UNTSO. There were, though, enough offers of contingents from other member states to permit the formation of the force. As usual the majority of contributors were from the traditional middle powers, with troops sent from Canada, Finland, Ireland, the Netherlands, Norway and Sweden.

France also provided troops. Its participation was comparable to that of Britain in the Cyprus operation. In both cases a particular post-colonial relationship was involved. France had been responsible for the administration of Lebanon under a League of Nations mandate after the dismantling

of the Ottoman Empire at the end of the First World War. Paris had subsequently maintained a special relationship after the creation of a Lebanese
state during the Second World War. But as with Britain in Cyprus, France
was somewhat compromised by a traditional affinity with one of the
Lebanese factions. Although Britain's historical leaning towards the Turkish
community in Cyprus did not significantly affect its standing in the UN
force, perceptions of French sympathy for the Maronite Christians became
a problem for UNIFIL. After a series of controversial incidents the major part
of the French contribution was withdrawn (Verrier, 1981).

UNIFIL was deployed in southern Lebanon in the first days of April 1978
and within a month a force of 6000 (some 2000 more than originally
planned) was on the ground. Its area of operations was in principle the
southern fifth of the country north of the Israeli border. In reality the actual
locale of UNIFIL control was pockmarked with enclaves controlled by local
factions. Although the Israelis handed over to UNIFIL the northernmost part
of the territory they had occupied in 1978, they became less cooperative
as they withdrew south. Along the area adjacent to its frontier Israel passed
control not to the UN but to local Christian militias. The fearsomely anti-
Palestinian stance of these irregular forces provided Israel, in the view of its
leaders, with a more reliable buffer in its self-declared 'security zone' than
any UN peacekeeping force could be trusted to provide.

These local conditions posed a serious challenge to the traditional concept
of UN peacekeeping and raised questions about UNIFIL's capacity to carry
out the tasks in hand. How appropriate was a lightly armed, interposition
force in the tortuous international and domestic cross-currents of southern
Lebanon in 1978? How effective was the moral presence of UN forces in this
situation? It is possible that a more strongly armed force mandated to protect
Israel's border might have persuaded the Israeli government to permit
UNIFIL's full deployment and allow it freedom of movement. But, of course,
such a force would have meant that the UN was involved in an enforcement
rather than a traditional peacekeeping operation. It would have required
force contributors to give a freer hand (and heavier weapons) to the UN. But
more significantly, it would probably have required a mandate unequivocally
based in Chapter VII of the Charter which would almost certainly have been
vetoed by the Soviet Union. In this way the Lebanon situation provided
a sharp illustration of the central dilemma of UN military intervention in the
(re-emerging) cold war. There would always be a play-off between what
would be operationally effective and what was politically feasible.

The difficulties for UNIFIL did not come from the Israeli side alone. The
Palestinian forces in southern Lebanon insisted on maintaining various positions within the UN zone. More substantially, they also demanded that they
should retain control of the port city of Tyre on the Mediterranean coast south

of the Litani. From the beginning, therefore, UNIFIL did not have full freedom of movement in its own operational area. This was a fatal weakness for any peacekeeping operation, one well-recognised since the Congo experience in the early 1960s. Even before this it had been identified as a prerequisite for effective peacekeeping by Hammarskjöld in his 1958 Summary Study. At the outset, therefore, UNIFIL's operations were hampered by fundamental strategic and tactical shortcomings. A lack of effective superpower backing for the UN's efforts at the strategic level was aggravated by restricted freedom of movement and limited firepower at the tactical level (Thakur, 1987).

Yet with these handicaps taken into consideration, UNIFIL was in many respects quite successful during its first years of deployment. It provided a buffer if not directly between Israel and its enemies, then certainly between pro-Israeli and anti-Israeli factions in Lebanon itself. UNIFIL could not, though, impose a peace on this cockpit of regional tensions and four years after its deployment it was effectively brushed aside as the principal players crashed back into the arena (Skögmo, 1989).

Israel's invasion of June 1982 – which it referred to as 'Operation Peace for Galilee' – eventually reached to the southern outskirts of Beirut. It was provoked by an increase in cross-border attacks into northern Israel and, more specifically, the attempted murder of the Israeli ambassador in London by the PLO. Israel was now determined to settle the 'Palestinian problem' in Lebanon once and for all. In this they were largely successful, though at a considerable cost in national prestige. The UNIFIL commander was informed by the Israelis of their intentions only ninety minutes before the first tanks crossed the border. While UNIFIL attempted as far as possible to obstruct the Israeli advance merely by its physical presence, as a peacekeeping force it could do little when its moral authority was simply disregarded. The 1982 invasion might be seen to mark a tipping point in western public opinion towards Israel. Before this, Israel had been widely regarded as a victim of Arab aggression, particularly in the wars of 1967 and 1973. After 1982, in contrast, Israeli behaviour came increasingly to be seen as part of the region's problems. In the short-term the PLO was effectively expelled from Lebanon, but this was achieved with much apparently indiscriminate violence on the part of Israel. Artillery attacks on Palestinian areas of West Beirut and Israeli complicity in factional atrocities – which the UN proved incapable of preventing – badly damaged Israel's standing in western opinion.

For the three years following this second Israeli invasion UNIFIL's *raison d'être* was unclear. It could perform no significant peacekeeping function, interposition being meaningless in an area now dominated by the Israeli occupation forces and their local allies. Nevertheless, every six months the Security Council voted to renew its mandate with a view to the eventual resumption of its peacekeeping role.

When the Israelis withdrew once again in 1985 they left behind an expanded security zone which further restricted UNIFIL's authority. In one respect, though, the force's general political position was improved. As the cold war succumbed to another, this time final, thaw as a result of the fundamental changes taking place under Mikhail Gorbachev's leadership in Moscow, the Soviet Union abandoned its policy of abstention on votes extending UNIFIL's mandate. Henceforward the operation would have the unanimous support of the permanent members of the Security Council. This did not, however, bring any obvious change in its position on the ground. UN troops remained vulnerable to physical attack and political recrimination from the tangle of factions they were forced to confront. UNIFIL did, however, have an important humanitarian role in its areas of operation, often in the wake of violent outbreaks which it had been unable to prevent. In this sense it became, in the developing language of peace operations, a **'humanitarian intervention'** as much as a traditional peacekeeping mission. It also provided an international witness to events in the region (the traditional function of military observation) and therefore acted as something of a constraint on the behaviour of the protagonists. This role was in evidence after the end of the cold war, in 1996 and again in 2006, when the Israelis launched cross-border attacks against their Islamist enemies of the Hezbollah. This more fundamentalist Muslim opposition had come to replace the PLO as Israel's principal foe in Lebanon. In common with peacekeeping operations generally, the pertinent question over UNIFIL was perhaps not what it had 'done' in a positive sense but rather what would have happened in its absence.

Humanitarian intervention: Peace operations undertaken specifically with a humanitarian purpose; contrasted with traditional peacekeeping which was largely concerned with the management of conflict in the interests of international stability.

7

The 'Second' Cold War: Peace Suspended?

For ten years after the formation of the Interim Force in Lebanon no new peacekeeping operation or military observer mission was established by the United Nations. The Lebanon venture was perched on the cusp of the shift from détente peacekeeping and a return to the rigidities of the cold war and it prefigured the effective suspension of new military interventions by the UN. Conceived in the dying days of détente, UNIFIL was required to operate throughout the ensuing resumption of hostilities between Washington and Moscow. The behaviour of local clients would no longer be controlled by the two superpowers for the greater good of their own bilateral relationship (Halliday, 1987).

While no new UN peace operations were created during this extended period, this did not mean that 'international peacekeeping' as a whole went into hibernation. Multilateral operations were still mounted, but in both purpose and composition they were now sectional rather than truly global undertakings. These new forces were for the most part substitutes for (or extensions of) operations previously undertaken by the UN.

NON-UN PEACEKEEPING IN THE MIDDLE EAST

As we have seen, Soviet alienation from the US-driven peace process between Egypt and Israel led to the winding up of UNEF II in 1979. Yet a peace operation was still required to oversee the agreed Israeli withdrawal from the Sinai and then to maintain a watching brief in the area. The Camp David agreement itself had assumed the continuation of the UN presence, and the United States was now put on the spot. President Carter, anxious to avoid any obstacle to the final completion of the very delicate process of agreement, indicated that if necessary, America would itself organise a peace operation to replace UNEF II. In the meantime United States personnel took on the task of military observation while all possibilities of a further UN mission were explored. By 1981, however, with détente now more or less non-existent, the effort was abandoned; it had become clear that the Soviet Union would veto any attempt to re-engage UN peacekeepers in the region.

Consequently, the US negotiated with both Israel and Egypt to work out the terms for the recruitment and deployment of 2500-strong non-UN operation: the **Multinational Force and Observers (MFO)**. This grouping eventually consisted of US allies from NATO, Australasia and Latin America. Lacking the clear identity of a UN operation, the MFO faced a number of structural problems when eventually deployed in April 1982 (on the day that Israel formally handed the Sinai back to Egyptian sovereignty). Despite – or perhaps more correctly because of – its essentially western character it proved difficult to gather an appropriate range of national contingents and to retain them. Potential European contributors in particular were wary of involvement in what was widely perceived as an American foreign policy project (James, 1990). But given the nature of its task – the supervision of a carefully negotiated and fully agreed peace treaty guaranteed by the United States – the MFO faced no great operational challenges. More than most UN operations, the conditions for success were present before the first boot was on the ground. Israeli-Egyptian relations remained strong after Camp David, at least at inter-governmental level, and there was no real concern that either side would attempt to change the terms of their agreement. There was, in short, a solid peace to keep and the effort involved in keeping it was minimal.

The same could not be said of another western-inspired venture which was designed as an alternative to wider UN involvement in Lebanon. When, following its 1982 invasion, Israel set about the expulsion of the Palestinians from their strongholds in West Beirut, there was an obvious danger of its forces clashing with the Syrian units present in the area since the intervention in 1976 and with the local armed factions. This threat of a reignition of full-scale war in the country seemed to call for a robust intervention.

An extension of the mandate of the UN Interim Force in Lebanon and its interposition between the opposing sides would have been one means of easing the situation. But with the crumbling of détente, Soviet support for UNIFIL which had never been enthusiastic was now non-existent. It was also unlikely that Israel would be willing to see the UN presence extended from the south of Lebanon. Crucially, in this regard, the United States was now more reluctant than during the era of détente to face down Israeli objections to the UN role. The days when the superpowers would restrain and direct their regional clients in pursuit of mutual self-interest had passed. Instead the

MFO: Multinational Force and Observers established formally in 1981 to oversee the Camp David agreement in the Sinai region between Israel and Egypt; effectively a successor to UNEF II whose mandate was terminated in 1979 after the withdrawal of Soviet support in the Security Council.

MNF: US-led Multi-national Force in the Beirut area of Lebanon established to deal with the upsurge of instability and violence in 1982 and 1983; operated simul-taneously with but wholly independent of the UN Interim Force in southern Lebanon.

Americans themselves took the initiative to form a non-UN multinational force (**MNF**). This operation went through two distinct phases. When first formed in August 1982 it consisted of 800 American, 800 Italian and 400 French troops. Initially the mission was successful in stabilising the situation in Beirut. Multi-party negotiations were held which resulted in the PLO agreeing to leave Lebanon and its leadership and fighters were transported to Tunisia. At the same time, the danger of a large-scale military clash between Israeli and Syrian forces in and around Beirut seemed to recede.

With a degree of self-congratulation, the MNF now began to wind up its operations. This would prove to be fatally premature, however. In the middle of September the Christian Lebanese president elect, Bashir Gemayal, was assassinated. In the violence that followed, hundreds of Palestinian civilians living in refugee camps in Beirut were murdered by Christian militia whose Israeli allies stood by. The resulting chaos led to US president Ronald Reagan arranging the deployment of what was effectively MNF II. Like its predecessor this consisted of US, Italian and French forces which were reinforced in early 1983 by a British contingent. MNF II was even less of a traditional 'peacekeeping' force than its recent predecessor. While it sought to interpose itself between hostile factions in order to control violence, it broke one of the golden rules of classical peacekeeping and of UN practice by identifying itself with a particular side. Its purpose was, in effect, to shore up the tottering Lebanese government and its weak and demoralised army. As a result, MNF II became a target for the tangle of factions and groups still involved in the Lebanese crisis, many of which sought the destruction of the remnants of central government authority.

This partisan objective of MNF II overlay its more traditional peace-keeping task of providing a buffer between the Israeli invasion force and its myriad enemies. Interposition of this type can work only if the neutrality and legitimacy of the buffer forces are accepted by all sides. Without the authority of a UN Security Council mandate this acceptance would inevitably be a problem in the fractured conditions of Lebanon. The American-dominated force was denounced by the Muslim militias as an instrument of pro-Israeli western imperialism. Throughout 1983 the situation in Beirut deteriorated and MNF II soon found itself in direct armed conflict with the militias. This, of course, transgressed another of the trinity of peacekeeping principles to add to the existing problem of the force's lack of neutrality: force was not being used only in self-defence and as a last resort. Nor could it possibly be said that the multinational force was deployed with the consent of the opposing sides. This broke the third of the fundamental rules of peacekeeping. While 'host state consent' could be claimed (even if the state in question was on the point of disintegration), the other actors involved utterly opposed the intervention.

In October 1983 coordinated suicide bomb attacks against the force killed over 300 American and French troops. Retaliation undertaken by the MNF II contributors in the form of air strikes and naval bombardment was directed exclusively at Syrian-backed groups, exposing further the weakness of the force's claim to be a peacekeeping mission in any traditional sense. The multinational force ended its operations at the beginning of 1984 as first the Italians, then the Americans and finally the French withdrew their contingents. Thereafter the situation in Beirut continued its downward spiral unhindered by peacekeeping efforts on the part of the UN or anyone else.

In the 1950s and 1960s peacekeeping had provided the UN with a means of sealing off superpower involvement in local conflicts on the peripheries of their main interests. In the 1970s, when cold war gave way to détente, it had offered the superpowers themselves a tool for the management of relationships between troublesome clients. Now, in the 1980s, with the second cold war underway, it appeared that no third phase of UN peacekeeping would emerge to meet the new situation.

PEACE OPERATIONS RESUME: THE NAMIBIA–ANGOLA ARRANGEMENT

The freezing of new UN peace operations began to thaw towards the end of the decade as the conditions which would bring a final end to the cold war began to move into place. During 1988, for example, a small **Good Offices Mission in Afghanistan and Pakistan (UNGOMAP)** was established to assist in the process of Soviet withdrawal from Afghanistan. The original intervention by the Soviet Union in 1979 had been a major factor in the crumbling of détente and the return to cold war. Now UN involvement there, however limited, at least hinted that the jealous protection of core interests by the superpowers which had hitherto kept out all third party intervention might be fading.

UNGOMAP: The UN Good Offices Mission in Afghanistan and Pakistan, formed in May 1988 following the withdrawal of Soviet forces from Afghanistan; mission ended in March 1990.

This impression was reinforced the following year with the creation of the first Angola Verification Mission (**UNAVEM**). The purpose of this was to supervise the withdrawal of the Cuban forces which had been in Angola since the time of its independence from Portugal in 1975. These Cuban 'internationalists', as they described themselves, had propped up the pro-Soviet MPLA (*Movimento Popular de Libertatação de Angola*) government in Angola (which had been in power since the country's independence from Portugal in 1975) against both South African incursions and the western-backed rebels of the UNITA (*União para a Independência Total de Angola*) movement. Another cockpit of the second cold war had moved into the range of UN peace operations (Fortna, 1993).

UNAVEM: The first United Nations Angola Verification Mission, formed in January 1989 to supervise the withdrawal of Cuban forces from Angola; mission ended successfully in May 1991.

The Cuban withdrawal overseen by UNAVEM was part of a linked agreement which was designed to bring Angola's southern neighbour Namibia to independence. The Namibian part of this process involved the deployment of a much larger UN force than UNAVEM and whose mandate was much wider than military observation alone. Namibia (previously South West Africa) had been a recurring issue in both the Security Council and the General Assembly since the 1960s. Originally a German colony, it had been passed as a League of Nations mandate to South Africa after the First World War. This arrangement continued when the UN **Trusteeship** Council supplanted the League Mandate Commission in 1945. Far from preparing the territory for self-determination and eventual statehood as required by the League and then the UN, the apartheid regime in South Africa had in essence annexed it. Namibia thus became the effective border between South Africa and Marxist Angola. Each of the two mutually hostile regimes supported guerrilla groups fighting against the other. South Africa regularly carried out direct military incursions into Angola while also supplying the UNITA rebels there. For its part Angola provided bases and support for the South West African People's Organization (SWAPO) which was fighting against South African rule in Namibia.

Worn down by international condemnation and faced with a growing crisis of military morale, South Africa eventually agreed, under American and United Nations pressure, to Namibia's independence with the withdrawal of Cuban forces from Angola as a *quid pro quo*. While UNAVEM was overseeing this, the **United Nations Transition Assistance Group (UNTAG)** was deployed in Namibia itself to replace South African security forces and to organise and oversee elections for a post-independence government. UNTAG was one of the UN's most ambitious undertakings to date. With about 8000 personnel (4500 troops, 1500 police and 2000 civilian officials), its role was similar to, though politically and diplomatically much more formidable than, that of UNTEA/UNSF in West New Guinea in 1962–63. In both places the UN was required to act as intermediary in the passage of a territory from colonial rule towards a post-imperial identity (absorption by Indonesia in the case of West New Guinea, full independence in that of Namibia).

The Angolan side of the arrangement was resolved largely without incident. UNAVEM was a small mission, consisting of seventy military observers. Its Security Council mandate required it to verify the withdrawal of all Cuban forces from Angola through agreed air and sea ports and this was achieved more than a month ahead of the June 1991 date fixed. UNTAG's task was more challenging. The UN operation was multifaceted and complex. It also faced persistent obstruction from South African officials in the territory as it became clear that the elections would result in a sweeping victory for SWAPO (Parsons, 1995). However, in March 1990,

Trusteeship: UN successor to the League of Nations mandate system by which colonial territories of the defeated countries of both world wars were held 'in trust' by UN member states responsible for preparing them for self-determination; overseen by the Trusteeship Council, a principal organ of the United Nations.

UNTAG: The UN Transition Assistance Group for Namibia, formed in April 1989 to oversee elections and the independence of Namibia from a disputed South African Trusteeship; mission successfully completed in March 1990.

in line with the original agreement Namibia became independent under a government elected by its people.

The Angola–Namibia process can be held up as a clear victory for United Nations peace efforts. It was one, sadly, of a very few in sub-Saharan Africa over the following decade. But just as those other and more familiar UN 'failures' in Africa were usually not failures of the institution but of its Security Council members, so success in Namibia was at least as much to do with big power cooperation as with UN performance on the ground. By the time that UNAVEM and UNTAG were approved by the Security Council, both Washington and Moscow were coming to terms with a new relationship. Just as détente followed cold war and a second cold war had succeeded détente, so it appeared by 1988, with Mikhail Gorbachev in power in the Kremlin, that the second cold war was giving way to a second détente. Over Namibia the two dominant powers in the Security Council seemed ready once again to direct their local clients (South Africa in the case of the United States, Angola in the case of the Soviet Union) towards cooperation in the interests of regional stability and to use the United Nations to facilitate this cooperation. The true, momentous extent of the changes then underway in global relationships was not yet clear; the cold war was not yet over. But the return to the rules of détente familiar in the 1970s in the Middle East was probably the crucial factor in the success of the Angola–Namibia arrangement. Fortuitously, in southern Africa itself momentous change was also approaching. The end of the apartheid regime in South Africa which followed hard on the independence of Namibia meant that the new state found itself in an unexpectedly benign regional environment with friendly governments in power in both South Africa to the south and Angola to the north.

The UN operations in Angola and Namibia prefigured a much larger shift in international relations, however. This 'détente' would give way not to a return to cold war but to the end of the bipolar structure of world politics which had been in place more or less since the United Nations came into being.

8

The End of the Cold War

The end of the cold war opened the way to a huge surge in new United Nations operations. The ten years from the Angola–Namibia missions up to 1998 saw the creation of about twenty new peacekeeping and military observer missions of significant size as well as a cluster of smaller ones. These were established across the world. There were no longer any areas of core superpower interest from which UN involvement was excluded. Some sense of the degree of this growth is given by the fact that even before the freeze on new undertakings during the second cold war in the 1980s, there had been only fifteen peace operations since the founding of the UN in 1945, and three of those involved observer missions with less than 100 personnel. Five of them (UNTSO in the Middle East, UNMOGIP in Kashmir, UNFICYP in Cyprus, UNDOF on the Golan Heights and UNIFIL in southern Lebanon) remained in place after the end of the cold war, swelling even further the number of UN commitments in the 1990s.

OPPORTUNITY AND DEMAND: THE NEW POST-COLD WAR WORLD

The extent and distribution of the new operations reflected not just the effect of the end of the cold war on relationships inside the Security Council, but also the altered geography of conflict that came with it. Six of the larger of the new post-cold war commitments were in Europe (five in various parts of the former Yugoslavia and one in Georgia). Two were in a new area of Middle East tension: the borders of Iraq. Of the others, eight were in Africa, three in Central America and the Caribbean, and one in Cambodia.

Whatever its origins, it was perhaps inevitable that this new dawn for peace operations (and for the standing of the United Nations more broadly) generated a great deal of optimism about a 'new world order' in which multilateral intervention would become the primary recourse in international conflicts. The political and security 'no-go areas' of the cold war were now opened up to UN involvement, and their problems, which remained intractable as long as they were the focus of superpower rivalry, would surely now be easily resolved with some support from the United Nations.

Moreover, the new setting in which peace operations were now to take place would not only be unpolluted by superpower rivalry; but these operations could now be immeasurably strengthened by the direct participation of the big powers at the operational level. The cold war rationale which required that peace operations be undertaken by middle powers in order to minimise the danger of big power interference in local conflicts simply no longer applied. If there was now no superpower competition then there was no reason to exclude superpower participation in peace operations.

Certainly, there were early signs that the prospects for future UN peacekeeping in this regard might have changed. In the period up until the fall of Mikhail Gorbachev and the disintegration of the Soviet Union at the end of 1991, the United States and the USSR appeared almost to be trying to outdo each other in their public commitment to a new multilateralism. Moscow, now in search of a post-cold war international identity, appeared to toy for a time with the idea of assuming the part of activist middle power. The UN offered the obvious stage for the role of international good citizen. A new world standing might be rescued in this way from the debris of the Soviet Union's evident 'defeat' in the cold war. A large proportion of the Soviet peacekeeping debts to the UN (the accumulation of unpaid assessments going back to the 1960s) which amounted to some US$200 million by the end of the 1980s was paid off. The United States committed itself to the payment of its own peacekeeping assessments which it had withheld since the mid-1980s during the Reagan administration which was generally ill-disposed towards the United Nations.

True to the perception of a new peacekeeping untrammelled by superpower rivalries, the first operations of the post-cold war period were undertaken in areas which would previously have been regarded as off-limits to multilateral intervention because of their cold war sensitivity (MacQueen, 2006). In March 1992 the **United Nations Transitional Authority in Cambodia (UNTAC)** was established to provide a temporary administration for the country pending UN-organised elections. The creation of the Transitional Authority followed the signing of an agreement in Paris in October 1991 between the internal factions which had been in conflict with each other and with various foreign forces in the country since the mid-1970s (Chesterman, 2004). Cambodia's misfortunes during these years had emerged from its geographical position. Its proximity to Vietnam – with which it shares a long border in the east – drew it into the maelstrom of ideological and strategic

UNTAC: The UN Transitional Authority in Cambodia, created in March 1992 to provide a temporary administration for Cambodia and to organise elections to determine its future government; mission ended in September 1993.

conflicts centred there during the cold war. UNTAC was a massive under-taking for the United Nations, consisting of some 22,000 military and civilian personnel. Its mandate, set by the Security Council with the full cooperation of the American and Russian delegations (the 'Soviet Union' having ceased to exist by the beginning of 1992), ended in September 1993 following elections for a new inter-party government (Doyle, 1995). The mission did not guarantee long-term peace and tranquillity for Cambodia; the country remained unstable after the winding up of UNTAC. But the UN's efforts certainly helped avoid a general political and security breakdown (Berdal and Leifer, 1996).

The difficulty in achieving a clear resolution to Cambodia's fundamental political problems even after the deployment of UNTAC illustrated the limits of post-cold war peace operations and the weakness of some of the more optimistic assumptions surrounding them. In a number of key areas the end of the cold war, far from liberating the peacekeeping project, in fact weakened it. Certainly no area was any longer out of bounds to UN peace-keeping. But the reason why peacekeeping was now unconstrained by superpower interests was, axiomatically, that the superpowers no longer *had* any especially strong interests in these areas. As a result they no longer managed the behaviour of client states and opposition movements as they had during the cold war. It was not simply that the end of the cold war and the shift away from superpower bipolarity offered a new opportunity for peace operations; the new circumstances of world politics also increased demand for UN intervention. The superpowers were no longer under any self-imposed pressure to maintain control of spheres of interest and a corol-lary to this was that they were equally no longer concerned about managing security or propping up particular regimes within these areas. As a result, previously suppressed tensions in various parts of the world which at one time had been held in check by the big powers now flared into violence. The assumption that the removal of the cold war dimension from regional conflicts would automatically resolve them was overly sanguine.

This view ultimately overestimated the importance of the big powers in regional conflicts. Many cold war conflicts on the periphery had been founded in – or had later acquired – real local dimensions. The passing of the cold war did not change this reality; it merely meant that the discipline which could once be imposed by strong external influences was no longer on offer. As the underlying conflicts persisted in Cambodia and elsewhere and as the superpowers no longer stretched themselves to control them, fundamental solutions were beyond the capacities of UN peace operations.

Angola provides a particularly sharp illustration of this situation. UNAVEM as we have seen was completely successful in overseeing the withdrawal of Cuban forces. But this operation had been established to serve the high politics of superpower diplomacy (in what appeared at the time to be a revival of détente). Angola, Cuba and South Africa, with the presence of the United States and the Soviet Union in the background, were committed to the process from the outset. They required only the formal presence of international observers at the designated points of departure. However, when the UN was later enlisted in the search for an overall settlement of Angola's civil war, the outcome was much less successful. **UNAVEM II**, which was established by the Security Council in May 1991, was given responsibility for the management of a peace agreement between the MPLA government and the UNITA rebel movement which had been brokered by the United States and the Soviet Union. Regardless of this powerful international pressure for a settlement and despite the long history of external interference which had been a feature of the civil war, UNAVEM II was an intervention in the internal politics of Angola. The international dimension of the Angolan crisis had, strictly speaking, been removed with the first UNAVEM and the withdrawal of Cuban forces. This conflation of the international and the domestic was not new to the peacekeeping process, but it became a major feature of the post-cold war period and a recurring political and operational problem for the UN.

UNAVEM II: The second UN Angola Verification Mission, established in 1991 to oversee implementation of an agreement to end Angola's civil war; withdrawn in 1995 after the collapse of the agreement.

Angolan presidential and parliamentary elections were to be held under the supervision of UNAVEM II. The underlying assumption was that with the passing of the cold war its local manifestations would merely wither away and in their absence the elections would move the country towards democratic stability. But underneath the exploitation of Angola's civil war as a cold war proxy conflict, the internal hostilities had always had deep roots in ethnic and regional divisions. The effect of years of external encouragement to the warring factions had simply been to deepen these local hostilities. The electoral process collapsed in October 1992 when UNITA withdrew its cooperation as its defeat at the polls became evident (Anstee, 1996). The resumption of fighting that followed was more destructive than anything that had preceded it during the cold war years. A chastened UN renewed its efforts with the creation of **UNAVEM III** in 1995 which approached its task with a fuller appreciation of the 'Angolan' character of the conflict and its potential intractability. But neither this nor a subsequent operation (the United Nations Observation Mission in Angola established in 1997) could make any headway against entrenched local positions. The UN withdrew in 1999 and the situation was finally resolved only when the leader of UNITA, Jonas Savimbi, was killed by government forces in 2002.

UNAVEM III: A third UN Angola Verification Mission, created in 1995 and mandated to oversee a new peace process for Angola; withdrawn amidst general failure of the process in 1997.

The limits of post-cold war peace missions and the shaky assumptions on which some of them were founded were also in evidence on the other side of Africa. In Somalia, between 1992 and 1995, local conflicts not only endured but worsened long after they had ceased to have a place in the cold war competition. Additionally, Somalia pointed up the disastrous consequences that could follow from direct superpower involvement in UN peace operations. Rather than the positive post-cold war development of big power participation in peacekeeping which had been anticipated by the optimists, American domination of the United Nations intervention in Somalia threatened to bring the peacekeeping project as a whole into disrepute.

Somalia had been drawn into the second cold war largely because of its strategic location on the Horn of Africa and its extensive coastline on the Indian Ocean. Soviet backing for the revolutionary regime in neighbouring Ethiopia in the 1970s and 1980s brought American support for the Somali regime of Siad Barre. With the end of the cold war, superpower interest in the region faded. Their respective client governments, both of which were authoritarian, corrupt and deeply unpopular, were now without their powerful patrons and could not survive on their own. In Somalia Siad Barre's government collapsed at the beginning of 1991. Its fall had been the result of the combined pressure of otherwise rival opposition groupings which, their common enemy gone, commenced to confront each other for the spoils. The result was chaotic civil war and humanitarian disaster.

The UN became involved in the macabre complexities of Somalia only reluctantly after it became clear in early 1992 that a million and a half people (a quarter of the population) were at risk of starvation (Lewis and Mayall, 1996). The **United Nations Operation in Somalia (UNOSOM)** was authorised by the Security Council in April 1992 with the objective of securing the delivery of emergency aid. The particular circumstances of the Somali crisis brought the term 'humanitarian intervention' into common use, sometimes as a description of a particular type of peacekeeping, sometimes as a synonym for peace operations in their entirety. Deployment of troops was initially deferred for several months, by which time about 5000 people were dying daily. Then, once on the ground, the 500-strong Pakistani contingent which spearheaded the operation was immediately faced with the hostility of Mohammed Farah Aideed, one of the most powerful of the clan warlords struggling for dominance in the Somali capital Mogadishu (MacQueen, 2002).

Overwhelmed by the violent and virtually incomprehensible web of local clan and factional politics, UNOSOM proved incapable of protecting aid supplies and ensuring their delivery. International public opinion, shaped by a stream of horrifying media images – the so-called **'CNN effect'** – now pressed for a more decisive intervention. In November the United States government offered 30,000 troops for a redoubled effort which would, it was hoped, simply overawe the local armed factions. Consequently, the Security Council voted at the beginning of December 1992 to authorise a **Unified Task Force (UNITAF)** of US troops to work alongside but

UNOSOM: The UN Operation in Somalia, established in April 1992 to oversee and protect the distribution of food aid; superseded in December 1992 by the US Unified Task Force and then re-established as UNOSOM II; finally withdrawn in March 1995.

CNN effect: The impact on public opinion of instant and graphic news coverage of foreign conflicts, which can create pressure on governments to intervene; named for the US-based Cable News Network.

UNITAF: The (non-UN) American Unified Task Force in Somalia, which operated between December 1992 and May 1993.

apart from UNOSOM. A force of 28,000 Americans landed by sea close to Mogadishu (in front of a battery of television cameras) before dawn a few days later.

The mere act of multiplying the number of international troops on the ground did not change the basic situation faced by the UN in Somalia. At the root of the country's ills was the absence of any central authority. From the peace-keeping perspective there was simply no 'host state'. Nor did the domination of the venture by the remaining superpower have any restraining effect. On the contrary, a strong residue of anti-Americanism remained in many parts of the global South. As the Americans were to find, accusations of neo-colonial interference were not put to rest by the end of the cold war.

In May 1993 the United Nations reclaimed the operation, at least in principle, by subsuming UNITAF in a second UNOSOM supposedly under UN rather than US command. But in reality American forces still dominated the operation and were subject to US and not UN control. Fighting between the multinational force and the Somali factions, particularly that of Mohammed Aideed, had led to the death of over 100 peacekeepers by the end of 1994, frequently in gruesome circumstances and with on-the-spot media coverage. Perhaps the critical point in this came with the incident later semi-fictionalised in Ridley Scott's film **Blackhawk Down**, when a US special forces operation against the Aideed faction in Mogadishu (of which the UN was not informed in advance) ended in catastrophe. Perhaps over a thousand Somalis, mostly civilians, were killed in the operation, but the focus of the outside world was firmly on the eighteen American servicemen who died in the incident. In the aftermath, Washington lost its enthusiasm for the venture and UNOSOM II withdrew from Somalia in March 1995 [**Doc. 23, p. 145**]. Its departure was followed immediately and emblematically by a battle between the local warlords for possession of the evacuated UN compound.

The fundamental dilemma for UNOSOM/UNITAF was that in the prevailing circumstances its objectives – the protection and distribution of emergency aid – required an enforcement operation rather than a traditional peacekeeping mission. In the absence of a consenting state subject to pressure from other states in the international system, and faced by the intense hostility of one of the dominant factions, moral authority and interposition alone could achieve nothing. The UN operation, while frequently taking offensive action, did not fully embrace this enforcement role. It avoided the essential but clearly perilous task of disarming the factions and relied instead on the vain hope that a show of force, both military and diplomatic, would of itself be enough to subdue opposition.

The United Nations also confronted a broadly similar set of post-cold war circumstances in the former Yugoslavia at this time. Once again, one of the

Blackhawk Down: 2001 film directed by Ridley Scott (starring Josh Hartnett and Ewan McGregor) presenting a partly fictionalised account of the 'Battle of Mogadishu' of October 1993 which led eventually to the end of UN operations in Somalia.

traditional preconditions for a successful peace operation – a responsive host state – was absent. Here, in contrast to Somalia, however, the United States resisted all pressure to commit its own ground forces to the UN's efforts. Instead, the American presence was felt through the parallel involvement of NATO. At the beginning of the crisis in 1991, when the component parts of Yugoslavia began to break away to form independent states, there was a widely held view in Europe and the United States that regional European bodies should take the lead in providing any intervention that might be judged necessary (Parsons, 1995). The United Nations itself, now heavily burdened by the demands of post-cold war interventions elsewhere, was happy to go along with this. But as repeated European efforts ran into the quicksand of Balkan politics, it became clear that the UN would be required to shoulder the burden.

UNPROFOR: The United Nations Protection Force in the former Yugoslavia; deployed originally in Croatia in February 1992 and subsequently in Bosnia (and for a time in Macedonia); dissolved in December 1995 after Operation Deliberate Force in Bosnia.

In February 1992 the **United Nations Protection Force (UNPROFOR)** was established. It was originally created to operate in Croatia but its responsibilities were later extended to Bosnia-Herzegovina, with the horrors of which UNPROFOR became most closely identified. Its mandate, to 'create the conditions of peace and security required for the negotiation of an overall settlement of the . . . crisis' (Security Council resolution 743, 21 February 1992) was based on the precepts of traditional interposition peacekeeping. But in Bosnia, as in Somalia, there was no peace to keep, and UNPROFOR's changing and frequently confused mandate came to reflect this (Roberts, 1995). Although the model for UNPROFOR seemed to be UNFICYP in Cyprus (the UN's only other European peacekeeping venture to date), the politico-military conditions were closer to those faced by ONUC in the Congo in the early 1960s. The Bosnian crisis, like that in central Africa thirty years before, was about a struggle for territorial and political control of an emergent state by competing ethnic forces. Local Muslims along with Croat and Serb minorities were engaged in a three-way fight for control of Bosnia which, following the other components of the former Yugoslavia, found itself impelled towards independence in the early 1990s. As in the Congo, the UN in Bosnia was continually pushed towards the frontier between interposition and enforcement.

Dual key: Inter-agency arrangement in Bosnia between the United Nations and NATO which required both to agree before air operations could be mounted by NATO in support of the UN Protection Force in Bosnia in 1994–95.

In August 1992 the Security Council explicitly invoked the enforcement powers of Chapter VII of the Charter in an attempt to establish UNPROFOR's credibility as guarantor of humanitarian aid supplies. But the culture shift from peacekeeping to enforcement proved a difficult one for UNPROFOR to make. The following year the way was prepared for the entry of a more enforcement-orientated agency when NATO became involved in maintaining a UN declared no-fly zone in contested areas. There now began two years of joint UN–NATO military involvement which was supposedly controlled by a **'dual key'** on decision-making. It was not an easy relationship (Economides

and Taylor, 1996). NATO, as a military alliance, had a fundamentally different view of multilateral intervention from that of UNPROFOR. Although it
was not necessarily more robust in its response to the many provocations
offered (especially from the Bosnian Serb minority), it was still unwilling to
act, in the words of its own secretary general, as a 'sub-contractor of the
United Nations' (Tharoor, 1992: 125).

Tensions in this inter-agency relationship became critical after the UN
abandoned its declared 'safe area' of Srebrenica to Bosnian Serb forces
in August 1995. The ensuing massacre of some 8000 civilians who had
supposedly been under the protection of a Dutch UNPROFOR unit saw the
United Nations effectively pushed aside when NATO, on the initiative of
the Clinton administration in Washington, began a sustained air and artillery
offensive against the Bosnian Serbs (**'Operation Deliberate Force'**). This
decisive abandonment of the myth of peacekeeping in Bosnia led for the
first time in the conflict to meaningful 'peacemaking' which resulted in
the **Dayton Accord** of November 1995 (Barnett, 1995).

> **Operation Deliberate Force:** US-led NATO enforcement operation in Bosnia against Serbian and Bosnian Serb forces in 1995; instrumental in creating conditions for the Dayton Accord.

At the root of this conflict between the UN and NATO lay the clash of two
quite distinct institutional – and historical – cultures. The peacekeeping
mindset of the UN was personified in Bosnia by the secretary general's representative, Yasushi Akashi from Japan, who was responsible for repeatedly
blocking proposals for tougher military action against the Bosnian Serbs.
NATO, in contrast, was in origin a cold war military alliance. While it had
recently been reinvented as a general regional security agency for the new
Europe, it was still guided by conventional military doctrine. Tellingly, perhaps, the international status of the 'non-peacekeeping' **Implementation
Force (I-FOR)** which replaced UNPROFOR after the watershed of Operation
Deliberate Force was left unclear. 'Authorised' by the Security Council in
December 1995 under Chapter VII of the Charter, it was effectively controlled by NATO. Ironically, this enforcement operation was conducted in
conditions which would have been much more appropriate to traditional
peacekeeping than those which had existed before the NATO campaign.
There was now a peace to keep and a clear space for third party interposition. This had been created, though, by military force.

> **Dayton Accord:** US-brokered agreement ending the Bosnian war following NATO's robust intervention in the form of Operation Deliberate Force in 1995.

> **I-FOR:** NATO Implementation Force deployed in Bosnia to implement the Dayton agreement of 1995.

COLLECTIVE SECURITY AT LAST? OPERATION DESERT STORM

The experience of these interventions of the early 1990s seemed to suggest
that UN peace operations had not, after all, been liberated from all constraints after the end of the cold war. Certainly, the demand for intervention

was high, but it appeared that the passing of the polarised international system had created new problems for the conduct of United Nations operations. One explanation of this is that, far from being restricted by the cold war, peacekeeping might more correctly be seen as a product of the cold war. The end of bipolarity meant the end of the international conditions which brought United Nations peacekeeping into being. Peace operations had emerged in part as a means of giving the UN an alternative military role in an environment which was simply incompatible with collective security. But, logically perhaps, there might have been a corollary to this. Could it not be that in a new, non-bipolar global structure the original conception of collective security could finally come into its own? (Weiss, 1994). Events in the Gulf in 1990 and 1991 could be seen at the time to point in this direction. The response to Iraq's invasion of Kuwait in August 1990 appeared to raise the prospect not of a new dawn for peacekeeping but of a delayed advent for full-blooded international enforcement as originally envisaged in the United Nations Charter.

Operation Desert Storm: US-led military action in 1991 to eject Iraqi occupation forces from Kuwait; authorised by the UN Security Council under resolution 678.

The 'optimistic' view of **Operation Desert Storm**, as it was known, saw it as a model for genuine collective security in a new world order. The Security Council decided on bold action under Chapter VII and, in the newly non-polarised environment, no veto was cast against it. A majority of the permanent members of the Council (the United States, Britain and France) then led a military alliance with broad regional and international participation to secure 'United Nations' objectives: Iraq's withdrawal from Kuwait. A more sceptical perspective, however, looked to the example of the Korean campaign rather than the spirit of the Charter for an explanation of Desert Storm. In this view, western foreign policy objectives were pursued by western-led forces with only a tendentious claim to UN legitimisation. The Soviet Union had been prevented from using its veto to protect its client (North Korea) in 1950 by its physical absence from crucial Security Council meetings. In 1990 it was also prevented from vetoing the undertaking against a client state (Iraq), but this time as a result of its general diplomatic weakness at a point when the very fabric of Soviet statehood was rending.

The role of the Security Council and the formal basis on which the United States and its allies took action were, in truth, far from clear-cut. A sequence of resolutions following the Iraqi invasion called for immediate, unconditional withdrawal and economic sanctions were also applied against Iraq. These resolutions culminated at the end of November 1990 with an authorisation for member states already cooperating with the (now exiled) government of Kuwait to use 'all necessary means' to implement previous resolutions after a deadline of 15 January 1991 [**Doc. 24, p. 146**]. Transparently the work of the United States and Britain, Security Council resolution 678 was an invitation to UN member countries to sign up to an anti-Iraqi alliance. Yet while this, like previous resolutions, made explicit reference to Chapter VII, it did not amount to a formal call to collective security under the Charter. There was no suggestion that article 43 which, it will be recalled, requires member states to provide military assistance at the behest of the Security Council, would be invoked. Resolution 678 merely provided the United States with the necessary permission to assemble a force of like-minded powers (Parsons, 1995).

Military operations began when the deadline set by resolution 678 passed without Iraq having backed down. The outcome was never in any real doubt. Air and land operations pushed the occupying forces back northwards across the Iraq border. Allied casualties were light, while those of the Iraqi armed forces were considerable. Military success aside, however, the inescapable fact was that this UN-legitimised force consisted largely of contingents from the United States and its NATO allies, just as the Unified Command in Korea had done. While no veto was cast against the authorisation of military action in the Security Council, Russia attempted to position itself as neutral honest broker and sought to mediate between Iraq and the 'UN' alliance even after fighting had begun. China, though also stopping short of vetoing UN support for military action, openly opposed Operation Desert Storm. In other words, although the Security Council authorised the operation and three of its permanent members took part in it, two others remained opposed, and this dividing line was drawn precisely along the old cold war cleavage. While the depth of this division was certainly not what it would have been ten years previously (when a veto of Security Council authorisation would have been virtually automatic), it clearly persisted.

This lack of wholesale commitment to the original machinery of collective security laid out in the Charter was an indication of the limits of the new consensus. But the difficulty was not merely one of residual cold war suspicions between east and west. A more profound resistance to 'muscular multilateralism' could be detected. Even in the vaunted 'new world order' (proclaimed by President George H.W. Bush), sovereign states proved resistant to the idea that they should not pursue their own foreign policy interests in their own ways. States alone, it seemed, would still determine how widely or how narrowly to conceive these interests. In short, the fundamental contradiction between sovereignty and collectivity which was clear in the League of Nations in the face of the security challenges of the 1930s had not been resolved. Bipolarity had perhaps just provided a false alibi for the deeper flaws of the UN's scheme for collective security by enforcement in an international system which was still constructed from independent sovereign states. The problems in the concept of collective security, in other words, went much deeper than the specific circumstances of the cold war.

BOUTROS-GHALI'S *AGENDA FOR PEACE*

Whatever the prospects for coercive collective security in the new world order, the demand for peace operations continued to grow at this time, as we have seen. Indeed, a conventional UN peace observation mission was put in place on the Iraq–Kuwait border immediately following the end of Desert Storm. The **Iraq-Kuwait Observation Mission (UNIKOM)** was deployed by the Security Council to monitor a demilitarised zone between the two countries and, by its presence, discourage any violation of the peace imposed by Desert Storm. There was, however, little pretence that this mission was neutral between the protagonists. In the first months of 2003 the demilitarised zone was comprehensively violated by the massing of the American-led invasion force which would shortly launch itself across the border against Saddam's Iraq. There was, needless to say, no question of Security Council action in response to this. Here, the veto assuredly would have been used.

Faced with the surge in demand for more and often complex peace operations, the first UN secretary general of the post-cold war era, Boutros Boutros-Ghali of Egypt, attempted to focus the attention of the UN membership on the questions (both political and resource-related) raised by the new situation. In June 1992, four months after the creation of UNPROFOR and a year after Operation Desert Storm, when optimism about developments in UN military capacities was still strong, he produced a major report on peace operations, **An Agenda for Peace**: *Preventive Diplomacy, Peacemaking and Peacekeeping*. This explored the future prospects for peace operations in the wake of a special Security Council summit held the previous January.

The basic purpose of *An Agenda for Peace* was to reconsider UN peace operations in light of the end of the cold war which was described by Boutros-Ghali as the collapse of 'the immense ideological barrier that for decades gave rise to distrust and hostility' (Boutros-Ghali, 1992: para. 8). While it sought to exploit the momentum of the new interest in peacekeeping, the report showed a fair appreciation of limitations as well as possibilities. The new optimism had, for example, to be conditioned by the fact that some 800 million dollars was still owed to the UN from arrears in members' peacekeeping assessments. With the new demands, operational commitments for the current year (1992) were running at almost 3 billion dollars. On this central issue of financing, Boutros-Ghali noted that 'a chasm has developed between the tasks entrusted to (the UN) and the financial means provided to it' (Boutros-Ghali, 1992: para. 69).

National contributions of peacekeeping forces, he argued, should be put on a more formal and reliable basis. Member states should enter long-term agreements regarding 'the kind and number of skilled personnel they will be prepared to offer the United Nations as the needs of new operations arise'

UNIKOM: The UN Iraq-Kuwait Observer Mission, established in April 1991 in the aftermath of Operation Desert Storm; mandated to monitor the security of the border between Kuwait and Iraq; withdrawn in 2003 following US-led invasion of Iraq.

An Agenda for Peace: 1992 report and recommendations by secretary general Boutros Boutros-Ghali on the challenges facing UN peace operations in the immediate post-cold war period.

(Boutros-Ghali, 1992: para. 51). This, of course, had no connection with the notional requirements of article 43 of the Charter which related to the obligation to participate in enforcement action. But voluntary agreements relating to peacekeeping operations would free the UN Secretariat from some of the burden of *ad hoc* recruitment from members after an operation had been authorised but before it could be deployed.

The possibility for the realisation of the UN's original scheme for enforcement was not completely dismissed. Forces made available under Chapter VII article 43 might never, Boutros-Ghali conceded, 'be sufficiently large or well enough equipped to deal with a threat from a major army equipped with sophisticated weapons' (Boutros-Ghali, 1992: para. 43). Nevertheless, he urged the Security Council to explore all the possibilities of Chapter VII. To this end he proposed that the Military Staff Committee, originally envisaged by article 47 of the Chapter to consist of the chiefs of military staff of the five permanent members of the Security Council, should be revived.

Beyond this, it was conceivable that a semi-enforcement mechanism could be created even without the full application of Chapter VII powers. **'Peace enforcement units'**, formed from volunteers and more heavily armed than traditional peacekeeping operations, could be deployed to implement by force if necessary ceasefires and peace agreements which had already been formally agreed by the antagonists in a conflict and which were then deliberately broken [**Doc. 25, pp. 146–7**]. Existing observer and peacekeeping missions had been insufficient when faced with this situation, most recently, for example, in Angola.

Moving on from the Chapter VII question, Boutros-Ghali also approached an area of some political complexity which nevertheless could have important implications for resources and the UN's capacity to meet the rush of new demands for intervention. Chapter VIII of the Charter, which dealt with 'regional arrangements' in the maintenance of peace and security, was also revisited [**Doc. 4(ii), p. 121**]. Although originally envisaged as an adjunct to centralised collective security, the utilisation of regional organisations in peacekeeping functions should be encouraged, although concrete proposals to this end were explicitly forsworn by the secretary general. The problems of inter-agency operations in Bosnia, where the UN–NATO relationship was often less than productive, have already been discussed. In the coming years the UN would enter joint arrangements with other regional organisations in both West Africa and the former Soviet Union which were often less than satisfactory.

Challenging though much of *An Agenda for Peace* undoubtedly was, it was a product of a particular – and essentially temporary – phase in the early post-cold war period. Boutros-Ghali's approach was predicated on the existence of a new post-bipolar consensus among the big powers which

Peace enforcement units: Form of peace operation proposed by Boutros-Ghali in *An Agenda for Peace* (1992) which would involve limited enforcement action to ensure compliance with previously agreed settlement plans; never implemented.

would endure to create a new type of world politics. In this he was merely reflecting the *zeitgeist* – and the rhetoric of national leaders – of the early 1990s. Inherent in this approach were the assumptions, first, that this new international relationship between the big powers would indeed become embedded and, second, that the smaller powers would be willing to put themselves unquestioningly behind the policies of the permanent members of the Security Council. In the afterglow of the success of Operation Desert Storm these assumptions may have been understandable, but they inferred a fundamental shift in the nature of international relations on rather slim historical evidence (Bertrand, 1993). As we have seen, Desert Storm was in many respects no more a genuine UN collective security undertaking than Korea had been. The fragmentation of the Security Council's anti-Iraq stance even as fighting continued and then the deep divisions among the permanent members on policies to be pursued towards Saddam Hussein's regime in Baghdad in the aftermath of the 1991 war, and on the long march towards the 2003 invasion, exposed the fragility of any supposed new consensus.

In the event, little of *An Agenda for Peace* was implemented in any concrete way (MacQueen, 2006). No sustained attempt was made in the Security Council to rehabilitate the Military Staff Committee. Article 43 remained dormant. The 'peace enforcement units' proposed by Boutros-Ghali seemed tailor-made for subsequent operations from Bosnia to Somalia, but they did not materialise. It was never likely that member states would be willing to commit their personnel to operations with such an explicit combat function. Instead, these crises were subject to various distortions of the traditional peacekeeping model which usually did not meet the demands of the situations. There were some developments on UN–regional agency cooperation. But the process was not always a happy one, as we have observed. Such inter-agency relationships – not only in Bosnia but in Liberia and Sierra Leone where 'partnerships' were established between the UN and the military arm of the Economic Community of West African States – tended to be led by the regional organisation with the United Nations assuming a loose supervisory and legitimising role. The resulting operations were not always conducted to 'UN standard'.

An Agenda for Peace marked the high tide of post-cold war optimism and its value lies in the perspective it provides on a particular historical conjuncture. It was significant less perhaps for any tangible changes it precipitated, than for its unintended exposure of the limits of the new world order.

Part 3

ASSESSMENT

9

Peace Operations and the Cold War: A Balance Sheet

T he role played by United Nations peace operations in the cold war had a number of separate facets. Peacekeeping, broadly defined, involved three more or less distinct areas of political activity: institutional, international and national. First, it had a major role in the interior politics of the United Nations itself. Second, and more obviously, peacekeeping had a part to play in the relationship between the superpowers in both the cold war and the interlude of détente. Simultaneously, peace operations had an impact on the international relations of the various regions in which they took place. Third, peacekeeping operations were instrumental in shaping the domestic politics of a number of host states. At the state level too, though it was perhaps a less obvious effect, peacekeeping was often important in the national politics of the peacekeeper as well as the 'peacekept'.

PEACE OPERATIONS AND THE STATUS OF THE UNITED NATIONS

As an institutional device, non-enforcement peace operations went some way to rescue the United Nations from irrelevance in the military sphere. The obvious effect of the cold war on the fabric of international relationships was a clustering in the international state system around the respective poles of the superpowers. This polarisation fractured the collectivism which was the minimal prerequisite for the adoption and operation of the ambitious security system on which the UN Charter was based. The Korean War merely underlined the futility of pursuing this collective security ideal in a fundamentally divided world. Hailed by the west as a victory for bold enforcement by the UN, the Unified Command in Korea was simultaneously denounced by the Soviet Union as a western-devised anti-communist crusade.

In consequence, by the early 1950s the UN faced an uncertain future as a security organisation. With its collective security ambitions unrealised, it seemed probable that the UN would drift into one of two equally unattractive futures. It could have declined, via platitude and piety, into an anodyne irrelevance in an increasingly dangerous international system. Alternatively, it might simply have become absorbed into the emerging western alliance system. The United States and its supporters dominated the General Assembly, and with the Uniting for Peace resolution in 1950 it was clear that they were willing to use this power to undermine the supremacy of the Security Council. As this supremacy (underscored by the permanent members' power of veto) had effectively been a condition for Moscow's participation in the UN in the first place, to undermine it could only deepen, perhaps fatally, Soviet alienation.

In the event, the huge expansion of UN membership which followed the rapid process of decolonisation in the 1960s probably saved the UN from these threatened futures. The new balance of power in the General Assembly that came with this growth diluted the force of the western states and shifted the UN's agenda away from the pointless repetition of cold war arguments towards more immediate issues of decolonisation and racism. But even then, by the 1960s the UN would already have been a much less significant organisation if its credibility had not been enhanced by its development of peacekeeping as an alternative to coercive collective security. It would clearly be an exaggeration to say that the peacekeeping enterprise saved the UN from the post-Korea alternative of irrelevance or disintegration, but its peace operations provided some much needed institutional buoyancy through the most threatening years of the cold war.

The importance of peacekeeping in the politics of the UN was enhanced by the fact that it developed as an institutional device rather than one imposed on it by the big powers. The Suez crisis of 1956 gave the organization an opportunity to rethink its military function. Partly improvised and partly drawn from the experience of existing military observation missions in the Middle East and Kashmir, the UN Emergency Force was a 'UN' initiative rather than one driven by self-interested states. The support of a group of middle powers like Canada, Sweden and India in both the planning and execution of peace operations was obviously essential, but the nature of the project was determined by the institution.

This was not, of course, always a wholly positive situation. The 'leave it to Dag' (Hammarskjöld) attitude which followed after the success of UNEF would lead a few years later to considerable problems in the Congo. Here the two overarching events of the time were intertwined: the cold war and decolonisation. What ensued was not positive for either the Congo or the United Nations. The peacekeeping concept, however impartial in theory, was still vulnerable to political misuse in the rigid bipolarity of the 1950s and 1960s, the more so when the high political stakes of colonialism, decolonisation and post-colonial relationships became involved. The management of the Congo operation provided the justification for Khrushchev's troika proposals in 1960 which challenged one of the fundamental tenets of the UN: the possibility of a disinterested international civil service. Paradoxically, rather than peacekeeping fencing off a local crisis from superpower involvement, the Congo operation seemed itself to provoke that involvement. Similarly, the wrangles over the financing of peacekeeping – which at their root were about institutional power rather than money – generated another major crisis for the UN over the implementation of sanctions under article 19 of the Charter in 1964. The institutional benefits of its peace operations for the UN did not, therefore, come free of an institutional price.

PEACE OPERATIONS AND REGIONAL STABILITY

These conflicts inside the United Nations often appeared to aggravate east–west relations rather than ease them, and in this sense peacekeeping might seem at key points to have been counterproductive. But, at least in part, the disputes over peace operations were often *casus belli*, excuses for a fight, in the fundamentally hostile relationship between east and west. If the grievances over peacekeeping had not existed, others would assuredly have been found. Overall, the superpower relationship gained from the existence of peacekeeping, with the UN working to seal off local conflicts from their potentially disastrous involvement. How much worse might the crisis over the Congo have been if, in the absence of the UN operation, the Soviet Union had intervened directly in support of Lumumba and the United States in support of Kasavubu and Mobutu? Bad though the situation in the Congo in the early 1960s obviously was, it was not as intractable or destructive as the conflict in neighbouring Angola in the 1980s where the superpowers simply backed their own local clients and did not consider a UN option.

This function of United Nations peacekeeping – the distancing of conflicts from superpower involvement – reached its high point during the period of détente in the 1970s. The United States and the Soviet Union now seemed to take over control of the UN peacekeeping process from the institution itself to exploit it in the interests of stability in their own relationship. The creation of UNEF II and UNDOF in the aftermath of the 1973 Middle East war and, to a lesser extent, the advent of the Interim Force in Lebanon in 1978, saw the UN acting more or less at the behest of the United States with the complicity of the Soviet Union. Unhappily, the disintegration of détente and reversion to cold war in the 1980s brought an end to this type of peace-keeping without any corresponding return to the earlier cold war form. UN peace operations seemed no longer to have a place in conflict resolution, leaving afflicted countries like Angola to their own devices. The second cold war appeared to mark the end of UN peace forces as a palliative in super-power rivalry. The resumption of peacekeeping – in the process of Namibian independence – came only at the point at which that rivalry began to dissolve as the end of the cold war itself approached.

Beyond the east–west dimension, peace operations had an obvious role in the management of regional international crises. The Middle East conflict in its various aspects (Egyptian-Israeli, Lebanese-Syrian, Egyptian-Saudi, Syrian-Israeli, Lebanese-Israeli) was a constant object of peacekeeping attention. The fundamental problems of the region's international relations remained unsolved but that was a failure of peacemaking, not of peace-keeping. The contribution of the various United Nations operations in the Middle East cannot be assessed on the basis of their positive achievements but only on inference about the likely consequences if they had not existed. It is an unprovable hypothesis but nevertheless a reasonable one that these consequences would have been very grave at different times and places.

The regional stability of other parts of the world was also aided by the presence of UN peacekeepers. Again, the basic deficiencies in the relation-ships between India and Pakistan over their shared borders or between Greece and Turkey over Cyprus were not solved by the peace operations put in place by the UN. But the regional international relations of south Asia and the eastern Mediterranean would certainly not have been improved by the absence of those operations.

PEACE OPERATIONS AND THE STATE

It is at the local level that judging the success of United Nations peace operations during the cold war becomes problematical. Partly, of course, this is because UN peacekeeping has, strictly speaking, no direct role to play in the resolution of internal conflicts. Article 2(7) of the Charter specifically states that the UN is not authorised 'to intervene in matters which are essentially within the domestic jurisdiction of any state' (United Nations Charter, 1945). Formally at any rate then, states are significant in the peace-keeping process only as sub-systems of the broader international system. It is with the security of the latter that the UN is properly concerned. But the peacekeeping principle of neutrality and non-interference in local politics has always been more apparent than real. It is beyond any sensible dispute that the United Nations presence helped shape the politics of the Congo in the early 1960s. It is obviously impossible to construct an alternative history for the Congo had the UN not been involved. We cannot judge whether many more would have died without ONUC. Similarly we cannot say whether the three decades of dictatorship, corruption and misgovernment to which the country was subjected after the UN intervention might have been even worse if ONUC had not existed. But we can say with full confidence that things would have been different.

Less positively, in West New Guinea the United Nations operation was complicit in the denial of self-determination to the local population and its transfer to the rule of a state which the majority of its population considered alien and oppressive. The subsuming of the Papuan people into Indonesia which was facilitated by UNTEA/UNSF brought no moral credit to the United Nations. But, as we have said, the UN's primary function was the management of international relations, not the safeguarding of individual rights. In the circumstances of the early 1960s the outcome of the intervention in New Guinea was probably positive in this respect. The security of the Asia-Pacific region was strengthened and the demands of a powerful bloc in the General Assembly were met.

The overall effect of UN intervention in Cyprus is also difficult to assess. UNFICYP carried out what was in many ways a model peacekeeping role with considerable success. Even though the conflict was, narrowly speaking, an internal rather than an international one, the geopolitics of Cyprus meant that the UN operation could deploy as a classic interposition force. It is unclear, though, whether it was actually a positive force in Cyprus over the decades of its operation. Unable to prevent either the Turkish invasion of 1974 or the Greek manoeuvrings which provoked it, UNFICYP may merely have become a part of the problem it was created to manage. In the absence of effective peacemaking, the UN in Cyprus was left to keep (with some success) a peace which was fundamentally unsatisfactory.

The impact of peacekeeping on the national politics of the contributing rather than the host states has been less ambiguous. Ostensibly, participation in peacekeeping operations is about altruism, national sacrifice and international good citizenship. In reality, the role of peacekeeper often brought distinct advantages to contributing states. For the original middle powers and later the growing number of third world states which contributed forces, United Nations service conferred a particular international status. During the cold war at least, participation in UN peace operations implied stable domestic politics, disciplined and well-trained armed forces and diplomatic sophistication. Indeed for some states during this period (Canada, Ireland, India and Sweden prominent among them) activism at and on behalf of the United Nations became a central component of national foreign policy. Later, smaller less developed states like Bangladesh, Fiji and Nepal would acquire an international prestige disproportionate to their tangible national resources through their peacekeeping contributions. Contributing countries could gain from participation at the most practical level too. UN service provided operational experience otherwise unavailable to the armed forces of most peaceful states. While obviously secondary to the purposes of peacekeeping, this symbiotic distribution of benefits between the undertaking and those who carried it out was an important element in maintaining the supply of peacekeepers apparently in defiance of the expectations of self-interested international behaviour.

Despite the spectacular growth in the number of new commitments established from the late 1980s onwards, a great deal of the optimism surrounding the prospects for peace operations in the post-cold war world – whether traditional inter-state peacekeeping or the newer forms of humanitarian intervention – proved misplaced. Much of the new world order thinking which informed discussion of the UN's role in the 1990s failed to make a distinction between enforcement and peacekeeping. Aggressive action and interposition were often conflated in a loose assumption that UN military intervention of whatever variety was now liberated from the prison of the cold war and would provide the key to a new global security system. In reality there were major obstacles to the further development of both coercive collective security and peacekeeping.

Like the Unified Command in Korea forty years previously, Operation Desert Storm against Iraq in 1991 could be interpreted from a certain perspective as the dawn of 'real' collective security. But the truth is that, as with the Korean affair in the early 1950s, Desert Storm drew on a temporary military alliance that had procured a limited legitimisation through Security Council resolutions. The passage of these resolutions – in 1950 as in 1990 – was merely a function of the balance of national power among the permanent members of the Security Council at these particular historical points. The central flaw of collective security remained the same in 1990 as it had been in 1951. It was essentially the same flaw that had caused the 'failure' of the League of Nations in the 1930s: sovereign states will always reserve to themselves the power to make decisions about their national interests and will tend to do so according to narrow political and geographical criteria. Cold war bipolarity may have rendered UN collective security unworkable – but only in the sense that a lack of fuel for a wrecked engine makes it unworkable. The larger problem remains under the hood. United Nations peace operations developed in part to meet those flaws in collective security which derived from the more superficial problem – the empty fuel tank of bipolarity. The forms and practices of cold war peacekeeping were contrived to work round the obstacles of superpower competition. It was, in this sense at least, a product of the cold war. There was no obvious reason, therefore, why the end of the cold war should enhance its effectiveness. On the contrary, the passing of superpower competition brought a retraction of superpower interests and consequently the end of their influence over local clients. This control of local behaviour by the big powers had been an essential component in successful cold war peace operation from Suez to Namibia.

The peacekeeping model, with certain modifications, remained at the centre of the UN's approach to intervention after the cold war in the absence of an effective system of collective enforcement. It remains the most viable form of international military involvement in local conflicts. Fundamental problems will persist between the model and the reality. In the real world the division between interposition and enforcement will frequently be unclear, the presence of a peacekeeping force will inevitably impact on local politics, and the separation of national crises from international ones will often be impossible. And, the passing of the cold war probably brought as many operational drawbacks for peace operations as it did improvements in the political setting in which they were created. In short, United Nations peace operations remain largely as they were in the cold war: an imperfect yet still invaluable tool for the local management of conflict. The international system in which they operate may be much more diffuse than the polarised one of the cold war; the violence they confront has changed little.

Part 4

DOCUMENTS

Document 1   THE LEAGUE OF NATIONS INTERNATIONAL FORCE IN THE
SAAR TERRITORY

*The League of Nations international force established to oversee the 1935
plebiscite on the future of the Saar had many of the characteristics and faced
many of the challenges that would become familiar to UN peace operations
after the Second World War. The force was 3300-strong, consisting of troops
from Britain (1500), Italy (1300), Holland (250) and Sweden (250). The
involvement of the Netherlands and Sweden looked ahead to the special
role that would be performed by 'middle powers' in UN operations in the
cold war period. The tactical and strategic emphases in the report on force
mobility and relations with the civil authority also presage future peacekeeping by the United Nations.*

In pursuance of the resolution of the Council that an international force
should be sent to the Saar territory, the following recommendations are made
by the Sub-Committee:

1. The contingents will be composed of infantry, armoured cars, and
    ancillary troops. It is important that this force should be highly mobile
    and should be equipped with motor transport up to approximately
    50 per cent of the infantry's strength.

2. The governing commission of the Saar Territory shall continue to bear
    the responsibility for the maintenance of law and order in the Territory.
    Subject to the military requirements of the situation, and without pre-
    judice to the immediate action which may be necessary in the event of
    emergency, the Commander-in-Chief will comply with such requests
    as may be made to him by the chairman of the Governing Commission
    for the intervention of the force for the purpose of maintaining or restor-
    ing order.

3. The Commander-in-Chief of the international force and staff officers
    of the national contingents shall proceed as soon as possible to the Saar
    Territory and concert measures with the Governing Commission for
    the distribution, accommodation, and maintenance of the force in the
    Territory. Each of the governments furnishing a contingent will appoint
    an officer to the staff of the Commander-in-Chief.

4. All other questions arising out of the distribution, accommodation, and
    maintenance of the international force will be settled direct between
    the Governing Commission and the Commander-in-Chief of the inter-
    national force.

*Source: Report of the Sub-Committee of the League of Nations Council on the International
Force for the Saar, 12 December 1934.*

———————◄◆►———————

COLLECTIVE SECURITY AND THE LEAGUE OF NATIONS   **Document 2**

The League of Nations first attempted to introduce a general system of collective security in the aftermath of the First World War. The basic principle remained at the centre of subsequent attempts by the United Nations to regulate international relations. The 'failure' of the League's system was considered by the architects of the UN as due at least in part to the limited character of the commitments to be undertaken by member states, particularly in the military field, and to the fact that all action had to be agreed unanimously. The Covenant (basic constitution) of the League of Nations outlines the terms of collective security in articles 10 and 16.

Article 10

The Members of the League undertake to respect and preserve as against external aggression the territorial integrity and existing political independence of all Members of the League. In case of any such aggression or in case of any threat or danger of such aggression, the Council shall advise upon the means by which this obligation shall be fulfilled.

Article 16

1. Should any Member of the League resort to war in disregard of its covenants . . . it shall *ipso facto* be deemed to have committed an act of war against all other Members of the League, which hereby undertake immediately to subject it to the severance of all trade or financial relations, the prohibition of all intercourse between their nationals and the nationals of the Covenant-breaking state . . .

2. It shall be the duty of the Council in such case to recommend to the several governments concerned what effective military, naval or air force the Members of the League shall severally contribute to the armed forces to be used to protect the covenants of the League.

3. The Members of the League agree, further, that they will mutually support one another in the financial and economic measures which are taken . . . in order to minimise the loss and inconvenience resulting . . . and they will take the necessary steps to afford passage through their territory to the forces of any Members of the League which are co-operating to protect the covenants of the League.

Source: Covenant of the League of Nations.

Document 3   THE ATLANTIC CHARTER: WAR-TIME POINTERS TO A NEW SECURITY
ORGANISATION

*The League of Nations became marginal to issues of international security
long before the outbreak of the Second World War. But from an early stage in
that conflict there was an assumption among the allied leadership that a new
attempt would be made to regulate post-war international relations on a
collective basis. In August 1941 the British prime minister Winston Churchill
and US president Franklin Roosevelt met aboard a warship off the Canadian
coast. The joint declaration which emerged from this – the 'Atlantic Charter'
– set out the basic principles for post-war international relations to be pursued
by the signatories.*

First, their countries seek no aggrandizement, territorial or other;

Second, they desire to see no territorial changes that do not accord with
the freely expressed wishes of the people concerned;

Third, they respect the right of all peoples to choose the form of government under which they will live; and they wish to see sovereign rights
and self-government restored to those who have been forcibly deprived of
them;

(. . .)

Sixth, after the final destruction of the Nazi tyranny, they hope to see
established a peace which will afford to all nations the means of dwelling
in safety within their own boundaries, and which will afford assurance
that all men in all the lands may live out their lives in freedom from fear
and want;

(. . .)

Eighth, they believe that all of the nations of the world, for realistic as well
as spiritual reasons must come to the abandonment of the use of force. Since
no future peace can be maintained if land, sea or air armaments continue to
be employed by nations which threaten, or may threaten, aggression outside
of their frontiers, they believe, pending the establishment of a wider and
permanent system of general security, that the disarmament of such nations
is essential. They will likewise aid and encourage all other practicable
measures which will lighten for peace-loving peoples the crushing burden
of armaments.

Source: US Department of State, *The Foreign Relations of the United States, 1941*, Vol. I
(New York: Kraus, 1972), pp. 368–9.

INTERNATIONAL SECURITY AND THE UNITED NATIONS CHARTER **Document 4**

The Charter is the basic constitution of the United Nations which has the legal force of an international treaty on its signatories (all member states).

(i) The UN's wide-ranging and legally binding collective security machinery is outlined in Chapter VII – 'Action with Respect to Threats to the Peace, Breaches of the Peace, and Acts of Aggression'. This should be compared with the extracts from the League Covenant in Document 2.

Article 39

The Security Council shall determine the existence of any threat to the peace, breach of the peace, or act of aggression and shall make recommendations, or decide what measures should be taken in accordance with Articles 41 and 42, to maintain and restore international peace and security.

Article 40

In order to prevent an aggravation of the situation, the Security Council may, before making the recommendations or deciding upon the measures provided for in Article 39, call upon the parties concerned to comply with such provisional measures as it deems necessary or desirable. . . . The Security Council shall duly take account of failure to comply with such provisional measures.

Article 41

The Security Council may decide what measures not involving the use of armed force are to be employed to give effect to its decisions, and it may call upon the Members of the United Nations to apply such measures. These may include interruption of economic relations and of rail, sea, air, postal, telegraphic, radio and other means of communication, and the severance of diplomatic relations.

Article 42

Should the Security Council decide that measures provided for in Article 41 would be inadequate or have proved to be inadequate, it may take such action by air, sea or land forces as may be necessary to maintain or restore international peace and security. Such action may include demonstrations, blockade, and other operations by air, sea and land forces of Members of the United Nations.

Article 43

1. All Members of the United Nations, in order to contribute to the maintenance of international peace and security, undertake to make available to the Security Council, on its call and in accordance with a special agreement or agreements, armed forces, assistance and facilities, including

rights of passage, necessary for the purpose of maintaining international peace and security.

2. Such agreement or agreements shall govern the numbers and types of forces, their degree of readiness and general location, and the nature of the facilities and assistance to be provided.

3. The agreement or agreements shall be negotiated as soon as possible on the initiative of the Security Council. They shall be concluded between the Security Council and Members or between the Security Council and groups of Members and shall be subject to ratification by the signatory states in accordance with their respective constitutional processes.

Article 44

When the Security Council has decided to use force it shall, before calling on a Member not represented on it to provide armed forces in fulfilment of the obligations assumed under Article 43, invite that Member, if the Member so desires, to participate in the decisions of the Security Council concerning the employment of contingents of that Member's armed forces.

Article 45

In order to enable the United Nations to take urgent military measures, Members shall hold immediately available national air-force contingents for combined international enforcement action. The strength and degree of readiness of these contingents and plans for their combined action shall be determined . . . by the Security Council with the assistance of the Military Staff Committee.

(. . .)

Article 47

1. There shall be established a Military Staff Committee to advise and assist the Security Council on all questions relating to the Security Council's military requirements for the maintenance of international peace and security, the employment and command of forces placed at its disposal, the regulation of armaments, and possible disarmament.

2. The Military Staff Committee shall consist of the Chiefs of Staff of the permanent members of the Security Council or their representatives . . .

3. The Military Staff Committee shall be responsible under the Security Council for the strategic direction of any armed forces placed at the disposal of the Security Council. Questions relating to the command of such forces shall be worked out subsequently.

4. The Military Staff Committee, with the authorization of the Security Council and after consultation with appropriate regional agencies, may establish regional sub-committees.

Article 48

1. The action required to carry out the decisions of the Security Council for the maintenance of international peace and security shall be taken by all Members of the United Nations or by some of them as the Security Council may determine . . .

Article 49

The Members of the United Nations shall join in affording mutual assistance in carrying out the measures decided upon by the Security Council.
(. . .)

Article 51

Nothing in the present Charter shall impair the inherent right of individual or collective self-defence if an armed attack occurs against a Member state of the United Nations, until the Security Council has taken measures necessary to maintain international peace and security. Measures taken by Members in the exercise of this right of self-defence shall be immediately reported to the Security Council and shall not in any way affect the authority and responsibility of the Security Council under the present Charter to take at any time such action as it deems necessary in order to maintain or restore international peace and security.

(ii) Collective Security as originally conceived had a regional dimension. According to Chapter VIII – 'Regional Arrangements' – local inter-governmental agencies might act as an enforcement arm of the Security Council. In the post-cold war years some joint operations have taken place but inter-agency relationships can be difficult – as was clear from the UN–NATO arrangement in Bosnia.

Article 52
(. . .)

3. The Security Council shall encourage the development of pacific settlement of local disputes through such regional arrangements or by such regional agencies either on the initiative of the states concerned or by reference from the Security Council. . . .

Article 53

1. The Security Council shall, where appropriate, utilize such regional arrangements or agencies for enforcement action under its authority. But no enforcement action shall be taken under regional arrangements or by regional agencies without the authorization of the Security Council . . .

(iii) In contrast to collective security, the concept of peacekeeping is not specifically recognised in the Charter. It has been suggested that some legal base to peacekeeping might be found in Chapter VI – 'The Pacific Settlement of Disputes'.

Article 33

1. The parties to any dispute, the continuance of which is likely to endanger the maintenance of international peace and security, shall, first of all, seek a solution by negotiation, enquiry, mediation, conciliation, arbitration, judicial settlement, resort to regional agencies or arrangements, or other peaceful means of their choice.
2. The Security Council shall, when it deems necessary, call upon the parties to settle their dispute by such means.

Article 34

The Security Council may investigate any dispute, or any situation which might lead to international friction or give rise to a dispute, in order to determine whether the continuance of the dispute or situation is likely to endanger the maintenance of international peace and security.

    (. . .)

Article 36

1. The Security Council may, at any stage of a dispute . . . recommend appropriate procedures or methods of adjustment. . . .

Article 37

1. Should the parties to a dispute of the nature referred to in Article 33 fail to settle it by the means indicated in that Article, they shall refer it to the Security Council.
2. If the Security Council deems that the continuance of the dispute is in fact likely to endanger international peace and security, it shall decide whether to take action under Article 36 or to recommend such terms of settlement as it may consider appropriate.

(iv) The crisis over the financing of peacekeeping operations which came to a head in the early 1960s turned on interpretations of Chapter IV of the Charter which dealt with the powers of the General Assembly. The Soviet Union (along with France) refused to accept that peacekeeping costs should be distributed according to article 17 as security matters were the sole responsibility of the Security Council. In response the United States threatened to invoke article 19 which deprived those in default of voting rights in the Assembly.

Article 17

1. The General Assembly shall consider and approve the budget of the Organization.
2. The expenses of the Organization shall be borne by the Members as apportioned by the General Assembly.

(. . .)

Article 19

A member of the United Nations which is in arrears in the payment of its financial contributions to the Organization shall have no vote in the General Assembly if the amount of its arrears equals or exceeds the amount of the contributions due to it for the preceding two full years. The General Assembly may, nevertheless, permit such a member to vote if it is satisfied that the failure to pay is due to conditions beyond the control of the member.

Source: Charter of the United Nations, 1945.

THE SOVIET UNION AND THE VETO   **Document 5**

Throughout the planning process for the United Nations the Soviet Union insisted that power should be concentrated in the Security Council. In the following document the Soviet representative at San Francisco (and future long-serving Soviet foreign minister), Andrei Gromyko, recalls his determination to resist any attempt by the west and the smaller powers to readjust the internal balance of power in the UN in favour of the General Assembly.

The USSR argued that all important issues of war and peace should go to the Security Council. Washington and London – supported by the representatives of many, mostly smaller, countries – argued for the division that would give the General Assembly more rights and the Security Council fewer. This attempt to hand over many of the Security Council's powers to the General Assembly was based on America's confidence that it could easily obtain a majority there and so put through any resolutions it liked. The clear result of this tendency would be to shift the balance of responsibility for the preservation of peace from the Security Council to the General Assembly, and the line separating each body hence became a major issue.

Tension grew steadily at the five power meetings as it became clear that President Truman had issued directives which cut straight across the Yalta agreements, and the US-British position on the division of powers was not going to be reconciled with the Soviet position unless one side gave way.

A host of resolutions now poured forth giving the General Assembly the right to review virtually any question that was not concerned with sanctions against a state. But Stettinius [the US secretary of state] was basically sympathetic to the Soviet Union's position that there should be a proper division of powers, and, after some tough talking, a possible agreement emerged: the Assembly would be able to discuss any question put by any state or group of states, but it could only issue a consultative opinion, and it would be for the Council to take binding decisions.

The Soviet delegation further declared: 'Our country will not agree to any UN Charter that might sow the seeds of a new military conflict.' The opponents of the [Security Council] veto then gave in. Everyone relaxed; jokes became more frequent. In just a few days the climate had changed. Clause 10 of chapter IV of the Charter appeared, limiting the powers of the General Assembly . . .

Source: Andrei Gromyko, *Memories* (London: Hutchinson, 1989), p. 120.

Document 6   THE UNIFIED COMMAND IN KOREA

The 'UN' identity of the anti-North Korean alliance was distinctly ambiguous. In all essentials it was an American-led coalition – as is clear from this memo of 13 September 1950 from the US state department to the American mission at the UN on the processing of offers of military assistance to South Korea. Effectively, the UN was merely a message carrier between the US and its allies.

1. Offers of military assistance from member gvts will be transmitted to the SYG [secretary general] of the UN who, in turn, will transmit the offers to the Unified Command (USG) [United States Government] through the US mission to the UN. Requests from the Unified Command (USG) for additional effective assistance in Korea may be transmitted to SYG for communication to the permanent delegations of the member govts.

2. Upon receipt of the offer the Unified Command (USG) will enter into direct negotiations with the member govts concerned regarding details of the offer and its utilization or in respect to other effective assistance which the member govt might be in a position to provide.

3. Upon completion of direct negotiations the Unified Command (USG) will inform the SYG of their results. The SYG will transmit this info to the delegation of the member govt concerned and, in consultation with the Unified Command (USG) and the delegation concerned, will release this info to the press.

Source: US Department of State, *The Foreign Relations of the United States, 1950*, Vol. VII (Washington, DC: US Government Printing Office, 1976), p. 776.

Document 7   THE 'UNITING FOR PEACE' RESOLUTION

The return of the Soviet delegation to the Security Council in August 1950 ended the interlude in which the western powers could make decisions unhindered by the veto. In response the United States sought to open the way for issues blocked in the Security Council to be passed to the General Assembly for determination through a so-called 'Uniting for Peace' procedure. This amounted to a de facto *amendment to the Charter in an area of primary concern to the Soviet Union (see Document 5).*

The General Assembly

1. *Resolves* that if the Security Council, because of lack of unanimity of the permanent members, fails to exercise its primary responsibility for the maintenance of international peace and security in any case where there appears to be a threat to the peace, breach of the peace, or act of aggression, the General Assembly shall consider the matter immediately with a view to making appropriate recommendations to Members for collective measures, including in the case of a breach of the peace or act of aggression the use of armed force when necessary, to maintain or restore international peace and security. If not in session at the time, the General Assembly may meet in emergency special session within twenty-four hours of the request therefor. Such emergency special session shall be called if requested by the Security Council on the vote of any seven members, or by a majority of the members of the United Nations.

2. *Adopts* for this purpose . . . amendments to its rules of procedure . . .

Source: General Assembly resolution GA/RES/377A [V], 3 November 1950.

INTER-WAR PRECURSORS OF UN PEACE OPERATIONS   **Document 8**

At the beginning of 1948 after Britain announced its intention to relinquish its mandate for Palestine, the UN sought a means by which it could deal with the likely consequences. Part of this exercise involved an exploration of international forces which had been set up by the League of Nations and other multilateral agencies in the inter-war years to help resolve territorial disputes in Europe. The document offers a corrective to the assumption that 'peacekeeping' was an invention of the United Nations.

UNITED NATIONS PALESTINE COMMISSION
PRECEDENTS CONCERNING THE CREATION OF AN INTERNATIONAL FORCE
(Working Paper Prepared by the Secretariat)

The object of this paper is merely to show that immediately after the first World War and again in 1935 it was possible to create international forces with a view toward assisting international commissions to fulfil the functions assigned to them (in each case the holding of plebiscites in disputed regions).

The following are precedents concerning the creation of international forces:

1. Plebiscite in Schleswig (1920)

Under the authority of an International Commission composed of five members; 2 United Kingdom, 1 France, 1 Norway, 1 Sweden. (The United States did not appoint a Commissioner. For this reason Great Britain appointed two).

(. . .)

2. Plebiscites in Allenstein and Marienwerder (1920)

Under the authority of an International Commission composed of five members in theory and four practically: 1 British, 1 French, 1 Italian, 1 Japanese.

(. . .)

3. Plebiscite in the Klagenfurt Basin (1920)

Under the authority of an International Commission composed of five members nominated respectively by the United Kingdom, France, Italy, Austria and the Serb-Groat-Slovene State [sic].

(. . .)

4. The Plebiscite of Upper Silesia (1921)

Under the authority of an International Commission composed of three members designated by the United Kingdom, France and Italy.

(. . .)

5. The attempted Plebiscite in Vilna (1921)

Under the authority of a Commission of five army officers – British, Italian, Japanese, Spanish and French (President). (The Council of the League of Nations also appointed a Committee of three of its own members – French, Japanese, Spanish – to keep in touch with the question).

(. . .)

6. Plebiscite in the Saar Territory (1935)

Agreement establishing International Force: Resolution of the Council of the League of Nations, 8 December 1934. (See Document 1)

(. . .)

Source: General Assembly document A/AC.21/W.18, 22 January 1948.

Document 9   THE TRUCE SUPERVISION ORGANIZATION AND THE ASSASSINATION OF COUNT BERNADOTTE

The United Nations Truce Supervision Organization in Palestine could in some respects be described as the first UN 'peacekeeping' operation. It was established in June 1948 on the initiative of the UN Mediator for Palestine, Count

Folke Bernadotte, who shortly afterwards was murdered by Jewish extremists. Here the UN's first secretary general, Trygve Lie, recalls this first peace mission and the death of its founder.

Count Bernadotte had requested me earlier to supply some military personnel to assist him in truce control functions, and I arranged with the three governments represented on the Security Council's Truce Commission – Belgium, France, and the United States – to assign officers from their armed forces for duty as United Nations military observers. During the second truce the number reached five hundred. They were stationed at strategic points along the cease-fire line and in the capitals of Israel and the Arab states. No story of United Nations effort in Palestine would be complete without a tribute to these gallant men who, without any previous experience in international teamwork, welded themselves in a matter of days into an effective team of United Nations officials. Their only protection was the modest blue-and-white armband added to their national uniform to identify them as United Nations observers. There was no risk they refused to take in the service of peace.

(. . .)

The shock was inexpressible. Ralph Bunche [a senior UN official in Palestine who was to succeed Bernadotte as Mediator] cabled that Count Bernadotte had been 'brutally assassinated by Jewish assailants of unknown identity in a planned, cold blooded attack in the new city of Jerusalem at 14.05 GMT today, Friday 17 September'. The terrorism which had stained the Zionist cause had taken its noblest victim . . . I knew the Count and his family personally, and this was enough to give a special edge to my sorrow. But my pain was refined by the reflection that the Count had died for the cause of the United Nations.

The bodies of Count Bernadotte and Colonel Serot [a French military observer who had died with him] were flown to Paris and that of the Count on to Stockholm. There was a memorial service at Orly airport for him and Colonel Serot, and for six other United Nations personnel who had been killed in Palestine either by the Arabs or by the Israelis. I flew to Stockholm for the funeral. The ceremonies were deeply moving. Count Bernadotte's uncle, the ninety year-old King was in attendance. Countess Bernadotte bore the tragedy of her husband's death with a dignity and nobility which seemed to symbolise the dedications to public service so characteristic not only of Count Bernadotte himself, but of his whole family.

Source: Trygve Lie, *In the Cause of Peace: Seven Years with the United Nations* (New York: Macmillan, 1954), pp. 187, 190–1.

———◆———

Document 10   LESTER PEARSON AND THE UNITED NATIONS EMERGENCY FORCE

The foreign minister of Canada, Lester Pearson, played a key role leading up to the establishment of the United Nations Emergency Force for Suez in 1956. Here he describes the delicate behind-the-scenes diplomacy in New York which prefigured the General Assembly vote.

We had to sense the atmosphere in New York and, particularly, find out what the British were thinking. (The French were standing pat.) I had seen the British Acting High Commissioner [ambassador] in Ottawa the evening before I left for New York. Now I saw Sir Pierson Dixon, the British Ambassador to the United Nations, an old friend for whom I had great admiration, and told him we were contemplating some kind of initiative. I also talked by telephone with Norman Robertson [Canadian High Commissioner in London] who . . . had told Kirkpatrick [the Permanent Under-Secretary of the British Foreign Office] that I was turning over in my mind the possibility of proposing a cease-fire . . . He had also told him that, as part of this approach, it would be essential to set up an adequate UN military force to separate the Egyptians from the Israelis pending a stable and peaceful settlement of outstanding Middle Eastern questions.

We had learned in advance of Eden's intention to state in the British House of Commons that 'police action . . . must be to separate the belligerents and to prevent the resumption of hostilities between them. If the UN were willing to take over the physical task of maintaining peace, no one would be better pleased than we.' It was not much but it was something. We took it to mean that Britain and France would be prepared to hand over the 'police task' they had assumed to a UN force. . . . I knew that we would have to have something more to offer than just a diplomatic gimmick to meet Anglo-French requirements; another observer corps would not do. . . .

By midnight [on 1 November] we had a fairly good idea that a UN peacekeeping intervention would be well-supported. If you like we had begun to mount a diplomatic operation on the assumption that we might decide to introduce a resolution for a cease-fire, to be policed by a United Nations emergency force . . .

Source: John A. Munro and Alex I. Inglis (eds), *Mike: The Memoirs of the Right Honourable Lester B. Pearson, Vol.2 1948–1957* (Toronto: University of Toronto Press, 1973), pp. 245–6.

THE WITHDRAWAL OF UNEF FROM EGYPT, 1967   **Document 11**

One of the essential principles guiding traditional peacekeeping is that of 'host state consent'. During the cold war years peace operations were considered to be legitimate only as long as the country on whose territory they operated agreed to their presence. When Egypt (or the United Arab Republic, as it was formally known at the time) withdrew its consent to the presence of the United Nations Emergency Force in May 1967, its action was widely – and correctly – seen as a preliminary to war with Israel. Although attracting criticism at the time, secretary general U Thant had little choice but to comply with Egypt's instruction. Evidently stung by the criticism, he later devoted a considerable part of his memoirs to explaining his dilemma.

At 5.30 p.m. on May 16, 1967 I received a message from the commander of UNEF, a message that would set in motion events that would change the course of history in the Middle East. General Indar Jit Rikhye notified me (at 10.00 p.m. local time) that he had been requested by the chief of staff of the U.A.R. armed forces to withdraw 'all UN troops which install observer posts along our borders'.

(. . .)

I then plunged into one of the most intensive periods of diplomatic activity in my ten years as Secretary General. After taking the series of steps outlined below, I met informally the next afternoon with the representatives of countries providing contingents to UNEF (Brazil, Canada, Denmark, India, Norway, Sweden and Yugoslavia) to inform them of the seriousness of the situation, as it was then known to me. I told them how I intended to proceed, observing that, in my view, if a formal request for the withdrawal of UNEF were to be made by the government of the United Arab Republic, I would have to comply with it, since the force was on United Arab Republic territory only with the consent of the government and could not remain there without it. I informed the group that it was my intention to report my action to the General Assembly immediately. I also said, however, that 'if there is any request from the government of the United Arab Republic for withdrawal or deployment of UNEF, the first action I propose to take is to appeal to the government to reconsider, without immediately complying with the request'.

Two representatives (Brazil and Canada) expressed serious doubts about the consequences of agreeing to a peremptory request for the withdrawal of UNEF, and raised questions of possible consideration by the General Assembly of such a request and a possible appeal to the United Arab Republic not to request the withdrawal.

Two other representatives (India and Yugoslavia), who jointly contributed approximately one half of the UNEF contingent expressed the view that the

United Arab Republic was entitled to request the removal of UNEF at any moment, and that the request would have to be respected regardless of what the General Assembly might have to say in the matter, since the agreement for UNEF's presence had been concluded between the then Secretary General (Dag Hammarskjöld) and the government of Egypt.

Source: U Thant, *View from the UN* (New York: Doubleday, 1978), pp. 220–21.

Document 12   HAMMARSKJÖLD'S 'SUMMARY STUDY' – PEACEKEEPING CONCEPTUALISED

In 1958, two years after the establishment of UNEF, the UN secretary general Dag Hammarskjöld submitted a lengthy report to the General Assembly on the experience and lessons of the operation. This 'Summary Study' set out a series of principles relating to key aspects of the peacekeeping process such as host state consent, the appropriate type of contributing state, freedom of movement, political neutrality and financing. These, in Hammarskjöld's view, should form the basis of a future peacekeeping 'model'.

B. *Basic Principles*

155. As the arrangements discussed in this report do not cover the type of force envisaged under Chapter VII of the Charter, it follows from international law and the Charter that the United Nations cannot undertake to implement them by stationing units on the territory of a Member State without the consent of the Government concerned. It similarly follows from the Charter that the consent of a Member nation is necessary for the United Nations to use its military force or *materiel*. These basic rules have been observed in the recent United Nations operations in the Middle East. They naturally hold valid for all similar operations in the future.

(. . .)

160. Another point of principle which arises in relation to the question of consent refers to the composition of United Nations military elements stationed on the territory of a Member country. While the United Nations must reserve for itself the authority to decide on the composition of such elements, it is obvious that the host country, in giving its consent, cannot be indifferent to the composition of these elements. In order to limit the scope of possible difference of opinion, the United Nations in recent operations has followed two principles: not to include units from any of the permanent members of the Security Council; and not to include units from any country which, because of its geographical position or for other reasons, might be considered as possibly having a special interest in the situation which has

called for the operation. I believe that these two principles should also be considered as essential to any stand-by arrangements.

(. . .)

164. Another principle in the UNEF status Agreement which should be retained is that the United Nations activity should have freedom of movement within its area of operations and all such facilities regarding access to that area and communications as are necessary for successful completion of the task. . . .

165. . . . (A)uthority granted to the United Nations group cannot be exercised within a given territory either in competition with representatives of the host Government or in co-operation with them on the basis of any joint operation. Thus a United Nations operation must be separate and distinct from activities by national authorities . . .

166. A rule closely related to the one last mentioned, and reflecting a basic Charter principle, precludes the employment of United Nations elements in situations of an essentially internal nature. As a matter of course, the United Nations personnel cannot be permitted in any sense to be a party to internal conflicts. Their role must be limited to external aspects of the political situation as, for example, infiltration or other activities affecting international boundaries.

167. Even in the case of UNEF, where the United Nations itself had taken a stand on decisive elements in the situation which gave rise to the creation of the Force, it was explicitly stated that the Force should not be used to enforce any specific political solution of pending problems or to influence the political balance decisive to such a solution. This precept would clearly impose a serious limitation on the possible use of United Nations elements, were it to be given general application to them whenever they are not created under Chapter VII of the Charter. However, I believe its acceptance to be necessary, if the United Nations is to be in a position to draw on Member countries for contributions in men and *materiel* to United Nations operations of this kind.

(. . .)

179. . . . It should be generally recognized that [a right of self-defence for peacekeeping forces] exists. However, in certain cases this right should be exercised only under strictly defined conditions. A problem arises in this context because of the fact that a wide interpretation of the right of self-defence might well blur the distinction between operations of the character discussed in this report and combat operations, which would require a decision under Chapter VII of the Charter . . . A reasonable definition seems to have been established in the case of UNEF, where the rule is applied that men engaged in the operation may never take the initiative in the use of armed force, but are entitled to respond with force to an attack with arms . . . The basic element involved is clearly the prohibition against any *initiative*

in the use of armed force. This definition of the limit between self-defence, as permissible for United Nations elements of the kind discussed, and offensive action, which is beyond the competence of such elements, should be approved for future guidance.

(. . .)

189. I believe that . . . it should be established that the costs for United Nations operations of the type in question, based on decisions of the General Assembly or Security Council, should be allocated in accordance with the normal scale of contributions. The United Nations in this way should assume responsibility for all additional costs incurred by a contributing country because of its participation in the operation, on the basis of a cost assessment which, on the other hand, would not transfer to the United Nations any costs which would otherwise have been incurred by a contributing Government under its regular national policy.

Source: Summary Study of the Experience Derived from the Establishment and Operation of the [UN Emergency] Force: Report of the Secretary-General. General Assembly document A/3943, 9 October 1958.

Document 13   THREE SECURITY COUNCIL RESOLUTIONS ON THE CONGO

The rapidly shifting complexities of the Congo crisis and the UN's intervention in it are reflected in these successive Security Council mandates.

(i) When the operation was established in July 1960 the UN's role was seen simply as facilitating the withdrawal of Belgian forces and the provision of technical assistance.

The Security Council

Considering the report of the Secretary-General on a request for a United Nations action in relation to the Republic of the Congo,

Considering the request for military assistance addressed to the Secretary-General by the President and Prime Minister of the Congo

1. *Calls upon* the Government of Belgium to withdraw its troops from the territory of the Republic of the Congo;
2. *Decides* to authorize the Secretary-General to take the necessary steps, in consultation with the Government of the Congo, to provide the Government with such military assistance as may be necessary until, through the efforts of the Congolese Government with the technical assistance of the United Nations, the national security forces may be able, in the opinion of the Government, to meet fully their tasks;

3.   *Requests* the Secretary-General to report to the Security Council as appropriate.

Source: Security Council resolution S/RES/143, 14 July 1960 [Passed 8 : 0 with China, France and UK abstaining].

(ii) By the following February prime minister Lumumba had been murdered in Katanga whose mercenary-backed secession from the Congo seemed, particularly to the Afro-Asian bloc, to be insufficiently opposed by the UN. A more robust response on the part of ONUC was now approved by the Security Council. The border between peacekeeping and enforcement was now becoming blurred.

The Security Council

   (. . .)

1.   *Urges* that the United Nations take immediately all appropriate measures to prevent the occurrence of civil war in the Congo, including arrangements for cease-fires, the halting of all military operations, the prevention of clashes and the use of force, if necessary, in the last resort;

2.   *Urges* that measures be taken for the immediate withdrawal and evacuation from the Congo of all Belgian and other foreign military and paramilitary personnel and political advisers not under the United Nations Command, and mercenaries;

3.   *Calls upon* all states to take immediate and energetic measures to prevent the departure of such personnel for the Congo from their territories, and for the denial of transit and other facilities to them;

4.   *Decides* that an immediate and impartial investigation be held in order to ascertain the circumstances of the death of Mr Lumumba and his colleagues and that the perpetrators of these crimes be punished . . .

Source: Security Council resolution S/RES/161, 21 February 1961 [Passed 9 : 0 with France and USSR abstaining].

(iii) In November 1961, following the death of Hammarskjöld, the Security Council responded to the continuing defiance of separatist Katanga with a still stronger enforcement-orientated resolution.

The Security Council

   (. . .)

1.   *Strongly deprecates* the secessionist activities illegally carried out by the provincial administration of Katanga, with the aid of external resources and manned by foreign mercenaries;

2.   *Further deprecates* the armed action against United Nations forces and personnel in pursuit of such activities;

3.   *Insists* that such activities shall cease forthwith, *and calls* upon all concerned to desist therefrom;

4. *Authorizes* the Secretary-General to take vigorous action, including the use of the requisite measure of force, if necessary, for the immediate apprehension, detention pending legal action and/or deportation of all foreign military and paramilitary personnel and political advisers not under the United Nations Command, and mercenaries;

    (. . .)

8. *Declares* that all secessionist activities against the Republic of the Congo are contrary to . . . Security Council decisions and specifically *demands* that such activities that are now taking place in Katanga shall cease forthwith . . .

Source: Security Council resolution S/RES/169, 24 November 1961 [Passed 9 : 0 with France and UK abstaining].

Document 14   EXCHANGE OF LETTERS BETWEEN CONGO PRIME MINISTER PATRICE LUMUMBA AND UN SECRETARY GENERAL DAG HAMMARSKJÖLD ON THE PURPOSE OF THE UN OPERATION IN THE CONGO

Relations between the Congolese prime minister Patrice Lumumba and secretary general Dag Hammarskjöld deteriorated very quickly after the arrival of UN forces in the Congo. At particular issue was the breakaway province of Katanga which Lumumba demanded (with the support of the Soviet Union) should be brought to heel by the UN. His insistence that 'in its intervention in the Congo the United Nations is not to act as a neutral organisation but rather that the Security Council is to place all its resources at the disposal of my Government', went to the heart, not just of the UN's dilemma in the Congo, but to the fundamental principle of impartiality which guided United Nations peace operations at this time. The tone of both Lumumba's letter and Hammarskjöld's reply the following day gives a measure of the breakdown in the relationship.

(i) From Lumumba to Hammarskjöld, 14 August 1960

. . . the Government of the Republic of the Congo can in no way agree with your personal interpretation, which is unilateral and erroneous, as the resolution of 14 July 1960 expressly states that the Security Council authorizes you 'to provide the Government [of the Republic of the Congo] with such military assistance as may be necessary'. This text adds that you are to do so 'in consultation with' my Government. It is therefore clear that in its intervention in the Congo the United Nations is not to act as a neutral organization but rather that the Security Council is to place all its resources at the disposal of my Government. From these texts it is clear that, contrary to your personal interpretation, the United Nations Force may be used to subdue the rebel government of Katanga, that my Government may call upon the United Nations services to transport civilian and military representatives of the central Government to Katanga in opposition to the provincial government of Katanga and that the United Nations Force has the duty to protect the civilian and military personnel representing my Government in Katanga.

(. . .)

My Government also takes this opportunity to protest against the fact that upon your return to New York *en route* to Katanga, you did not consult it, as prescribed in the resolution of 14 July 1960 [see Doc. 13(i)], despite the formal request submitted to you by my Government's delegation in New York before your departure and despite my letter replying to your cable on this subject. On the contrary, you have dealt with the rebel government of Katanga in violation of the Security Council's resolution of 14 July 1960. That resolution does not permit you to deal with the local authorities until after you have consulted with my Government. Yet you are acting as though my Government, which is the repository of legal authority and is alone qualified to deal with the United Nations, did not exist.

The manner in which you have acted until now is only retarding the restoration of order in the republic, particularly in the province of Katanga, whereas the Security Council has solemnly declared that the purpose of the intervention is the complete restoration of order in the republic of the Congo . . .

(ii) From Hammarskjöld to Lumumba, 15 August 1960

I have received your letter of 14 August. In it I find allegations against the Secretary-General as well as objections to the Secretary-General's interpretation of the resolutions with the implementation of which he has been entrusted. In your letter you also submit certain requests which appear to derive from a position contrary to my interpretation of the resolutions.

There is no reason for me to enter into a discussion here either of those unfounded and unjustified allegations or of the interpretation of the Security Council's resolutions.

(. . .)

Source: Security Council document S/4417/Add.7. Official Record for July–September 1960, pp. 71–6.

KHRUSHCHEV AND THE 'TROIKA' PROPOSAL   **Document 15**

Within a few months of its creation, the United Nations operation in the Congo seemed to have aggravated rather than eased east–west relations.

Moscow claimed that the UN led by secretary general Hammarskjöld had become an instrument of western 'imperialism' in the Congo. The Soviet leader, Nikita Khrushchev, called for a fundamental reform of the organisation's management. In a speech to the General Assembly in September 1960 he proposed the replacement of the office of secretary general with a 'troika' composed of representatives of the west, the eastern bloc and the Afro-Asian group.

280. The Soviet Union considers that if a correct approach is taken to the utilization of . . . international armed forces, they may indeed be useful. But the experience of the Congo puts us on our guard. That experience indicates that the United Nations forces are being utilized exactly in the way against which we warned, a way we emphatically oppose. Mr Hammarskjöld . . . has taken a position of purely formal condemnation of the colonialists. In actual practice, however, he is following the colonialists' line, opposing the lawful government of the Congo and the Congolese people and supporting the renegades who, under the guise of fighting for the independence of the republic of the Congo, are actually continuing the policy of the colonialists and are evidently receiving some reward from them for their treachery.

281. What is to be done in this case? If this is how the international armed forces are to be used in practice, to suppress liberation movements, it will naturally be difficult to reach agreement on their establishment, since there will be no guarantee that they will not be used for reactionary purposes that are alien to the interests of peace. Provision must be made to ensure that no state falls into the predicament in which the Republic of the Congo now finds itself. We are convinced that other States also realize this danger. Solutions must therefore be sought which would preclude similar occurrences in the future.

282. The Soviet Government has come to a definite conclusion on this matter and wishes to expound its point of view before the United Nations General Assembly. Conditions have clearly matured to the point where the post of Secretary-General, who alone directs the staff and alone interprets and executes the decisions of the Security Council and the sessions of the General Assembly, should be abolished. It would be expedient to abandon the system under which in all practical work in the intervals between General Assembly sessions and Security Council meetings is determined by the Secretary-General alone.

283. The executive organ of the United Nations should reflect the real situation that obtains in the world today. The United Nations includes States which are members of the military blocs of the Western Powers, socialist States and neutralist [Non-Aligned] countries. It would therefore

be completely justified to take that situation into account, and we would be better safeguarded against the negative developments which have come to light in the work of the United Nations, especially during the recent events in the Congo.

284. We consider it reasonable and just for the executive organ of the United Nations to consist not of a single person – the Secretary-General – but of three persons invested with the highest trust of the United Nations, persons representing the States belonging to the military block of the Western Powers, the socialist States and the neutralist States. This composition of the United Nations executive organ would create conditions for a more correct implementation of the decisions taken.

285. In brief, we consider it advisable to set up, in the place of a Secretary-General who is at present the interpreter and executor of the decisions of the General Assembly and the Security Council, a collective executive organ of the United Nations consisting of three persons each of whom would represent a certain group of States. That would provide a definite guarantee that the work of the United Nations executive organ would not be carried on to the detriment of any one of these groups of States. The United Nations executive organ would then be a genuinely democratic organ; it would really guard the interests of all States Members of the United Nations irrespective of the social and political system of any particular Member State. This is particularly necessary at the present time, and it would be even more so in the future.

Source: General Assembly document A/PV.869, 23 September 1960.

THE CONGO – CONOR CRUISE O'BRIEN AND THE KATANGA QUESTION   **Document 16**

The military operations ordered by Conor Cruise O'Brien, the UN representative in Katanga, against the western-backed secessionists in August and September 1961 led indirectly to Hammarskjöld's death when he travelled to the Congo to deal with the ensuing crisis. Following the abrupt end of his UN service after these events, O'Brien wrote an elegant apologia *for his actions. Refuting accusations that he had acted without authorisation, he suggested that Hammarskjöld himself had supported firm action against Katanga. Here he recalls his initiation by Rajeshwar Dayal into the fraught international politics surrounding the Katanga affair.*

By any reckoning there were storms ahead. The captain's problem in setting his course was to decide which storm-centre presented on the whole the lesser risk. In deciding as he did on the 'Afro-Asian interpretation' – the vigorous implementation of the February resolution [authorising the use of force by ONUC 'to prevent the occurrence of civil war'] – Mr Hammarskjöld decided to head for the storm centring on the English Channel – that is to say, to risk the hostility of England, France and Belgium. He may have under-estimated the dangers of this course; he was surely right in considering it less dangerous – to the United Nations, to the Congo and to general peace – than the alternative of drifting towards collapse.

At the time I was aware of these storm signals, but that does not mean that I had much idea of what the fury of the storm, when actually experienced, would be like. . . . There were some whitened bones around . . . which should have brought things home to me.

Mr Dayal was just leaving . . . to rejoin the Indian Foreign Service. He was leaving at his own request, following his 'controversial' term of office as UN Special Representative in the Congo . . . He explained without rancour, but as things important for me to know, the basic reasons for his departure. Every great power, he explained, wished to turn the United Nations into an instrument of its own policy, but some powers were in a better position than others to do so. In his time in Leopoldville . . . the powers in the best position to make this use of the United Nations were the United States and, secondarily, Britain. Ambassadors of these powers, effectively – though not always in unison – controlled President Kasavubu and General Mobutu, and they were therefore most anxious that the United Nations should accept these gentlemen's nominees as being the Government of the Congo. As the legality of all this was highly questionable, and as it represented the viewpoint of only one group of powers within the United Nations, Mr Dayal had held out against it and in favour of the con-vening of parliament and the election of a government of unquestioned legality. In this stand he was supported by the Secretary-General.

Source: Conor Cruise O'Brien, *To Katanga and Back: A UN Case History* (London: Hutchinson, 1962), pp. 63–4.

Document 17   HAMMARSKJÖLD AND THE CONGO – THE PRESSURES OF OFFICE

Assailed from all sides over the Congo, the stress on the solitary and cerebral Hammarskjöld over the year leading up to his death in September 1961 was immense. Some indication of his state of mind can be detected in the verse he wrote at the time and which was published after he died.

July 6th, 61
Tired
And lonely,
So tired
The heart aches.
Meltwater trickles
Down the rocks,
The fingers are numb,
The knees tremble.
It is now,
Now, that you must not give in.
On the path of the others
Are resting places,
Places in the sun
Where they can meet.
But this
Is your path,
And it is now,
Now, that you must not fail.
Weep
If you can,
Weep,
But do not complain.
The way chose you –
And you must be thankful.

Source: Dag Hammarskjöld [trans. Leif Sjöberg and W.H. Auden], *Markings* (London: Faber & Faber, 1964), p. 175.

FORMING THE CYPRUS FORCE   **Document 18**

In March 1964 secretary general U Thant encountered initial wariness on the part of potential contributors to UNFICYP. Behind this lay the experience of the Congo and a perception that the Cyprus crisis might be even more militarily and politically dangerous. There was also concern at the uncertainty over financing. These worries are evident in the reply from the Irish Minister for External Affairs, Frank Aiken, to U Thant's initial request for troops. In addition to misgivings held in common with all potential contributors, Ireland had a special concern over the prospect of the partition of Cyprus.

13 March 1964

Excellency,

I have received your telegram this morning about your efforts to implement the resolution of the Security Council of 4 March 1964, dealing with the establishment of a United Nations peace-keeping force in Cyprus. I have also received the text of replies you have given to the requests for clarification made to you by some of the countries asked to participate in the force.

As your telegram so generously recognises, Ireland as a faithful member of the United Nations has invariably given its whole-hearted support to the peace-keeping efforts of the United Nations. It was in this spirit that my Government examined sympathetically your request for an Irish contingent for the United Nations peace-keeping force in Cyprus. I am authorised to give you the following reply to your request.

The Government of Ireland have agreed in principle, subject to the adoption by Dáil Eireann [the Irish parliament] of the resolution required by Irish law, to comply with the Secretary-General's request to contribute a battalion of approximately 500 men to the United Nations peace-keeping force in Cyprus.

This decision is conditional on the Government's understanding:

1) that the function of the force will be to maintain peace while the process to achieve an agreed solution of the problem confronting Cyprus is in progress and that the force will have no function in influencing the character of the settlement to be made or its subsequent enforcement;

2) that an assurance will be forthcoming from the Governments of Great Britain, Greece and Turkey that, during the presence of the force in Cyprus, they will not intervene or attempt to impose by force, or by threat of force, a solution of the problem – and, particularly, a solution by partition;

3) that every effort will be made by the Secretary-General to ensure that the Greek and Turkish Governments will place under the command of the United Nations their troops now stationed in Cyprus; and

4) that if it should be agreed to be necessary to keep a United Nations force in Cyprus after the expiration of three months,
   a) other member countries of the United Nations would be asked to provide contingents and
   b) the Government would be free to withdraw the Irish contingent, irrespective of the progress of the mediation and the state of affairs in Cyprus at that time.

The Irish Government view with regret the decision to raise funds on a voluntary basis for a United Nations peace-keeping force. They regard it as a grave and unwise departure from the principle of collective responsibility.

Subject to Dáil approval the Government would pay the usual United Nations overseas allowances to our troops and would accept no reimbursement from the United Nations unless it were levied on all members of the United Nations in the normal way.

Subject to the foregoing and as soon as you inform me that you have received the assurance referred to in paragraph 4 above, my government will take the earliest opportunity of seeking the approval of the Dáil for sending a battalion to join the United Nations peace-keeping force in Cyprus.

Accept, Excellency, the renewed assurance of my highest consideration.
Frank Aiken
Minister for External Affairs

Source: Bulletin of the Department of External Affairs of Ireland, No. 653, 23 March 1964.

THE INTERNATIONAL COURT OF JUSTICE ADVISORY OPINION ON THE   **Document 19**
FINANCING OF PEACEKEEPING

The deepening crisis over how peace operations should be paid for led to the issue being sent to the International Court of Justice for an advisory opinion in 1962 on the applicability of article 17(ii) of the Charter [see Doc. 4(iv)]. The Court, after detailed consideration of the legal bases of UNEF and ONUC, upheld by a majority decision the western position that peacekeeping was a 'normal' cost of the UN.

It is not possible to find in (the) description of the functions of UNEF, as outlined by the Secretary-General and concurred in by the General Assembly without a dissenting vote, any evidence that the force was to be used for purposes of enforcement. Nor can such evidence be found in the subsequent operations of the force, operations which did not exceed the functions ascribed to it.

It could not therefore have been patent on the face of the [General Assembly enabling] resolution that the establishment of UNEF was in effect 'enforcement action' under Chapter VII which, in accordance with the Charter, could be authorized only by the Security Council.

On the other hand, it is apparent that the operations were undertaken to fulfil a prime purpose of the United Nations . . . This being true, the Secretary-General properly exercised the authority given to him to incur financial obligations of the Organization and expenses resulting from such obligations must be considered 'expenses of the Organization within the meaning of Article 17, paragraph 2'.

(. . .)

The operations in the Congo were initially authorized by the Security Council in the resolution of 14 July 1960 [Doc. 13(i)] which was adopted without a dissenting vote.

(. . .)

In the light of (this) . . . it is impossible to reach the conclusion that the operations in question usurped or impinged upon the prerogatives conferred by the Charter on the Security Council. . . .

It is not necessary for the Court to express an opinion as to which article or articles of the Charter were the basis for the resolutions of the Security Council but it can be said that the operations of ONUC did not include a use of armed force against a State which the Security Council, under Article 39, determined to have committed an act of aggression or to have breached the peace. The armed forces which were utilized in the Congo were not authorized to take military action against any State under Chapter VII and therefore did not constitute 'action' as that term is used in Article 11.

For the reasons stated; financial obligations which, in accordance with the clear and reiterated authority of both the Security Council and the General Assembly, the Secretary-General incurred on behalf of the United Nations, constitute obligations of the Organization for which the General Assembly was entitled to make provision under Article 17 . . .

For these reasons,

THE COURT IS OF THE OPINION

by nine votes to five,

that the expenditures authorized . . . constitute 'expenses of the Organization' within the meaning of Article 17, paragraph 2, of the Charter of the United Nations.

Source: 'Certain Expenses of the United Nations (Article 17, paragraph 2 of the Charter), Advisory Opinion of 20 July 1962', *ICJ Reports 1962*.

Document 20   DÉTENTE AND THE 1973 MIDDLE EAST WAR – THE US PERSPECTIVE

In the 1970s détente brought a new appreciation of mutual interests between the superpowers and they achieved a considerable degree of cooperation over the Middle East war in 1973. Here Henry Kissinger, US secretary of state at the time, describes the initial coordination of policy with the Soviet Union which would eventually lead to the creation of UNEF II. It is clear in the extract, though, that national advantage was never far from the calculations of the superpowers.

A message was received from Brezhnev [the Soviet leader] early Monday, October 8: 'We have contacted the leaders of the Arab states on the question of cease-fire. We hope to get a reply shortly. We feel that we should act in cooperation with you, being guided by the broad interests of maintaining peace and developing the Soviet-American relations [*sic*]. We hope that President Nixon will act likewise'.

When Dobrynin [the Soviet ambassador in Washington – see Doc. 21] read me Brezhnev's message on the phone, I thought it served our immediate purpose very well. Since we did not intend to introduce a resolution and the Soviet Union was offering to coordinate with us, we were certain to get through the day without confrontation or embarrassing proposals. By the next day, we were convinced, the Israeli offensive would prevail; the Security Council would then call for a cease-fire in place. Our ally would have repulsed an attack by Soviet weapons. We could begin our peace process with the Arabs on the proposition that we had stopped an Israeli advance and with the Israelis on the basis that we had been steadfastly at their side in the crisis. I therefore did not hesitate to tell Dobrynin that we would act in the spirit of Brezhnev's message. We would put forward no resolution that day, nor without giving the Soviet Union several hours' advance warning. We would instruct Ambassador Scali [the US representative] to speak philosophically in the Security Council; we would avoid inflammatory statements. We expected the Soviet Union to follow a similar course. Dobrynin agreed.

Source: Henry Kissinger, *Years of Upheaval* (London: Weidenfeld and Nicolson, 1982), pp. 486–7.

DÉTENTE AND THE 1973 MIDDLE EAST WAR – THE SOVIET PERSPECTIVE   **Document 21**

The Soviet Union's reaction to the 1973 Middle East war and the implications for superpower détente are here recalled by Anatoly Dobrynin, Moscow's veteran ambassador to Washington.

Kissinger was already in New York for the annual session of the United Nations General Assembly [when the war began], and he wanted to convoke the Security Council. He wanted both the Soviet and the American representatives to be instructed to take a measured position without siding entirely with their traditional clients. The United States, he said, intended to propose a resolution calling for a cease fire . . .

Moscow replied promptly: 'The Soviet Union received reports about the beginning of hostilities in the Middle east [*sic*] simultaneously with you. . . . We are considering, like you, possible steps to be taken to remedy the situation. We hope to communicate with you soon to coordinate our actions.'

Source: Anatoly Dobrynin, *In Confidence: Moscow's Ambassador to America's Six Cold War Presidents* (New York: Times Books, 1995), p. 290.

Document 22   KURT WALDHEIM ON THE LEBANON FORCE

Here Kurt Waldheim, secretary general in 1978, recalls the process of formation of UNIFIL and some of the political problems around its composition.

Speed was of the essence. The nearest available troops were the Austrian and Iranian contingents serving in UNDOF, the disengagement force on the Golan Heights. They could be transported overland by truck convoy and reach their new deployment area within a few hours. However, I could not transfer them without the consent of their governments.

I first contacted the Austrian government, which let me know that they rather preferred to have their troops stay where they were. So I turned to the Iranians. The Shah was still in power and had been most helpful in previous peace-keeping activities. I reached him easily on the telephone, he gave his assent, and within twenty-four hours the Iranian contingent was on its way. We withdrew the Swedes from UNEF and soon reached the approved strength of 4,000 men. General Erskine of Ghana was in command and strongly recommended an increase to 6,000. It was a prudent request. The force was operating in two largely separate and extensive areas, in rugged terrain and often in situations of great danger. Over the months, the Security Council agreed to a further reinforcement of up to 7,000 men.

(. . .)

The Netherlands government, traditionally friendly to the Israelis, provided a contingent, yet, when they began to take casualties in skirmishes with Major Haddad's Christian militia and the PLO, the Dutch began to criticise the Israelis for failing to control their satellite. The Netherlands government found it necessary to pacify growing domestic opposition over the casualties and over embroilment with the Israelis. Their contingent was finally withdrawn.

The French played an important part in UNIFIL from the first. They furnished more men for the force than any other single nation. An elite group of French paratroopers arrived among the very first contingents under the command of Colonel Salvan, a wounded veteran of the climactic

Vietnam battle of Dien Bien Phu. He was appointed chief of staff to General Erskine, but a few months later his car was ambushed and he was seriously injured.

Source: Kurt Waldheim, *In the Eye of the Storm* (London: Weidenfeld and Nicolson, 1985), pp. 189–90.

BOUTROS BOUTROS-GHALI ON THE END OF THE SOMALIA OPERATION   **Document 23**

Secretary general Boutros-Ghali oversaw some of the most important and controversial peace operations in the immediate post-cold war period, including those in Bosnia, Rwanda and Somalia. His relationship with the United States – always a critical one for UN secretaries general – gradually deteriorated, in large part as a result of his complaints about what he saw as Washington's self-serving approach to UN operations. Here he describes what he saw as American cynicism surrounding the abandonment of the Somalia intervention.

Secretary of State Warren Christopher, Secretary of Defense Les Aspin, and [National Security Advisor] Anthony Lake were called before the Congress on October 5 and criticized harshly for the debacle of the U.S. Rangers in south Mogadishu [the *Blackhawk Down* incident]. At 8.30 that night, Robert Oakley who was a dinner guest at the Syrian embassy in Washington, received a call asking him to come to the White House immediately. Oakley, who had overseen the US-led Unified Task Force phase in Somalia from December 1992 to March 1993, had been back in Washington for six months but had been neither debriefed nor consulted by the Clinton administration, now it wanted him to return to Somalia. . . . (I)t was decided that the U.S. forces must withdraw from Somalia but that Oakley would be sent back to Mogadishu as a sign that the United States was in charge of events. As a cover for the American withdrawal, another U.S. task force, under another U.S. general, would be sent in as a show – but only a show – of strength.

On October 7, 1993, President Clinton spoke to the American people. He announced that U.S. forces in Somalia would be more than doubled and 'will be under American command', as if that were a change in status. Clinton's inclination was to blame the United Nations for what had been entirely an American disaster. The United States had run into trouble and it wanted out.

Source: Boutros Boutros-Ghali, *Unvanquished: A U.S.–U.N. Saga* (New York: Random House, 1999), p. 105.

Document 24   OPERATION DESERT STORM

Military action against Iraq to force its withdrawal from Kuwait was approved by the Security Council in November 1990. Although referring to Chapter VII of the Charter, the Council did not invoke its legally binding collective security powers under article 43. Operation Desert Storm was essentially the work of an independent alliance acting with UN authorisation rather than a 'UN force'.

The Security Council
Acting under Chapter VII of the Charter;

1. *Demands* that Iraq comply fully [with previous resolutions calling for its withdrawal from Kuwait] and decides, while maintaining all its decisions, to allow Iraq one final opportunity as a pause of goodwill to do so;
2. *Authorizes* member States co-operating with the Government of Kuwait, unless Iraq on or before January 15, 1991 fully implements the foregoing resolutions, to use all necessary means to uphold and implement Security Council Resolution 660 and all subsequent relevant resolutions and to restore international peace and security in the area;
3. *Requests* all States to provide appropriate support for the actions undertaken in pursuance of paragraph 2 of this resolution;
4. *Requests* the States concerned to keep the Council regularly informed of the progress of actions undertaken pursuant to paragraphs 2 and 3 of this resolution;
5. *Decides* to remain seized of the matter.

Source: Security Council resolution S/RES/678, 29 November 1990 [Passed 12 : 2 with Cuba and Yemen voting against and China abstaining].

Document 25   *AN AGENDA FOR PEACE*

In his major 1992 analysis of the current state and future prospects for peace-keeping, secretary general Boutros Boutros-Ghali proposed the creation of a new type of UN force with a role between interposition and enforcement.

Peace-enforcement units
44. The mission of forces under Article 43 would be to respond to outright aggression, imminent or actual. Such forces are not likely to be available for some time to come. Cease-fires have often been agreed to but not complied with, and the United Nations has sometimes been called upon to send forces

to restore and maintain the cease-fire. This task can on occasion exceed the mission of peace-keeping forces and the expectations of peace-keeping force contributors. I recommend that the Council consider the utilization of peace-enforcement units in clearly defined circumstances and with their terms of reference specified in advance. Such units from Member States would be available on call and would consist of troops that have volunteered for such service. They would have to be more heavily armed than peace-keeping forces and would have to undergo extensive preparatory training within their national forces. Deployment and operation of such forces would be under the authorization of the Security Council and would, as in the case of peace-keeping forces, be under the command of the Secretary-General. I consider such peace-enforcement units to be warranted as a provisional measure under Article 40 of the Charter. Such peace-enforcement units should not be confused with the forces that may eventually be constituted under Article 43 to deal with acts of aggression or with the military personnel which Governments may agree to keep on stand-by for possible contribution to peace-keeping operations. (See Document 4(i))

Source: Security Council document S/24111, 17 June 1992.

Further reading

The starting point for an exploration of UN peace operations during the cold war lies in general studies of international organisation and the history of the United Nations. At the broadest level LeRoy Bennet's *International Organization: Principles and Issues* (Englewood Cliffs, 1994) provides a thorough introduction to the concept of international organisation – including the United Nations – in contemporary world politics. Similar ground is covered, though more concisely, by Clive Archer in *International Organizations* (London, 2001). Another general but more historically orientated study is provided by David Armstrong, Lorna Lloyd and John Redmond's *International Organization in World Politics* (London, 2004).

At the level of specific institutions, F.P. Walters' *A History of the League of Nations* (single volume edition, Oxford, 1960) is an immensely detailed study of the UN's predecessor institution written by a former League deputy secretary general. Wide-ranging studies of the United Nations as an institution include Amos Yoder's *The Evolution of the United Nations System* (London, 1997) and, more comprehensively, *The Oxford Handbook on the United Nations* edited by Sam Daws and Thomas Weiss (London, 2008). *The United Nations: an Introduction* (London, 2005) by Sven Bernhard Gareis and Johannes Varwick, originally published in German, is perhaps not aptly named as it engages with the topic at a relatively advanced level, but it deals in interesting detail with collective security and peacekeeping. There is as yet no political and diplomatic history of the first decades of the UN to compete with Evan Luard's authoritative *A History of the United Nations*. The first of the two volumes of this work covers *The Years of Western Domination, 1945–55* (London, 1982) and the second *The Age of Decolonization, 1955–65* (London, 1989). A closer focus on the very early development of the UN is provided by Ruth Russell in her detailed *A History of the United Nations Charter* (Washington, DC, 1958). Another relatively early work, coordinated by Leon Goodrich, *Charter of the United Nations: Commentary and Documents* (New

York, 1969), provides a political and legal analysis which gives particular attention to the UN's international security functions and the use of force.

A number of studies of the use of military forces by the United Nations were written during the cold war which, though now limited in their range, nevertheless provide historical insights into contemporary thinking. Among the more interesting of these are: *Peacekeeping by UN Forces from Suez to the Congo* by Arthur Burns and Nina Heathcote (London, 1963); Joel Larus (ed.), *From Collective Security to Preventive Diplomacy* (New York, 1965); Arthur M. Cox, *Prospects for Peacekeeping* (Washington, DC, 1967) and Alan James, *The Politics of Peacekeeping* (London, 1969). David Bowett provides an early legal exploration of peacekeeping in *United Nations Forces* (London, 1964).

Another category of books on peacekeeping offering a special perspective are the memoirs of former military commanders and civilian officials in the field. The Canadian commander of UNEF in Suez, General E.L.M. Burns, published his account in *Between Arab and Israeli* (London, 1962) and the Swedish general, Carl von Horn, who was chief of staff of the Truce Supervision Organization in the Middle East, provided his account of the operation in *Soldiering for Peace* (London, 1966). The British peacekeeper Michael Harbottle and his Indian colleague Indar Jit Rikhye, who between them had very wide experience of a range of cold war operations, together produced *The Thin Blue Line* (New Haven, 1974). Among civilian field officers' accounts, the book by the Irish UN official Conor Cruise O'Brien, *To Katanga and Back* (London, 1962) on his (ill-)fated time as Hammarskjöld's representative in Katanga, is both controversial and extremely readable. Another, less heated, account of the Congo operation from the inside is offered by his Indian colleague Rajeshwar Dayal in *Mission for Hammarskjöld* (London, 1976). Two books from the field dealing with episodes from the immediate post-cold war years of peacekeeping are both important in different ways. Margaret Anstee's *Orphan of the Cold War* (London, 1996) provides an account of the failure of the Angolan peace process in 1992 which was overseen by the UNAVEM II operation. Anstee was the secretary-general's representative in Angola at the time. The Canadian General Roméo Dallaire, commander of the UN force in Rwanda, provides a coruscating account of the 1994 genocide and the UN's impotence in the face of it in *Shake Hands with the Devil* (London, 2004).

Most of the UN's successive secretaries general have themselves produced memoirs in retirement. All of these have revealing sections on the peace operations which took place during the terms in office of their authors. These began with the first secretary general Trygve Lie's *In the Cause of Peace* (New York, 1954) which covers the early peace observation missions and, of course, the Korean War. U Thant's *View from the UN* (New York, 1978) embraces a significant part of the UN's cold war operations including the

Congo, West New Guinea, Cyprus and the final phase of the Emergency Force in Suez. Thant's successor, the Austrian Kurt Waldheim, was in office during the range of 'détente' UN operations in the Middle East (in Sinai, the Golan Heights and Lebanon). His accounts of these are offered in his memoir *In the Eye of the Storm* (London, 1985). Javier Pérez de Cuéllar of Peru followed Waldheim on the 38th Floor of the UN Building in 1982 and remained in post for ten years through the greater part of the 'second' cold war and then during the tectonic shift which saw the end of global bipolarity. Given the drama of his period in office his memoir, *Pilgrimage for Peace* (London, 1997), is perhaps a little lacking in colour. Nevertheless, he offers an important account of the important linked operations in Namibia (UNTAG) and Angola (UNAVEM I) at the end of the 1980s. In contrast, his post-cold war successor Boutros Boutros-Ghali's record of his time in office (from 1992 until his involuntary departure in 1997) could hardly be accused of being colourless. But *Unvanquished: A U.S.–U.N. Saga* (New York, 1999) focuses, as the title suggests, on a specific area of his experience as secretary-general: the relationship with the United States. While the book exudes a strong impression of self-justification and score-settling, it offers very revealing accounts of the international politics behind the high-profile UN 'failures' in Bosnia, Somalia and Rwanda.

The secretary general most closely associated with the development of UN peace operations during the cold war, Dag Hammarskjöld, was effectively killed in action while directly pursuing peace in the Congo in 1961. However, his faithful subordinate, the Briton Brian Urquhart, who represented him in the Congo (and later became under-secretary general with responsibility for peacekeeping) produced a detailed insider, but largely uncritical, account of his mentor's period in office: *Hammarskjöld* (London, 1972). A less thorough but no less admiring study of the UN's second secretary general was published by the journalist Joseph Lash: *Dag Hammarskjöld: Custodian of the Brushfire Peace* (London, 1962).

There are several general studies of UN peace operations, though many of the more recent of them approach the subject from the perspectives of political science and peace studies rather than contemporary history. Among those with a relatively strong historical orientation are Norrie MacQueen's *Peacekeeping and the International System* (London, 2006), which follows the narrative of multilateral military intervention from the nineteenth century until the beginning of the twenty-first. The same author deals specifically with peace operations in sub-Saharan Africa in *United Nations Peacekeeping in Africa since 1960* (London, 2002). A comprehensive approach is also taken by Alan James in *Peacekeeping in International Politics* (London, 1990), though the time-frame is obviously shorter. A relatively critical perspective on UN operations during the cold war and détente is offered by Anthony Verrier in *International Peacekeeping: United Nations Forces in a Troubled World* (Harmondsworth, 1981). *The Evolution of Peacekeeping* (New York, 1993), edited by William Durch, is a multi-authored work which traces, operation-by-operation, the development of UN interventions up until the transition in peace operations at the end of the cold war. The later cold war years and the period immediately following are explored in a short and accessible book written by a former British ambassador to the UN, Sir Anthony Parsons: *From Cold War to Hot Peace: UN Interventions 1975–1995* (Harmondsworth, 1995). *Understanding Peacekeeping* (Cambridge, 2010) by Alex Bellamy and Paul Williams, although not primarily a history, nevertheless provides a good sense of historical perspective on peace operations.

The monumental multi-volume series by Rosalyn Higgins, *United Nations Peacekeeping 1946–67: Documents and Commentary* (London, 1969, 1970, 1980, 1981) occupies a class of its own. Volume 1 deals with the Middle East; volume 2 Asia, volume 3 Africa, and volume 4 (which covers the period 1946–79) Europe. Dame Rosalyn Higgins, an international lawyer by training, ended her career as the first female president of the International Court of Justice (2006–9).

References

Abi-Saab, George (1978) *The United Nations Operation in the Congo, 1960–1964*. Oxford: Oxford University Press.

Anstee, Margaret (1996) *Orphan of the Cold War: The Inside Story of the Collapse of the Angolan Peace Process, 1992–93*. London: Macmillan.

Archer, Clive (2001) *International Organizations*, 3rd edn. London: Routledge.

Armstrong, David (1982) *The Rise of the International Organization: A Short History*. London: Macmillan.

Ashton, S.R. (1989) *In Search of Détente: The Politics of East-West Relations since 1945*. London: Macmillan.

Barnett, Michael (1995) 'Partners in peace? The UN, regional organizations and peace-keeping', *Review of International Studies*, 21(4), 411–33.

Bell, Coral (1977) *The Diplomacy of Détente: The Kissinger Era*. London: Martin Robertson.

Bellamy, Alex and Williams, Paul (2010) *Understanding Peacekeeping*, 2nd edn. Cambridge: Polity.

Bennett, A. LeRoy (1994) *International Organization: Principles and Issues*, 6th edn. Englewood Cliffs, NJ: Prentice Hall.

Berdal, Mats and Leifer, Michael (1996) 'Cambodia', in James Mayall (ed.), *The New Interventionism 1991–1994: United Nations Experience in Cambodia, Former Yugoslavia and Somalia*. Cambridge: Cambridge University Press, pp. 25–58.

Bertrand, Maurice (1993) 'The historical development of efforts to reform the UN', in A. Roberts and B. Kingsbury (eds), *United Nations, Divided World*. Oxford: Oxford University Press, pp. 420–36.

Bloomfield, Lincoln *et al.* (1964) *International Military Forces: The Question of Peacekeeping in an Armed and Disarming World*. Boston, MA: Little Brown.

Boutros-Ghali, Boutros (1992) *An Agenda for Peace: Preventive Diplomacy, Peacemaking and Peacekeeping*. New York: United Nations.

Boyd, Andrew (1971) *Fifteen Men on a Powder Keg: A History of the UN Security Council*. London: Methuen.

Burns, A.L. and Heathcote, Nina (1963) *Peacekeeping by UN Forces from Suez to the Congo*. London: Pall Mall.

Calvocoressi, Peter (2008) *World Politics since 1945*, 9th edn. London: Longman.

Chesterman, Simon (2004) *You, the People: the United Nations, Transitional Administrations, and State-Building*. London: Oxford University Press.

Comay, M. (1976) *UN Peace-Keeping in the Arab-Israeli Conflict, 1948–1975*. Jerusalem: Hebrew University.

Crockatt, Richard (1996) *The Fifty Years War: The United States and the Soviet Union in World Politics 1941–1991*, 2nd edn. London: Routledge.

Dayal, Rajeshwar (1976) *Mission for Hammarskjöld: The Congo Crisis*. Oxford: Oxford University Press.

Divine, Robert A. (1974) *Foreign Policy and US Presidential Elections, 1940–1948*. New York: New Viewpoints.

Doyle, Michael W. (1995) *UN Peacekeeping in Cambodia: UNTAC's Civil Mandate*. London: Lynne Rienner.

Economides, Spiros and Taylor, Paul (1996) 'Former Yugoslavia', in James Mayall (ed.), *The New Interventionism 1991–1994: United Nations Experience in Cambodia, Former Yugoslavia and Somalia*. Cambridge: Cambridge University Press, pp. 59–93.

Fabian, Larry L. (1973) *Soldiers without Enemies: Preparing the UN for Peace-keeping*. Washington, DC: Brookings Institute.

Fortna, Virginia Page (1993) 'The United Nations Angola Verification Mission I', in William Durch (ed.), *The Evolution of UN Peacekeeping: Case Studies and Comparative Analysis*. New York: St Martin's Press, pp. 376–405.

Gaddis, John L. (1997) *We Know Now: Rethinking Cold War History*. Oxford: Clarendon Press.

Garthoff, Raymond L. (1985) *Détente and Confrontation: American-Soviet Relations, Nixon to Reagan*. Washington, DC: Brookings Institute.

Goodrich, Leon M. *et al.* (1969) *Charter of the United Nations: Commentary and Documents*. New York: Columbia University Press.

Gordenker, Leon (1967) *The UN Secretary General and the Maintenance of Peace*. New York: Columbia University Press.

Halliday, Fred (1987) *The Making of the Second Cold War*. London: Verso.

Harbottle, Michael (1970) *The Impartial Soldier: A Study of the UN Operation in Cyprus*. Oxford: Oxford University Press.

Harbottle, Michael (1971) *The Blue Berets: The Story of United Nations Peacekeeping Forces*. London: Leo Cooper.

Hastings, Max (1988) *The Korean War*. London: Michael Joseph.

Higgins, Rosalyn (1969) *United Nations Peacekeeping 1946–67: Documents and Commentary*, Vol. 1 *The Middle East*. Oxford: Oxford University Press.

Higgins, Rosalyn (1970) *United Nations Peacekeeping 1946–67: Documents and Commentary*, Vol. 2 *Asia*. Oxford: Oxford University Press.

Higgins, Rosalyn (1980) *United Nations Peacekeeping 1946–67: Documents and Commentary*, Vol. 3 *Africa*. Oxford: Oxford University Press.

Higgins, Roslyn (1981) *United Nations Peacekeeping: Documents and Commentary 1946–79*, Vol. 4 *Europe*. Oxford: Oxford University Press.

Hoskyns, Catherine (1965) *The Congo since Independence, January 1960– December 1961*. Oxford: Oxford University Press.

Ikambana, Peta (2008) *Mobutu's Totalitarian Political System*. London: Routledge.

Isaacson, Walter (1992) *Kissinger: A Biography*. London: Faber & Faber.

James, Alan (1989) 'The UN Force in Cyprus', *International Affairs*, 65(3), 481–500.

James, Alan (1990) *Peacekeeping in International Politics*. London: Macmillan.

Kedourie, Elie (1992) *Politics in the Middle East*. Oxford: Oxford University Press.

Khrushchev, Nikita (1974) *Khrushchev Remembers: The Last Testament*, ed. Strobe Talbott. London: André Deutsch.

Kissinger, Henry (1982) *Years of Upheaval*. London: Weidenfeld & Nicolson.

Kyle, Keith (1991) *Suez*. London: Weidenfeld & Nicolson.

Lash, Joseph P. (1962) *Dag Hammarskjöld: Custodian of the Brushfire Peace*. London: Cassell.

Lefever, E.W. (1967) *Uncertain Mandate: The Politics of the UN Congo Operation*. Baltimore, MD: Johns Hopkins University Press.

Lewis, Ioan and Mayall, James (1996) 'Somalia', in James Mayall (ed.), *The New Interventionism 1991–1994: United Nations Experience in Cambodia, Former Yugoslavia and Somalia*. Cambridge: Cambridge University Press, pp. 94–124.

Litwak, Robert S. (1986) *Détente and the Nixon Doctrine: American Foreign Policy and the Pursuit of Stability, 1969–1976*. Cambridge: Cambridge University Press.

Louis, W.R., Stookry, R.W. and Wilson, R. (1986) *The End of the Palestine Mandate*. London: Tauris.

Louis, William Roger and Owen, Roger (1989) *Suez 1956: The Crisis and its Consequences*. Oxford: Clarendon Press.

Luard, Evan (1982) *A History of the United Nations*: Vol. I *The Years of Western Domination, 1945–55*. London: Macmillan.

Luard, Evan (1989) *A History of the United Nations*: Vol. II *The Age of Decolonization, 1955–65*. London: Macmillan.

MacQueen, Norrie (2002) *United Nations Peacekeeping in Africa since 1960*. London: Longman.

MacQueen, Norrie (2006) *Peacekeeping and the International System*. London: Routledge.

Mahoney, Richard (1983) *JFK: Ordeal in Africa*. Oxford: Oxford University Press.

Northedge, Frederick S. (1985) *The League of Nations: Its Life and Times, 1920–1946*. Leicester: Leicester University Press.

Ovendale, Ritchie (1989) *Britain, the United States and the End of the Palestine Mandate 1942–48*. London: Royal Historical Society.

Ovendale, Ritchie (1992) *The Origins of the Arab-Israeli Wars*. London: Longman.

Padelford, Norman (1962) *The Financing of Future Peace and Security Operations under the United Nations*. Washington, DC: Brookings Insitute.

Parsons, Anthony (1995) *From Cold War to Hot Peace: UN Interventions 1975–1995*. Harmondsworth: Penguin.

Pearson, Lester (1973) *Memoirs, Vol. 2 1948–1957*. Toronto: University of Toronto Press.

Pipes, Richard (1981) *US–Soviet Relations in the Era of Détente*. Boulder, CO: Westview.

Quandt, William B. (1986) *Camp David: Peacemaking and Politics*. Washington, DC: Brookings Institute.

Rees, David (1967) *The Age of Containment: The Cold War 1945–65*. London: Macmillan.

Reyntjens, Filip (2009) *The Great African War: Congo and Regional Geopolitics, 1996–2006*. Cambridge: Cambridge University Press.

Roberts, Adam (1995) 'Communal conflict as a challenge to international organization: the case of the former Yugoslavia', *Review of International Studies*, 21(4), 389–410.

Rosner, Gabriella (1963) *The United Nations Emergency Force*. New York: Columbia University Press.

Russell, Ruth B. (1958) *A History of the United Nations Charter*. Washington, DC: Brookings Institute.

Saltford, John (2002) *The United Nations and the Indonesian Takeover of West Papua, 1962–1969*. London: Routledge.

Shlaim, Avi (1997) 'The Protocol of Sèvres 1956: anatomy of a war plot', *International Affairs*, 73(3), 509–30.

Skögmo, Bjørn (1989) *UNIFIL: International Peacekeeping in Lebanon*. London: Lynne Rienner.

Stegenga, James (1968) *The United Nations Force in Cyprus*. Columbus, OH: Ohio State University Press.

Stoessinger, John G. *et al.* (1964) *Financing the United Nations System*. Washington, DC: Brookings Institute.

Thakur, Ramesh (1987) *International Peacekeeping in Lebanon*. Boulder, CO: Westview.

Thant, U. (1978) *View from the UN*. New York: Doubleday.

Tharoor, Sashi (1992) 'United Nations peacekeeping in Europe', *Survival*, 37(2), 121–34.

Thomas, Hugh (1967) *The Suez Affair*. London: Weidenfeld & Nicholson.

Urquhart, Brian (1973) *Hammarskjöld*. London: Bodley Head.

United Nations Charter (1945) found at: http://www.un.org/en/documents/charter/index.shtml.

Vadney, T.E. (1998) *The World since 1945*, 3rd edn. Harmondsworth: Penguin.

Verrier, Anthony (1981) *International Peacekeeping: United Nations Forces in a Troubled World*. Harmondsworth: Penguin.

Wainhouse, D.W. *et al.* (1966) *International Peace Observation: A History and a Forecast*. Baltimore, MD: Johns Hopkins University Press.

Waldheim, Kurt (1985) *In the Eye of the Storm*. London: Weidenfeld & Nicolson.

Walters, F.P. (1960) *A History of the League of Nations*. Oxford: Oxford University Press.

Weiss, Thomas G. (1994) *Collective Security in a Changing World*. London: Lynne Rienner.

Weissman, Stephen R. (1974) *American Foreign Policy in the Congo, 1960–64*. Ithica, NY: Cornell University Press.

Whelan, Richard (1990) *Drawing the Line: The Korean War, 1950–1953*. Boston, MA: Little Brown.

White, N.D. (1997) *Keeping the Peace*. Manchester: Manchester University Press.

Williams, Andrew (2007) *Failed Imagination? The Anglo-American New World Order from Wilson to Bush*, 2nd edn. Manchester: Manchester University Press.

Yalta Agreement, found at: http://www.h-net.org/~hst203/documents/YALTA.html.

Yoder, Amos (1997) *The Evolution of the United Nations System*, 3rd edn. London: Taylor & Francis.

Zacher, Mark W. (1969) *Dag Hammarskjöld's United Nations*. New York: Columbia University Press.

Index